The Politics of Foster Care
Administration in the United States

Government-by-proxy and intergovernmental relations profoundly affect the public administration of foster care. Using examples from foster care systems in the states of Delaware, Michigan, New York, and Rhode Island, Rebecca Padot eloquently combines a rigorous methodology and theory work to expose the conditions under which foster care outcomes can be improved. The cases selected suggest that the federal government has increased its focus on measuring the performance of state programs while simultaneously decreasing its funding of state foster care programs and offering the states very little management or mentorship. Padot turns the page and recommends administrators place a greater priority on building community partners, integrating the advice of mentors, providing leadership from public managers, and cultivating relationships with the federal government.

An original and timely resource for scholars and practitioners, this book represents a significant contribution to our understanding of how leadership and management variables may be associated with more positive foster care practices and performance in the United States.

Rebecca H. Padot is a Non-Resident Senior Fellow at PRRUCS at the University of Pennsylvania. She has previously held the titles of Bradley Fellow, Earhart Fellow, Fox Distinguished Graduate Fellow, and Mumford Fellow.

Routledge Research in Public Administration and Public Policy

1 **A Complexity Theory for Public Policy**
Göktuğ Morçöl

2 **Network Governance in Response to Acts of Terrorism**
Comparative Analyses
Naim Kapucu

3 **Leadership and Policy Innovations – From Clinton to Bush**
Countering the Proliferation of Weapons of Mass Destruction
Joseph R. Cerami

4 **Disaster Resiliency**
Interdisciplinary Perspectives
Edited by Naim Kapucu, Christopher V. Hawkins, Fernando I. Rivera

5 **Paying Our High Public Officials**
Evaluating the Political Justifications of Top Wages in the Public Sector
Teun J. Dekker

6 **The Politics of Regulatory Reform**
Stuart Shapiro and Debra Borie-Holtz

7 **Block Granting Medicaid**
A Model for 21st Century Health Reform?
Edward Alan Miller

8 **Toward Resilient Communities**
Examining the Impacts of Local Governments in Disasters
Christopher L. Atkinson

9 **Local Disaster Resilience**
Administrative and Political Perspectives
Ashley D. Ross

10 **Does Government Need to be Involved in Primary and Secondary Education**
Evaluating Policy Options Using Market Role Assessment
Michael T. Peddle

11 **Environmental Justice through Research-Based Decision-Making**
William M. Bowen

12 **The Politics of Foster Care Administration in the United States**
Rebecca H. Padot

The Politics of Foster Care Administration in the United States

Rebecca H. Padot

NEW YORK AND LONDON

First published 2015
by Routledge
711 Third Avenue, New York, NY 10017

and by Routledge
2 Park Square, Milton Park, Abingdon, Oxon OX14 4RN

*Routledge is an imprint of the Taylor & Francis Group,
an informa business*

© 2015 Taylor & Francis

The right of Rebecca H. Padot to be identified as author of this work has been asserted by him/her in accordance with sections 77 and 78 of the Copyright, Designs and Patents Act 1988.

All rights reserved. No part of this book may be reprinted or reproduced or utilised in any form or by any electronic, mechanical, or other means, now known or hereafter invented, including photocopying and recording, or in any information storage or retrieval system, without permission in writing from the publishers.

Trademark Notice: Product or corporate names may be trademarks or registered trademarks, and are used only for identification and explanation without intent to infringe.

Library of Congress Cataloging-in-Publication Data
Padot, Rebecca.
  The politics of foster care administration in the United States /
by Rebecca Padot.
    pages cm. — (Routledge research in public administration and public policy ; 12)
  Includes bibliographical references and index.
  1. Foster home care—United States. I. Title.
  HV881.P33 2014
  362.73'3—dc23
  2014020626

ISBN: 978-1-138-02194-5 (hbk)
ISBN: 978-1-315-77741-2 (ebk)

Typeset in Sabon
by Apex CoVantage, LLC

Printed and bound in the United States of America by Publishers Graphics, LLC on sustainably sourced paper.

To the three kids I "fostered," a providential match resulting from our coincidental meeting that survived two decades. Thank you for inspiring these ideals.

I love you Maritza, Nato, and Jeremy.

Contents

List of Figures	ix
List of Tables	xi
Acknowledgments	xiii

1	A Public Administration Framework for Foster Care	1
2	A Quantitative and Qualitative Data Collection Approach	8
3	Delaware: A Small State with Stronger Performance	45
4	New York: A Larger State with Weaker Performance	67
5	Rhode Island: A Smaller State with Weaker Performance	90
6	Michigan: A Larger State with Stronger Performance	115
7	Case Research Results and Implications for Increasing Effectiveness	145
8	Improving Foster Care	173

Appendix	185
Index	189

Figures

2.1	Range of State performance in 2003 on Outcome Measure 1.1	15
2.2	Range of State performance in 2003 on Outcome Measure 2.1	16
2.3	Range of State performance in FY 2003 on Outcome Measure 3.1	16
2.4	Range of State performance in FY 2003 on Outcome Measure 3.4	17
2.5	Range of State performance in FY 2003 on Outcome Measure 4.1	17
2.6	Range of State performance in FY 2003 on Outcome Measure 4.2	18
2.7	Range of State performance in FY 2003 on Outcome Measure 5.1	18
2.8	Range of State performance in FY 2003 on Outcome Measure 6.1	19
2.9	Range of State performance on Outcome Measure 7.1	19
2.10	Factors Stronger Foster Care States Possess	30
2.11	Variable Presence in States	36
7.1	Federal Claims and Caseload History for Title IV-E Foster Care	150

Tables

2.1	Performance Measurement 2003: Stronger States	11
2.2	Performance Measurement 2003: Weaker States	13
2.3	Performance Improvement 2000 to 2003: Stronger States	21
2.4	Performance Improvement 2000 to 2003: Weaker States	23
2.5	2003 State Foster Care Caseload per Capita: NY, RI, MI, DE	26
2.6	2003 State Foster Care Caseload per Capita: UT, CO, TX	27

Acknowledgments

By sharing their experiences for this study, the following individuals will help to improve foster care and increase government effectiveness. In Delaware, I extend my gratitude to John Bates, Elizabeth Bouchelle, Tania Culley, Cari DeSantis, Del Failing, Vincent Giampeitro, Carlyse Giddens, Sandy Johnson, Michael Kersteter, Arkadi Kuhlmann, Chandlee Johnson Kuhn, Ruth Ann Minner, Leslie Newman, and Meghan Pasricha. In New York, I offer special thanks to Michael Arsham, Francis Ayuso, John Courtney, Kelly Garvey, Sarah Gerstenzang, Richard Hucke, Nancy Martinez, LaTrella R. Penny, Nicholas Pirro, and Deborah Rubien. In Rhode Island, I am grateful to Julie DiBari, Anne Fortier, Lisa Guillette, Dorothy Hultine, Patricia Martinez, Dana Mullen, Heidi Mulligan, Maureen O'Shea, Maureen Robbins, Kevin Savage, Jenifer Silva, Sarah St. Jacques, and Philip Steiner. In Michigan, I owe special thanks to Ishmael Ahmed, Mary Chaliman, Maura D. Corrigan, Kate Hanley, Patrick Heron, James Novell, Patrick Okoronokwo, Gayle Robbert, Janet Snyder, Vicki Thompson-Sandy, Victoria Tyler, Marianne Udow, and Jane Zehnder-Merrell. Hailing from all areas of the United States, I send my appreciation to Christine Craig, Lisa Pearson, Brent Thompson, Carole Thompson, Muna Walker, Barbara Wilson, and Harry Wilson.

I am grateful to many foundations and organizations for considering my research worthy of support. Thank you for granting me the following designations: PRRUCS Fellow, Earhart Fellow, Mumford Fellow, Bradley Fellow, and Fox Distinguished Graduate Fellow. Without these funders, this study would not have been possible.

The Pew Charitable Trusts taught me how to champion philanthropic performance measurement and return on investment community service, and for that I am grateful. Allowing me to serve on a portfolio of programs that assisted at-risk youth, universities, and other social impact endeavors was an extraordinary opportunity. Thank you to my supervisors Dr. Sulc and Dr. Lugo for your commitment to social science, performance measurement, and the social good. Much gratitude to Dr. Sulc for your feedback on an earlier draft of this study.

xiv *Acknowledgments*

To a public administration scholar who has written countless books upon which we now build our theories, I am grateful to Professor Donald F. Kettl, who served on my committee both during his time as executive director of the Fels Institute of Government at the University of Pennsylvania and also as professor and dean of the University of Maryland School of Public Policy. Both his assistance with the research design and implementation of this study and his mentoring in the fields of public policy and public administration research have been invaluable.

To Professor Jack Nagel, who served as associate dean for graduate studies and associate dean for the social sciences at the University of Pennsylvania during the bulk of this study, thank you for your profound role in shaping this study, some of which was during your time as committee chair. I thoroughly enjoyed serving as your teaching assistant and appreciated your dual commitment to students and research.

My greatest debt is to Professor John DiIulio, Frederic Fox Leadership Professor of Politics, Religion, and Civil Society and professor of political science, University of Pennsylvania, who guided me through multiple graduate programs and oversaw my research and teaching. He went well beyond what is required of an academic advisor and what one is generally rewarded for as a professor. His combination of leadership, commitment to students, partnership with his spouse, penchant for community service, and rigorous social science is a model I aspire to emulate.

To my University of Pennsylvania PRRUCS and Fox research families, much appreciation to Catherine W., David H., Sheria S., Cindy B., Lia F., Stephen D., Chuck B., Wilson G., Joe T., Hara S., Marc S., Mark H., Mary S., and Laura T. You have truly added the word "family" after the word "research."

I send heartfelt appreciation to Dr. Mulhern for his guidance during my studies at Penn's Fels Institute of Government. Countless thanks to junior fellows Jennifer S. and Miguel G. and to senior fellow Clinton O. Appreciation also to some of Penn's other faculty, Elizabeth Tuleja and Rogers Smith, for their roles in my academic development. Thanks to Pat K., Carlton J., Sergio S., Michael J., and Brian T. for their roles in shaping my academic journey.

Thanks to the White House Office of Faith-Based and Community Initiatives for allowing me to present initial findings. I am grateful to Carl Cannon for taking an interest in my research while he was at *The National Journal*.

Special thanks to Routledge Press, editor Natalja Mortensen, and to her team, Darcy Bullock, Colleen Roache, Kathleen Laurentiev and Lynne Askin-Roush. Special thanks to Natalja for championing this project. May many foster children be better served as a result of her and the board's decision.

Thanks to Peter Agree of the University of Pennsylvania Press for offering wonderful insights on an earlier draft. Also thanks to the PRRUCS editor for an earlier round of edits.

Acknowledgments xv

Thanks to Chapin Hall at the University of Chicago and The Casey Young Adult Survey for the findings cited in this book and for your overall contributions to the field of foster care.

My fondest thanks is reserved for my husband, Chris, whose love gives me the stamina to work so many hours on projects that serve the social good. I am truly honored to be your wife.

1 A Public Administration Framework for Foster Care

As political scientist Herbert Kaufman observed in his famous 1960 study of the U.S. Forest Service, public policy is "enunciated in rhetoric" but realized or not "in action."[1] Kaufman's point was echoed and elaborated upon by political scientists Donald F. Kettl and James W. Fesler in the opening of their classic textbook, *The Politics of the Administrative Process*: "Any road map of how government does what it does has to start with public administration. Policymakers might make policy, but their ideas, big and small, rarely have any meaning apart from their execution."[2]

Kettl and Fesler defined "public administration" as "the process of translating public policies into results."[3] Whether referred to as public administration, public management, or public bureaucracy, what political scientist James Q. Wilson has described as the systematic study of "what government agencies do and why they do it" has a long, distinguished tradition within political science and is very much alive today.[4]

From the Forest Service to the Federal Reserve,[5] from maximum-security prisons to public schools,[6] from big-city police departments to U.S. military special operations forces,[7] from the Securities and Exchange Commission to the myriad federal agencies that are responsible for health care finance,[8] and on issues ranging from homeland security to social welfare to environmental protection,[9] political scientists study how federal, state, and local government agencies succeed in "translating political decisions into practical steps."[10]

This study is offered in line with the tradition of political science research that focuses upon public administration, but with at least three distinctive features.

First, this study focuses on an important area of public policy and administration that political scientists have hitherto largely ignored, namely foster care, which is defined by the U.S. Department of Health and Human Services (HHS) as "24-hour substitute care for all children placed away from their parents or guardians and for whom the State agency has placement and care responsibility."[11]

The lack of attention that political scientists have given to foster care is difficult to understand. Each year 650,000 children are placed in the care

2 Politics of Foster Care Administration

and custody of public foster care agencies.[12] On any given day, government foster care employees are entrusted with making life and placement decisions for approximately 400,000 children.[13] Each year, about 250,000 children enter foster care, and roughly 250,000 exit the foster care system.[14] Foster care involves about $4.3 billion in annual federal spending,[15] and at least $4.1 billion in annual state and local spending.[16] More than 69,231 federal, state, and local public employees work directly for child welfare agencies that are involved with foster care.[17]

This study treats "government by proxy"[18] or "third-party government"[19] not as a theoretical construct, but as a hard empirical reality that profoundly affects the public administration of foster care in ways that cry out for preliminary description and analysis.

As recently as two decades ago, many scholars did not question the extent to which the federal government administered its programs largely through state and local governments, for-profit firms, and nonprofit organizations, nor did they question the significance of attendant financial and managerial arrangements.[20]

But today, only a public administration "doubting Thomas" could fail to recognize the vast extent and tremendous significance of Washington's proxy-government cast of characters, which now plainly goes far beyond mere "privatization" or "outsourcing" and reaches consequentially even to U.S. military organizations and intelligence operations abroad.[21]

In the same vein, this study considers "intergovernmental relations" and "administrative federalism" to be virtually synonymous with "public administration" when it comes to the actual, everyday implementation of public policies that are funded in whole or in part by the national government. As we shall see, even with the large role that HHS plays, foster care has been, and continues to be, administered mainly by state governments, with interesting and consequential differences in the public administration of foster care from state to state.

In addition, this study documents and zeroes in on state-to-state variance in the public administration of foster care in order to determine the conditions, if any, under which foster care outcomes can be improved. Further, it considers how, if at all, policymakers and practitioners can foster those conditions by making feasible changes in foster care administration (leadership and management) that would result in predictable and desirable consequences for children in foster care.

Many preliminary public administration studies of state or city agencies by political scientists have not been dedicated to mining variance in government performance in the hope of producing action-oriented, problem-solving approaches. For example, in *Varieties of Police Behavior* (1969), Wilson explicitly confined his inquiry to raising and preliminarily answering certain academic questions about three different "styles" of police administration that emerged from his data-gathering on eight different local police agencies.[22]

Public Administration Framework 3

By contrast, in *Governing Prisons* (1987), Wilson's student, John J. DiIulio, Jr., explicitly set out to explore different models of prison administration, in the hope of acquiring knowledge that policymakers and practitioners might use to improve prison "leadership" and "management" and thereby improve the "quality of life" in state prison systems.[23]

This study of foster care is in the action-oriented, problem-solving spirit of DiIulio's *Governing Prisons*, Stephen Kelman's work on federal government procurement,[24] Lawrence Mead's research on state welfare-to-work programs,[25] and the like.

Kettl's 2009 treatise *The Next Government of the United States* profiled numerous obstacles to improving public administration in America, and was aptly subtitled "Why Our Institutions Fail Us and How to Fix Them."[26] In the course of his analysis, Kettl identified the U.S. Coast Guard (USCG) as a public agency with leadership and management traditions that have long been associated with high performance and positive outcomes. The USCG succeeded in meeting the pressing human needs that followed Hurricane Katrina in 2005, even as the Federal Emergency Management Agency and most other government agencies at all levels failed to do so.[27]

Unfortunately, foster care does not have an administrative equivalent of the USCG. Newspaper archives are replete with reports of scandals, crises, and mistakes that have, in more than a few cases, exposed vulnerable children not only to bad home conditions but also to physical abuse and even death.[28] The *New York Times* noted:

> The state [of New Jersey], in response to a court action brought by *The New York Times*, released 2,000 pages of documents concerning seventeen different [foster care] children and that chronicled the mistakes, missed opportunities and other missteps that led to the deaths of four children and the sometimes brutal, prolonged abuse of thirteen more.[29]

Despite the prevalence of bad news, the fact is that state foster care agencies vary in interesting and consequential ways. Other things being equal, it appears that certain state foster care agencies are better than others when it comes to the safe, humane, and cost-effective care and placement of children in need.

This study focuses on the public administration of foster care systems in four states: Delaware, Michigan, New York, and Rhode Island. While these states may not be representative of all foster care administrative systems, my preliminary research persuaded me that they differ from one another administratively in interesting and potentially consequential ways. HHS federal quantitative data permitted me to select case states from both top-performing and bottom-performing state foster care systems so that I might come to understand what accounts for their differences.

Generally speaking, the foster care agencies in Delaware and Michigan have been by most measures more likely to produce safe, humane,

4 Politics of Foster Care Administration

and cost-effective foster care outcomes than corresponding agencies in New York and Rhode Island. As we shall see, these differences cannot be explained by the first two states having more personnel per capita, higher per capita budgets, or considerably lighter caseloads, because they do not.

This four-state public administration study is an effort by a political scientist to begin to identify the leadership and management variables that may be associated with more positive foster care practices and performance. In general, my research documents that in Delaware and Michigan, foster care administrators are considerably more likely than their counterparts in New York and Rhode Island to forge partnerships with community groups. They are also more likely to produce strong managers who build support networks both within and outside of their departments. Managers in Michigan used this approach so successfully that they developed a vast network of mentors and foundation relationships. These cases suggest that *better foster care administration is produced by public managers who operated as principled agents[30] to develop networks, partnerships, and strategies within and outside their states.*

The cases also offer insight into the changing roles of the federal and state governments with regard to foster care administration. These cases suggest that the *federal government has increased its focus on measuring the performance of state programs while simultaneously decreasing its funding of state foster care programs and offering the states very little management or mentorship.*

My academic research and a number of job experiences inspired me to pursue this particular study and encouraged me to believe that its preliminary findings might be of intellectual as well as practical and civic value. DiIulio's aforementioned 1987 study of prison administration contributed to leadership and management reforms in dozens of state prison systems that, according to the most recent study of the subject, resulted in improved conditions of confinement and dramatic reductions in prison violence.[31]

When I served as a program staff member for the Pew Charitable Trusts, I was responsible for the private foundation's involvement as a stakeholder in a generally well-regarded public–private social service delivery initiative anchored by the federal government and its public servants at HHS.[32] This Mentoring Children of Prisoners (MCOP) program was intended to provide a loving, caring, and nurturing nonparental adult mentor for as many of these children as possible. On any given day, America is home to some 2 million children of prisoners. I could not help but notice that many of the children who were involved in the MCOP program were also in foster care.

I observed that the MCOP program had its first and most notable successes in those states where public leaders and managers transcended public–private boundaries, forged relationships that were focused on serving children in need, and turned those relationships into reliable administrative partnerships. In due course, as my foundation and other groups shared information about what it took to make the program successful, several states that were

Public Administration Framework 5

once MCOP laggards (such as Texas) joined states that were leaders (such as Pennsylvania).

Recognizing fully that legal, budgetary, political, and other factors may frustrate this aspiration, I hope that the present study stimulates such active public administration learning and sparks measurable improvements in the design and delivery of foster care services that are received by more than 650,000 needy or neglected children each year.

NOTES

1. Herbert Kaufman, *The Forest Ranger: A Study in Administrative Behavior* (Baltimore: Johns Hopkins University Press, 1967), 3.
2. Donald F. Kettl and James W. Fesler, *The Politics of the Administrative Process*, 4th ed. (Washington, DC: CQ Press, 2009), xvii.
3. Ibid., 542.
4. James Q. Wilson, *Bureaucracy: What Government Agencies Do and Why They Do It* (New York: Basic Books, 1989).
5. Kaufman, *The Forest Ranger*; Donald Kettl, *Leadership at the Fed* (New Haven, CT: Yale University Press, 1986).
6. Charles Stastny and Gabrielle Tyrnauer, *Who Rules the Joint? The Changing Political Culture of Maximum-Security Prisons in America* (Lexington, MA: Lexington Books, 1982); John E. Chubb and Terry M. Moe, *Politics, Markets, and America's Schools* (Washington, DC: Brookings Institution Press, 1990).
7. James Q. Wilson, *Varieties of Police Behavior: The Management of Law and Order in Eight Communities* (Cambridge, MA: Harvard University Press, 1969); Susan L. Marquis, *Unconventional Warfare: Rebuilding U.S. Special Operations Forces* (Washington, DC: Brookings Institution Press, 1997).
8. Anne Khademian, *The SEC and Capital Market Regulation: The Politics of Expertise* (Pittsburgh, PA: University of Pittsburgh, 1992); John J. DiIulio, Jr., and Richard R. Nathan, *Making Health Reform Work: The View from the States* (Washington, DC: Brookings Institution Press, 1994).
9. Donald F. Kettl, *System under Stress: Homeland Security and American Politics*, 2nd ed. (Washington, DC: CQ Press, 2007); Lawrence Mead, *From Welfare to Work: Lessons from America* (London: Institute of Economic Affairs, 1997); Gerald J. Garvey, *Energy, Ecology, and Economy* (New York: W.W. Norton & Company, 1972).
10. Kettl and Fesler, *The Politics of the Administrative Process*, xvii.
11. U.S. Department of Health and Human Services, Administration for Children and Families, Administration on Children, Youth, and Families, Children's Bureau, "Child Welfare Policy Manual," http://www.acf.hhs.gov/j2ee/pro grams/cb/laws_policies/laws/cwpm/policy_dsp.jsp?citID=207. Note: All references to online works in this book were accessed at the time of research.
12. U.S. Department of Health and Human Services, Administration for Children and Families, Administration on Children, Youth, and Families, Children's Bureau, "Trends in Foster Care and Adoption—FY 2002–FY 2011," http:// www.acf.hhs.gov/sites/default/files/cb/trends_fostercare_adoption.pdf. Note: There were 664,000 foster children served in FY 2010 and 646,000 foster children served in FY 2011.
13. U.S. Department of Health and Human Services, Administration for Children and Families, Administration on Children, Youth, and Families, Children's

6 Politics of Foster Care Administration

Bureau, "Adoption and Foster Care Reporting System. The AFCARS (Adoption and Foster Care Analysis and Reporting System) Report #20," Preliminary FY 2012 Estimates as of November 2013.

14. Ibid. Note: This number varied from 288,778 in 2008 to a gradual decline of 240,923 by 2012.

15. U.S. Department of Health and Human Services, "Fiscal Year 2014 Budget in Brief. Administration for Children and Families: Mandatory Programs," http://www.hhs.gov/budget/fy2014/fy-2014/fy-2014-budget-in-brief.pdf.

16. U.S. Department of Health and Human Services, Office of the Assistant Secretary for Planning and Evaluation, Division of Children and Youth Policy, "Title IV-E Foster Care FY 2007 Expenditures as Reported by States, May 2, 2008," Office of the Assistant Secretary for Planning and Evaluation, Division of Children and Youth Policy, provided by Laura Radel, Senior Social Science Analyst, e-mail message to author, August 25, 2009. Note: The $4.1 billion mentioned here only refers to the HHS reported amount of state spending (including local spending) on foster care. State and local spending is significantly higher when including foster care expenses for non-Title IV-E eligible claims. HHS does not report overall data for state/local funded foster care, which is non-Title IV-E eligible.

17. National Data Analysis System, "Positions Authorized and Filled in the Child Welfare Agency, 2004," http://ndas.cwla.org. Note: The number of workers reported on this website—69,096—refers to the number of child welfare workers (including foster care workers) in 32 states. According to HHS, CWLA, and the Child Welfare Information Gateway, this CWLA report is the most comprehensive assessment of the number of child welfare workers. Nineteen states choose not to report their workforce data, so the actual number of child welfare workers is significantly higher; Kenneth J. Wolfe, U.S. Department of Health and Human Services, Administration for Children and Families, e-mail message to author, August 25, 2009. Note: 135 refers to the number of actual foster care federal workers working for the Children's Bureau in 2009. Taken together, 135 and 69,096 total 69,231 as referenced.

18. Donald F. Kettl, *Government by Proxy: (Mis?)Managing Federal Programs* (Washington, DC: CQ Press, 1988).

19. Lester M. Salamon, ed., *Beyond Privatization: The Tools of Government Action* (Washington, DC: The Urban Institute Press, 1989), 9.

20. James C. Musselwhite, Jr., "The Impacts of New Federalism on Public/Private Partnerships," *Publius: The Journal of Federalism,* Vol. 16, No. 1 (Winter 1986): 113–131; Louise G. White, "Public Management in a Pluralistic Arena," *Public Administration Review,* Vol. 49, No. 6 (1989): 522–532.

21. Paul Verkuil, *Outsourcing Sovereignty: Why Privatization of Government Functions Threatens Democracy and What We Can Do About It* (New York: Cambridge University Press, 2007), 189.

22. Wilson, *Varieties of Police Behavior.*

23. John J. DiIulio, Jr., *Governing Prisons: A Comparative Study of Correctional Management* (New York: The Free Press, 1987), 11, 95, 243.

24. Steven Kelman, *Procurement and Public Management: The Fear of Discretion and the Quality of Government Performance* (Washington, DC: AEI Press, 1990).

25. Mead, *From Welfare to Work.*

26. Donald F. Kettl, *The Next Government of the United States: Why Our Institutions Fail Us and How to Fix Them* (New York: W.W. Norton & Company, 2009).

27. Ibid., 186–198.

Public Administration Framework 7

28. Madelyn Freundlich et al., "Continuing Danger: A Report on Child Fatalities in New York City," http://www.childrensrights.org/wp-content/uploads/2008/06/continuing_danger_february_2003.pdf; Madelyn Freundlich, "Time Running Out: Teens in Foster Care," http://www.childrensrights.org/wp-content/uploads/2008/06/time_running_out_teens_in_foster_care_nov_2003.pdf.

29. Richard Lezin Jones and Leslie Kaufman, "New Jersey Opens Files Showing Failures of Child Welfare System," *New York Times*, April 15, 2003, A1.

30. John DiIulio Jr., "Principled Agents: The Cultural Bases of Behavior in a Federal Government Bureaucracy," *Journal of Public Administration Research and Theory,* Vol. 4, No. 3, (1994): 277–318.

31. Bert Useem and Anne Morrison Piehl, *Prison State: The Challenge of Mass Incarceration* (New York: Cambridge University Press, 2008).

32. Carl Cannon, "Stepchildren of Justice," *National Journal,* Vol. 38, No. 7 (February 18, 2006): 28–34; The White House, "Innovations in Compassion. The Faith-Based and Community Initiative: A Final Report to the Armies of Compassion," http://georgewbush-whitehouse.archives.gov/government/fbci/pdf/innovation-in-compassion.pdf.

2 A Quantitative and Qualitative Data Collection Approach

As explained in the last chapter, the goal of this research is twofold. First, it is intended to discover the conditions, if any, under which foster care outcomes can be improved. Second, it hopes to determine feasible changes that policymakers and practitioners can make to produce such conditions, thereby increasing predictable and desirable consequences for children in foster care.

This chapter presents a research framework that is poised to answer these questions by, first, identifying how cases were selected; second, outlining the variables (federal government, mentors, community partners, and leadership) to be tested in each of the states; and third, detailing the primary qualitative research approach.

The research was structured to test whether the following hypothesis is accurate: *Delaware and Michigan became stronger-performing states in the area of foster care by placing a greater priority than the lower-performing states of New York and Rhode Island on building community partners, integrating the advice of mentors, providing leadership from public managers, and cultivating relationships with the federal government.*

In other words, are we able to identify variables that contribute to producing better foster care? Was there greater leadership from public managers in the stronger foster care states? Did those states also build more community partners? Did they integrate the advice of mentors? Did they have stronger relationships with the federal government? The answers to those questions uncovered by this study should allow us to produce better foster care.

CASE STATE SELECTION

A mix of research methods was used to identify two states that had stronger foster care systems and two whose foster care programs were weaker. This was a necessary first step because there is no independent academic or policy source that ranks or classifies states according to the effectiveness of their foster care systems and policies. Some at-risk youth social welfare programs, such as the federal Mentoring Children of Prisoners program,

Data Collection Approach 9

have well-known model states and cities. At this study's inception, however, foster care had no such generally accepted classification, so additional measures were necessary to ensure that the four case states were properly selected.

I selected cases by first reviewing federal performance data and then taking into consideration state characteristics, to ensure that I had a mixture of small and large states. By culling the federal data for several measures of performance of quantitative data on annual outcome assessment, I was able to determine top and bottom performing states. To provide an understanding of a state's performance over a three-year period, I also assessed performance measures that impacted their improvement levels. Once a handful of states were identified, I then selected one large population state from the top-performing group (Michigan); one small population state from the top-performing group (Delaware); one large population state from the bottom-performing group (New York); and one small population state from the bottom-performing group (Rhode Island).

Federal Data

Foster care was a state fiscal responsibility until 1961, when it was partially shifted to the federal government under the Aid to Families with Dependent Children program (AFDC). Since 1980, it has been carried under Title IV-E Foster Care of the Social Security Act.[1] Title IV-E, an open-ended entitlement,[2] is the primary vehicle[3] for federal reimbursement to states for a portion of their foster care costs. Title IV-E eligibility is linked to the 1996 AFDC program and is based on children's eligibility for AFDC as it existed in their state's plan on July 16, 1996.[4] As a result, less than half of all foster care cases receive partial funding from the federal government.

The overseer of federal foster care is the Children's Bureau, which is housed within the Administration on Children, Youth and Families in the Administration for Children and Families of the U.S. Department of Health and Human Services (HHS). In 1995, the federal government began to collect federal performance measurement data under the Adoption and Foster Care Reporting System (AFCARS).[5] HHS conducted a light data scan as part of the Child and Family Services Review (CFSR) (implemented fully by 2004), as well as a less frequent but more rigorous data scan when it instituted the Child Welfare Outcomes Reports in 1998.

The present research design utilizes the "Child Welfare Outcomes 2003: Annual Report," which covers the years 2000 to 2003. This 2003 report was required by the Adoption and Safe Families Act of 1997, and was the sixth in a series of annual reports from the HHS. At the time of the research design and field research, this federal data provided the latest and most comprehensive published assessment of individual state performance on state child welfare systems over the three-year period.[6] The report utilized data from the AFCARS Foster Care File and the National Child Abuse and Neglect Data System (NCANDS).[7]

10 *Politics of Foster Care Administration*

The "Child Welfare Outcomes 2003: Annual Report" featured seven outcome indicators with submeasurements on each state for the years 2000 to 2003. These outcomes were determined after soliciting input from HHS, state and local child welfare agency administrators, child advocacy organizations, child welfare researchers, and other experts in the child welfare field.

The federal government set target performance goals for all states on each of these seven outcome indicators, although states struggled to meet these targets. In 2005, HHS reported the following to Congress: The current funding structure had not resulted in high quality outcomes; there were widely different claiming practices among states, ranging from claims of $4,200 to $41,400[8] per foster child;[9] and there was no relationship between state claims and service quality[10] or outcomes.[11] This report illuminated many significant problems with foster care policy, raised questions about the success of federal funding for foster care, and demonstrated each state's struggle to achieve the expected federal outcomes.

The federal government intentionally set its foster care outcome indicators high; as a result, no states have been performing at the expected levels.[12] Wade Horn, Assistant Secretary for Children and Families, reported in testimony before the U.S. House of Representatives Committee on Ways and Means that of the 14 outcomes and suboutcomes measured, the states reviewed have ranged from meeting only one to nine of the targets. Horn concluded that "significant weaknesses are evident in programs across the nation."[13]

The 2003 annual report did not offer an overall ranking of foster care states utilizing aggregate outcomes; rather, it measured states only across individual outcomes. No state consistently performed in the top five on every outcome measure. When taking into account seven outcome measures and multiple submeasures, each state provided mixed performance results. Consequently, the federal data did not clearly identify top and bottom performers.

Because HHS reported the median on each state's individual outcome, I was able to look for states that consistently performed above or below the median. To determine stronger states, I looked for patterns of consistency among the top performance data by tabulating the outcomes that specifically related to foster care performance. The next section describes four states that performed either near the top or the bottom of the aggregate foster care federal outcome data.

Quantitative Data: Outcome Assessment

This section details how I determined that two states, Delaware and Michigan, performed near the top of the states on foster care performance in 2003, while two other states, New York and Rhode Island, performed near the bottom.

Data Collection Approach **11**

First, I extracted the raw federal data from the "Child Welfare Outcomes 2003: Annual Report" that pertained to foster care performance. These data questions are outlined in the Appendix at the end of this book. When a state had a pattern of either poor or excellent performance on multiple individual outcomes, I tabulated their seven outcomes and compared them to the median, as shown in Tables 2.1 and 2.2.

Second, I classified an outcome as positive or negative based on whether the state performed worse (negative) or better (positive) than the median. When suboutcomes were included, they were averaged to arrive at one "positive" or "negative" figure for the overall outcome. A state that was performing very well would have seven positives across seven outcomes.

The federal data utilized percentages for outcome measurement. In Table 2.1, Outcome 1.1, Delaware (DE) achieved an outcome measurement of 3.0%, which is 4.7% better than the median of 7.7%, and Michigan (MI) achieved a measurement of 7.0%, which is 0.7% better than the median. Relative to the median, Delaware performed significantly better and Michigan performed slightly better, so Delaware's "positive" was not quite equivalent to Michigan's "positive."

As Table 2.1 reflects, the states of Michigan and Delaware performed well above the median for six or seven outcomes and thus were classified as stronger states.

Table 2.1 Performance Measurement 2003: Stronger States

Underlined number represents state success on that outcome/suboutcome.

Outcome*	Median (%)	DE (%)	DE as it relates to national median (%)	MI (%)	MI as it relates to national median (%)
1.1 Reduce recurrence of child abuse and/or neglect	7.7	<u>3.0</u>	+4.7 Positive	<u>7.0</u>	+0.7 Positive
2.1 Reduce incidence of child abuse and/or neglect in foster care	0.40	<u>0.14</u>	+0.26 Positive	<u>0.38</u>	+0.02 Positive
Increase permanency for children in foster care: 3.1 Exits of children from foster care	86.7	<u>89.0</u>	+2.3	<u>87.5</u>	+0.8
3.2 Exits of children with a diagnosed disability	78.2	73.8	−4.4	<u>80.6</u>	+2.4

(Continued)

Table 2.1 (Continued)

Outcome*	Median (%)	DE (%)	DE as it relates to national median (%)	MI (%)	MI as it relates to national median (%)
3.3 Exits of children older than age 12 at entry into foster care	72.2	<u>83.9</u>	+11.7	66.1	–6.1
3.4 Exits to emancipation for children age 12 or younger at entry	29.6	<u>16.4</u>	+13.2 Positive[1]	<u>28.6</u>	+1 Positive[1]
Reduce time to reunification without increasing reentry: 4.1 Time to reunification	72.1	<u>92.3</u>	+20.2	40.6	–31.5
4.2 Children reentering foster care	9.8	23.5	–13.7 Positive[1,2]	<u>3.1</u>	+6.7 Negative[1,2]
5.1 Reduce time in foster care to adoption	22.9	<u>32.4</u>	+9.5 Positive	<u>27.3</u>	+4.4 Positive
6.1 Increase placement stability: In care less than 12 months with no more than two placements	84.0	<u>97.7</u>	+13.7 Positive	<u>84.5</u>	+0.5 Positive
7.1 Reduce placements of young children in group homes or institutions	8.3	<u>6.1</u>	+2.2 Positive	<u>2.4</u>	+5.9 Positive
Summary of state performance compared to national median, assuming all outcomes are equivalent			Seven positives on seven outcomes		Six positives on seven outcomes

U.S. Department of Health and Human Services, Administration for Children and Families, Administration on Children, Youth and Families, Children's Bureau, "Child Welfare Outcomes 2003: Annual Report. Safety, Permanency, Well-Being," http://www.acf.hhs.gov/programs/cb/pubs/cwo03/cwo03.pdf.

Note: This table reflects the author's original model for finding top and bottom performing states based on raw data from the federal report.
* See appendix for full wording of outcomes.
[1] This is the total average positive/negative across all suboutcomes for this outcome.
[2] When there is one + and one –, then the percentage becomes a weighting factor.

Data Collection Approach 13

Table 2.1 shows that Delaware and Michigan are both considered strong case states because they each performed well above the median.[14] I selected these as stronger states because Delaware achieved a perfect score (seven out of seven outcomes above the median) and Michigan achieved a near perfect score (six out of seven outcomes above the median).

Two weaker states were also selected using the same approach. Table 2.2 reflects that New York (NY) and Rhode Island (RI) performed well below the median on all but one performance measure.

Table 2.2 Performance Measurement 2003: Weaker States

Underlined number represents state success on that outcome/suboutcome.

Outcome*	Median (%)	NY (%)	NY as it relates to national median	RI (%)	RI as it relates to national median
1.1 Reduce recurrence of child abuse and/or neglect	7.7	14.3	−6.6 Negative	11.1	−3.4 Negative
2.1 Reduce incidence of child abuse and/or neglect in foster care	0.40	.65	−0.25 Negative	1.52	−1.12 Negative
Increase permanency for children in foster care: 3.1 Exits of children from foster care	86.7	84	−2.7	83.1	−3.6
3.2 Exits of children with a diagnosed disability	78.2	No data	No data	78.1	−0.1
3.3 Exits of children older than age 12 at entry into foster care	72.2	69.7	−2.5	70.0	−2.2
3.4 Exits to emancipation for children age 12 or younger at entry	29.6	39.6	−10 Negative[1]	20.0	+9.6 Negative[1]

(Continued)

Table 2.2 (Continued)

Outcome*	Median (%)	NY (%)	NY as it relates to national median	RI (%)	RI as it relates to national median
Reduce time to reunification without increasing reentry: 4.1 Time to reunification	72.1	52.1	–20	68.3	–3.8
4.2 Children reentering foster care	9.8	10.7	–0.9 Negative[1]	20.3	–10.5 Negative[1]
5.1 Reduce time in foster care to adoption	22.9	5.1	–17.8 Negative	50.4	+27.5 Positive
6.1 Increase placement stability: In care less than 12 months with no more than two placements	84.0	91.3	+7.3 Positive	71.1	–12.9 Negative
7.1 Reduce placements of young children in group homes or institutions	8.3	8.8	–0.5 Negative	19.4	–11.1 Negative
Summary of state performance compared to national median, assuming all outcomes are equivalent			One positive on seven outcomes		One positive on seven outcomes

U.S. Department of Health and Human Services, Administration for Children and Families, Administration on Children, Youth, and Families, Children's Bureau, "Child Welfare Outcomes 2003: Annual Report. Safety, Permanency, Well-Being," http://www.acf.hhs.gov/programs/cb/pubs/cwo03/cwo03.pdf.

Note: This table reflects the author's original model for finding top and bottom performing states based on raw data from the federal report.

* See appendix for full wording of outcomes.

[1] This is the total average positive/negative across all suboutcomes for this outcome.

Table 2.2 shows that New York and Rhode Island are both considered weak states because nearly every outcome ranked near the bottom of state performance.[15] I selected both of these states because they achieved very weak scores (only one out of seven positive outcomes above the median).

The "Child Welfare Outcomes 2003: Annual Report" also offered figures of each outcome by state, in order to provide context on a state's performance. For these figures, I have inserted references to Delaware, Michigan, New York, and Rhode Island, as well as a median, and have underlined stronger state performance. Most states were represented on each figure. The median is represented by the 2003 median stated in the HHS executive summary of this report.[16] Although the aforementioned research included performance measures on Outcome 3.2 and Outcome 3.3, HHS did not provide figures for Outcome 3.2 and Outcome 3.3. However, these HHS figures (Figure 2.1, Figure 2.2, Figure 2.3, Figure 2.4, Figure 2.5, Figure 2.6, Figure 2.7, Figure 2.8, and Figure 2.9) still offer an overview of strong and weak states compared with other states.

These figures, for which HHS figures are available, show that on the majority of outcomes, Delaware and Michigan exhibit stronger performance and New York and Rhode Island exhibit weaker performance.

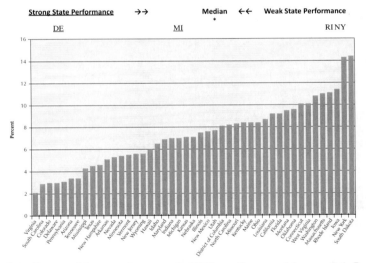

Figure 2.1 Range of State performance in 2003 on Outcome Measure 1.1: Percent of children experiencing a maltreatment recurrence within a 6-month period (N = 45)

U.S. Department of Health and Human Services, Administration for Children and Families, Administration on Children, Youth and Families, Children's Bureau, "Child Welfare Outcomes 2003: Annual Report. Safety, Permanency, Well-Being," Figure II-1 in original, http://www.acf.hhs.gov/programs/cb/pubs/cwo03/cwo03.pdf.

Note: Figure 2.1 is the actual figure distributed in the HHS report. I inserted notations regarding median, strong/weak performance, and case states. Strong state performance is underlined. Utah represents 7.7% and is equal to the median.

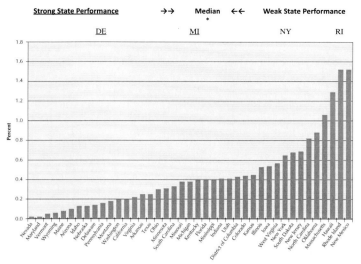

Figure 2.2 Range of State performance in 2003 on Outcome Measure 2.1: Percent of children in foster care who were victims of maltreatment by a foster parent or facility staff member (N = 41)

U.S. Department of Health and Human Services, Administration for Children and Families, Administration on Children, Youth and Families, Children's Bureau, "Child Welfare Outcomes 2003: Annual Report. Safety, Permanency, Well-Being," Figure II-2 in original, http://www.acf.hhs.gov/programs/cb/pubs/cwo03/cwo03.pdf.

Note: Figure 2.2 is the actual figure distributed in the HHS report. I inserted notations regarding median, strong/weak performance, and case states. Strong state performance is underlined. Florida represents 0.40% and is equal to the median.

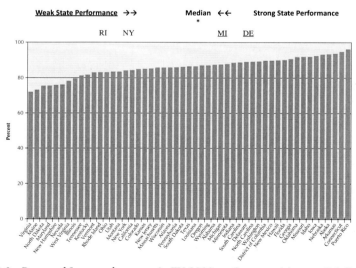

Figure 2.3 Range of State performance in FY 2003 on Outcome Measure 3.1: Percent of children exiting foster care who were discharged to a permanent home (N = 51)

U.S. Department of Health and Human Services, Administration for Children and Families, Administration on Children, Youth and Families, Children's Bureau, "Child Welfare Outcomes 2003: Annual Report. Safety, Permanency, Well-Being," Figure III-1 in original, http://www.acf.hhs.gov/programs/cb/pubs/cwo03/cwo03.pdf.

Note: Figure 2.3 is the actual figure distributed in the HHS report. I inserted notations regarding median, strong/weak performance, and case states. Strong state performance is underlined. Louisiana represents 86.5% and is the closest state to the median of 86.7%.

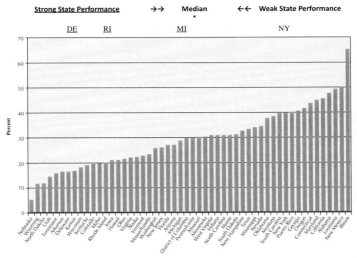

Figure 2.4 Range of State performance in FY 2003 on Outcome Measure 3.4: Percent of children emancipated from foster care who were age 12 or younger when they entered foster care (N = 52)

U.S. Department of Health and Human Services, Administration for Children and Families, Administration on Children, Youth and Families, Children's Bureau, "Child Welfare Outcomes 2003: Annual Report. Safety, Permanency, Well-Being," Figure III-2 in original, http://www.acf.hhs.gov/programs/cb/pubs/cwo03/cwo03.pdf.

Note: Figure 2.4 is the actual figure distributed in the HHS report. I inserted notations regarding median, strong/weak performance, and case states. Strong state performance is underlined. Pennsylvania represents 29.6% and is equal to the median.

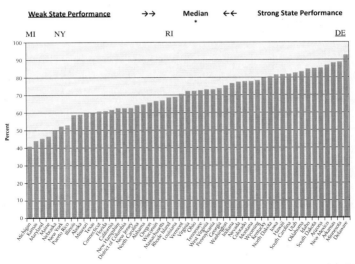

Figure 2.5 Range of State performance in FY 2003 on Outcome Measure 4.1: Percent of reunifications that occurred within 12 months of the child's entry into foster care (N = 51)

U.S. Department of Health and Human Services, Administration for Children and Families, Administration on Children, Youth and Families, Children's Bureau, "Child Welfare Outcomes 2003: Annual Report. Safety, Permanency, Well-Being," Figure III-3 in original, http://www.acf.hhs.gov/programs/cb/pubs/cwo03/cwo03.pdf.

Note: Figure 2.5 is the actual figure distributed in the HHS report. I inserted notations regarding median, strong/weak performance, and case states. Strong state performance is underlined. Ohio represents 72.1% and is equal to the median.

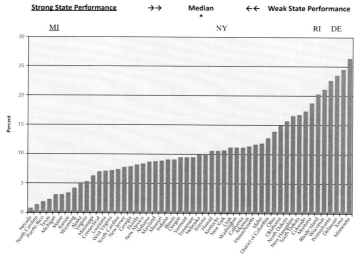

Figure 2.6 Range of State performance in FY 2003 on outcome measure 4.2: Percent of children entering foster care who were re-entering within 12 months of a prior foster care episode (N = 52).

U.S. Department of Health and Human Services, Administration for Children and Families, Administration on Children, Youth and Families, Children's Bureau, "Child Welfare Outcomes 2003: Annual Report. Safety, Permanency, Well-Being," Figure III-4 in original, http://www.acf.hhs.gov/programs/cb/pubs/cwo03/cwo03.pdf.

Note: Figure 2.6 is the actual figure distributed in the HHS report. I inserted notations regarding median, strong/weak performance, and case states. Strong state performance is underlined. Nebraska represents 10% and is the closest state to the median of 9.8%.

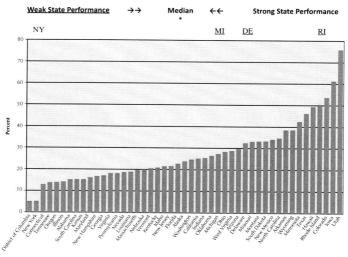

Figure 2.7 Range of State performance in FY 2003 on Outcome Measure 5.1

U.S. Department of Health and Human Services, Administration for Children and Families, Administration on Children, Youth and Families, Children's Bureau, "Child Welfare Outcomes 2003: Annual Report. Safety, Permanency, Well-Being," Figure III-6 in original, http://www.acf.hhs.gov/programs/cb/pubs/cwo03/cwo03.pdf.

Note: Figure 2.7 is the actual figure distributed in the HHS report. I inserted notations regarding median, strong/weak performance, and case states. Strong state performance is underlined. Florida represents 22.7% and is the closest state to the median of 22.9%.

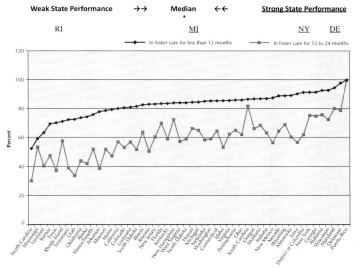

Figure 2.8 Range of State performance in FY 2003 on Outcome Measure 6.1: Range in percent of children in foster care for less than 12 months and for 12 to 24 months who had no more than 2 placement settings (N = 52)

U.S. Department of Health and Human Services, Administration for Children and Families, Administration on Children, Youth and Families, Children's Bureau, "Child Welfare Outcomes 2003: Annual Report. Safety, Permanency, Well-Being," Figure IV-1 in original, http://www.acf.hhs.gov/programs/cb/pubs/cwo03/cwo03.pdf.

Note: Figure 2.8 is the actual figure distributed in the HHS report. The data utilized for this research design is identified by the upper line representing "in foster care for less than 12 months with no more than two placements." I inserted notations regarding median, strong/weak performance, and case states. Strong state performance is underlined. North Dakota represents 84% and is equal to the median.

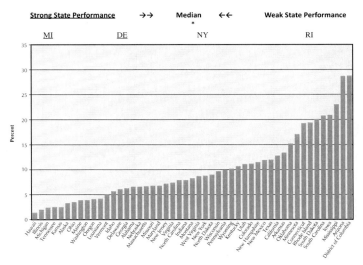

Figure 2.9 Range of State performance on outcome measure 7.1: Percent of children 12 and younger entering foster care in FY 2003 who were placed in a group home or institution (N = 49).

U.S. Department of Health and Human Services, Administration for Children and Families, Administration on Children, Youth and Families, Children's Bureau, "Child Welfare Outcomes 2003: Annual Report. Safety, Permanency, Well-Being," Figure IV-2 in original, http://www.acf.hhs.gov/programs/cb/pubs/cwo03/cwo03.pdf.

Note: Figure 2.9 is the actual figure distributed in the HHS report. I inserted notations regarding median, strong/weak performance, and case states. Strong state performance is underlined. Montana represents 8.3% and is equal to the median.

20   *Politics of Foster Care Administration*

In sum, these figures show that on the majority of outcomes for which figures are available, Delaware and Michigan exhibited stronger performance and New York and Rhode Island exhibited weaker performance.

Quantitative Data: Performance Improvement Assessment

This section surveys the four case states longitudinally by comparing the federal data from 2000 with that from 2003. In Tables 2.3 and 2.4, I classified an outcome as "increase" or "decrease" depending upon whether the state had an increase or decrease in performance from 2000 to 2003 on that particular outcome. When suboutcomes were included, they were averaged to arrive at one increase or decrease for the overall outcome. A state with significant improvement would have seven increases across seven outcomes.

The median performance improvement for states in 2000 compared to 2003 is also included to serve as a benchmark to the case states in Tables 2.3[17] and 2.4.

The federal data utilized percentages for outcome measurement. In Table 2.3, Outcome 2.1, Delaware's performance improvement was –27% and Michigan's performance improvement was –15%. Because the median for Outcome 2.1 was a 15% increase in performance, both Delaware and Michigan underperformed significantly in relation to this one outcome.

Table 2.3 shows that the median performance improvement among states when comparing 2003 to 2000 was 38% across all outcomes. Table 2.3 reflects that Delaware and Michigan exhibited no improvement in performance. Delaware improved its performance in two out of seven categories and Michigan in three out of seven. Overall, Delaware had a score of –53%, signifying a lack of improvement that is below the median, and Michigan had a score of –69%, signifying a lack of improvement that is below the median.

Delaware fared poorly when change in performance was measured between 2000 and 2003. Out of seven outcomes, Delaware showed increases or program improvements in only two areas. However, a quick perusal of the 2002 data suggests that 2002 was a stronger year for Delaware, and the state improved its performance overall between 2000 and 2002. Yet, when 2000 is compared to 2003, Delaware's data reflects a decline. Because Delaware is a small state and has a foster care caseload of only 800 children, few cases can significantly affect the outcome percentages.

Furthermore, obtaining an increase in significant improvement from 2000 to 2003 would be harder to obtain for a top performer in 2000, such as Delaware, than for a weaker performing state in 2000. Even with a decrease in performance, however, Delaware was still a top performer in 2003. Because of these statistics, Delaware is considered a major performer (Table 2.1), but not an improver (Table 2.3). Michigan is also considered a major performer (Table 2.1) but not an improver (Table 2.3).

Table 2.3 Performance Improvement 2000 to 2003: Stronger States

Underlined number represents state success on that outcome/suboutcome.

Outcome*	Median (%) change in performance from 2000 to 2003[1]	DE (%) change in performance from 2000 to 2003[2]	DE	MI (%) change in performance from 2000 to 2003[2]	MI
1.1 Reduce recurrence of child abuse and/or neglect	+3	No change	No change	–112	Decrease
2.1 Reduce incidence of child abuse and/ or neglect in foster care	+15	–27[6]	Decrease	–15	Decrease
Increase permanency for children in foster care: 3.1 Exits of children from foster care	+1	–3		+10	
3.2 Exits of children with a diagnosed disability	–2	–13		No data	
3.3 Exits of children older than age 12 at entry into foster care	–1	–2		+18	
3.4 Exits to emancipation for children age 12 or younger at entry	–17	–51	Decrease[3]	–20	Increase[3]
Reduce time to reunification without increasing reentry: 4.1 Time to reunification	+1	+10		–23	
4.2 Children reentering foster care	+8	–42	Decrease[3,4]	+38	Increase[3,4]

(*Continued*)

22 *Politics of Foster Care Administration*

Table 2.3 (Continued)

Outcome*	Median (%) change in performance from 2000 to 2003[1]	DE (%) change in performance from 2000 to 2003[2]	DE	MI (%) change in performance from 2000 to 2003[2]	MI
5.1 Reduce time in foster care to adoption	+16	<u>+65</u>	Increase	−22	Decrease
6.1 Increase placement stability: In care less than 12 months with no more than two placements	No change[5]	No change[5]	No change	−2	Decrease
7.1 Reduce placements of young children in group homes or institutions	+14	<u>+10</u>	Increase	<u>+59</u>	Increase
Summary of state performance change, assuming all outcomes are Equal	+38 Improvement median	−53 Improvement	Two increase	−69 Improvement	Three increase

U.S. Department of Health and Human Services, Administration for Children and Families, Administration on Children, Youth and Families, Children's Bureau, "Child Welfare Outcomes 2003: Annual Report. Safety, Permanency, Well-Being," http://www.acf.hhs.gov/programs/cb/pubs/cwo03/cwo03.pdf.

Note: This table reflects the author's original model for finding top and bottom performing states based on raw data from the federal report. Numbers have been rounded.
* See appendix for full wording of outcomes.
[1] The Child Welfare Outcomes 2003 Report noted the following on pg ii "Change in performance across years was assessed by calculating the percent change. This is calculated by subtracting "old" data from "new" data, dividing by "old" data and multiplying by 100."
[2] The author utlized the change in performance calculation method of original source. The author utilized negative values to reflect a decrease in improvement and a positive value to reflect an increase in improvement.
[3] This is the total average increase/decrease across all suboutcomes for this outcome.
[4] When there is one + and one −, then the percentage becomes a weighting factor.
[5] Less than .5%.
[6] No data available for 2000, so year 2001 data was utilized.

Table 2.4[18] offers data on performance improvement for the weaker states of New York and Rhode Island.

Table 2.4 shows that the median performance improvement among states when comparing 2003 to 2000 was 38% across all outcomes. Table 2.4 reflects that New York slightly improved its performance, but not above the

Table 2.4 Performance Improvement 2000 to 2003: Weaker States
Underlined number represents state success on that outcome/suboutcome.

Outcome*	Median (%) change in performance from 2000 to 2003[1]	NY (%) change in performance from 2000 to 2003[2]	NY	RI (%) change in performance from 2000 to 2003[2]	RI
1.1 Reduce recurrence of child abuse and/or neglect	+3	−11	Decrease	+10	Increase
2.1 Reduce incidence of child abuse and/or neglect in foster care	+15	+16	Increase	+8	Increase
Increase permanency for children in foster care: 3.1 Exits of children from foster care	+1	No change[3]		+11	
3.2 Exits of children with a diagnosed disability	−2	No data		+13	
3.3 Exits of children older than age 12 at entry into foster care	−1	+4		+18	
3.4 Exits to emancipation for children age 12 or younger at entry	−17	+14	Increase[4]	−17	Increase[4]
Reduce time to reunification without increasing reentry: 4.1 Time to reunification	+1	+5		+8	
4.2 Children reentering foster care	+8	−15	Decrease[4]	+2	Increase[4]

(*Continued*)

Table 2.4   (Continued)

Outcome*	Median (%) change in performance from 2000 to 2003[1]	NY (%) change in performance from 2000 to 2003[2]	NY	RI (%) change in performance from 2000 to 2003[2]	RI
5.1 Reduce time in foster care to adoption	+16	+11	Increase	+34	Increase
6.1 Increase placement stability: In care less than 12 months w/ no more than two placements	No change[5]	+1	Increase	−2	Decrease
7.1 Reduce placements of young children in group homes or institutions	+14	−13	Decrease	−14	Decrease
Summary of state performance change, assuming all outcomes are equal	+38 Improvement median	+12 Improvement	Four increase	+71 Improvement	Five increase

U.S. Department of Health and Human Services, Administration for Children and Families, Administration on Children, Youth and Families, Children's Bureau, "Child Welfare Outcomes 2003: Annual Report. Safety, Permanency, Well-Being," http://www.acf.hhs.gov/programs/cb/pubs/cwo03/cwo03.pdf.

Note: This table reflects the author's original model for finding top and bottom performing states based on raw data from the federal report. Numbers have been rounded.

* See appendix for full wording of outcomes.

[1] The Child Welfare Outcomes 2003 Report noted the following on pg ii "Change in performance across years was assessed by calculating the percent change. This is calculated by subtracting "old" data from "new" data, dividing by "old" data and multiplying by 100."

[2] The author utilized the change in performance calculation method of original source. The author utilized negative values to reflect a decrease in improvement and a positive value to reflect an increase in improvement.

[3] No change determined when less than 0.5.

[4] This is the total average increase/decrease across all suboutcomes for this outcome.

[5] Less than .5%.

Data Collection Approach 25

median, while Rhode Island significantly improved its performance, beating the median. New York increased its performance in four out of seven areas and Rhode Island improved its performance in five out of seven areas. New York's performance increased by only 12%, which places it below the median level of improvement; however, Rhode Island improved its performance by 71%, placing it above the median. Despite relative gains on its performance improvement from 2000 to 2003, Rhode Island earned some of the lowest scores of all the states in 2003. In other words, Rhode Island was such a weak performer that even with this significant improvement, the state still rested near the bottom of all fifty states in 2003.

Thus, based on performance indicators, New York is considered a weak performer (Table 2.2) and weak improver (Table 2.4). Rhode Island is considered a weak performer (Table 2.2) and major improver (Table 2.4).

To summarize the overall quantitative case state data from Tables 2.1 through 2.4:

Weak States

NY performance weak (+1) 2003, weak increase in improvement from 2000 to 2003 (+12%)
RI performance weak (+1) 2003, major increase in improvement from 2000 to 2003 (+71%)

Strong States

MI performance strong (+6) 2003, major decrease in improvement from 2000 to 2003 (–69%)
DE performance strong (+7) 2003, major decrease in improvement from 2000 to 2003

Quantitative Data: State Size

The previous sections identified best-performing and worst-performing states in the area of foster care. In order to demonstrate that state size and caseload size do not ultimately determine success in foster care administration, this section shows that these four case states represent a variety of state and caseload sizes.

The four case states represent one large population state from the best-performing group (Michigan), one small population state from the best-performing group (Delaware), one large population state from the worst-performing group (New York), and one small population state from the worst-performing group (Rhode Island).

Both Michigan and New York qualify as large states due to their large populations and large foster care caseloads. Ranked only behind California, New York had the second largest foster care population. Michigan had the

26   Politics of Foster Care Administration

seventh largest foster care population. In FY 2003, Michigan had 21,376 foster care children, representing 4.1% of the total foster care population, and New York had 37,067 foster care children, representing 7.1% of the total foster care population.[19]

Both Delaware and Rhode Island are considered small states due to their small populations and small foster care caseloads. In regard to foster care caseloads, Rhode Island was ranked 41st of the 50 states and Delaware ranked 50th. In FY 2003, Delaware had 814 foster care children, representing 0.2% of the total foster care population, and Rhode Island had 2,334 foster care children, representing 0.4% of the total foster care population.[20] Table 2.5 provides state population data, foster care caseload data, and foster care caseload per capita data.[21]

Table 2.5 shows that Delaware has a much lower per capita rate of foster care caseloads than any of the other three states. Delaware and Michigan are both stronger states, but with significantly different per capita rates. This suggests that success in foster care administration is unrelated to the size of the overall foster care caseload or foster care caseload per capita. A sampling of non-case states shows this pattern as well, as shown in Table 2.6. For 2003, Utah (UT), Colorado (CO), and Texas (TX) were also among the group of top performing states based on the same federal data in the "Child Welfare Outcomes 2003: Annual Report," yet they have vastly different foster care caseload sizes and per capita rates. In other words, Table 2.6 demonstrates that the per capita rates have little to do with predicting foster care administration success.

Because foster care caseload size and foster care cases per capita are not related to a state's success with foster care administration, this case research sets out to understand what *is* related to a successful foster care system in a given state. These four case states were intentionally selected to provide enough variance for this study to explore what factors contribute to a state's success with foster care administration.

Table 2.5   2003 State Foster Care Caseload per Capita: NY, RI, MI, DE

	Population Estimate[1]	Foster Care Caseload	Per Capita[2]
	2003	FY 2003	(per 100,000 people)
NY	18,600,527	37,067	199
RI	1,037,196	2,334	225
MI	9,825,840	21,376	218
DE	792,494	814	103

[1] U.S. Census Bureau, "2003 American Community Survey," http://www.census.gov.
[2] Estimate arrived at by dividing the foster care caseload by the population estimate and multiplying by 100,000.

Data Collection Approach 27

Table 2.6 2003 State Foster Care Caseload per Capita: UT, CO, TX

	Population Estimate[1]	Foster Care Caseload	Per Capita[2]
	2003	FY 2003	(per 100,000 people)
UT	2,309,555	2,033	88
CO	4,447,892	8,754	197
TX	21,547,821	22,191	103

[1] United States Census Bureau, "2003 American Community Survey," http://www.census.gov.
[2] Estimate arrived at by dividing the foster care caseload by the population estimate and multiplying by 100,000.

Qualitative Data: State Background

This section offers state background data that was available *prior to* field research so as to provide additional evidence for the selection of these four states as cases. However, in order to provide context, state administrative type as determined during field research was also included.

Michigan: Strong State

In Michigan, foster care is a state-run system. The state licenses the foster care homes and works with private agencies to place foster children throughout the state. In 2004, Michigan determined that its staff resources on foster care were not adequate. The state subsequently developed a dedicated unit that was assigned to monitor "not only the Program Improvement Plan and Child and Family Services Review process"[22] but also to operate as "a child welfare quality assurance unit within the Agency."[23]

Michigan's adoption process for foster children also improved. The number of children in the public foster care system waiting to be adopted in Michigan dropped from a high of 8,494 in FY 1999 to 6,164 by FY 2006.[24] Federal data for Michigan also showed that actual adoptions of children with public child welfare agency involvement increased from 1,717 in FY 1995 to 2,801 in FY 2004.[25]

The state also sought to improve foster care programs generally, and the well-being of foster care children more specifically. In 2005 alone, Michigan enacted two measures regarding smoking among foster children and their foster parents, three measures related to foster care administrative efficiency and effectiveness, one measure on disproportionate representation of minorities in child welfare, and created a task force to review services for youth.[26]

Michigan has received recognition for its commitment to improving foster care. The state was a 2003 finalist for the Harvard University

28   *Politics of Foster Care Administration*

Innovations in American Government Awards for creating a structured decision-making case management system that ties program outputs to child welfare outcomes.[27]

Delaware: Strong State

Foster care is a state-run system in Delaware, and the state licenses the homes. The state arranges regions by clusters so that foster care children have an extended foster family through the clusters in Delaware. Although Delaware holds the title as the state with the smallest foster care caseload, the state has still launched several foster care reform efforts. In 2001, the Delaware Cabinet Secretary of Department Services for Children, Youth, and Their Families stated, "We discovered very quickly that we have 21st century kids stuck in a 1970s foster care system."[28] In response, Delaware launched the Foster Care Task Force, commissioned by Governor Ruth Ann Minner in 2001, to follow up on a previous 1996 task force.[29] Along with approximately half a million dollars in additional funding, the governor endorsed 10 recommendations, including implementing a system for the growing group of hard-to-place foster care youth and strategies to increase foster care family recruitment.

Although the number of children on Delaware's adoption waiting list fluctuated, the number of foster children who were adopted increased. Between FY 1999/2000 and FY 2003, the number of children in the Delaware public foster care system waiting to be adopted dropped from a high range of 270–330 to 144; the number rose again between FY 2003 and 2006 to 302.[30] Federal data for Delaware also showed that actual adoptions of children with public child welfare agency involvement increased from 40 in FY 1995 to 70 in FY 2004, after peaking at 130 in FY 2002.[31]

Rhode Island: Weak State

Since 1997, Rhode Island has used a four region system. The system is centralized and the Rhode Island Department of Children, Youth, and Families creates policy and licenses foster care. Like Delaware, Rhode Island has a small foster care caseload. Between FY 1999 and FY 2006, Rhode Island had approximately 300 to 400 children in the public foster care system each year that were waiting to be adopted.[32] The number of foster children who were adopted did not improve. Federal data showed that in Rhode Island, actual adoptions of children with public child welfare agency involvement have fluctuated between 216 and 341 during the period from FY 1995 to FY 2004, with no consistent trend.[33]

There is an abundance of qualitative information that suggests that Rhode Island struggles with foster care. The state's agency-related website[34] devoted significantly less information to Rhode Island's foster care progress or commitment to improvement than did the foster care websites of Delaware and Michigan.

In 2004, two Rhode Island foster care parents who were undergoing licensing were charged with killing a 3-year-old toddler in their care, and one of the foster care parents was sentenced to life in prison.[35] In June 2007, Children's Rights filed a lawsuit against the Rhode Island Department of Children referring to this toddler and examples of other children who were being beaten or sexually abused.[36] Although Children's Rights also filed lawsuits against the state of Michigan and against New York City for their poor foster care practices,[37] Rhode Island was cited as having a long-term problem with the abuse of foster children. The complaint against the state notes that for "five of the six years from 2000 to 2005, Rhode Island had the highest rate of documented abuse or neglect of foster care children among all states that reported data."[38] Children's Rights considers Rhode Island to be the worst state for foster care children for the years 2000 to 2005.[39]

New York: Weak State

Like Rhode Island, New York did not devote much attention to performance improvement, state success, or policy change on its agency-based website.[40] New York foster care is state administered and county implemented. New York State is responsible for setting overall policy, foster care provider rates, and federal/state spending decisions. New York State incorporates a county-run system, with New York City as the largest segment. New York City manages its own foster care administration and handles approximately two-thirds of the foster care caseload for the state. New York City is divided into five boroughs and 59 service districts for foster care and other community services.

New York was the second-largest foster care state in FY 2003,[41] and the number of children waiting to be adopted in its public foster care system showed a consistent downward trend from a high of 16,138 in FY 1999 to 8,040 by FY 2006.[42] However, federal data reflect that in New York actual adoptions of children with public child welfare agency involvement hovered between 4,579 in FY 1995 and 4,258 in FY 2004.[43]

Between 2004 and 2006, the *New York Times* presented a bleak picture of the state's foster care system, including the heavy foster care caseload area of New York City. According to the *Times*, New York City had failed again in 2004 to fulfill its promise to get rid of the lowest-ranking private foster care agencies on its annual evaluations of child safety and child placement.[44] NYC had left 1,300 children in the care of problem agencies.

In 2005, New York City cancelled eight contracts with a long-established foster care agency after investigators found that it had systematically falsified case records for 50 case files.[45] In 2006, a 10-year employee of New York City's Administration for Children's Services was suspended after being charged with sexually abusing a teenager,[46] and the executive director of one of the city's midsize foster care agencies resigned after an audit found she had spent tens of thousands of dollars at luxury retailers.[47]

Amid this maelstrom, the New York legislature was very active on the issue of foster care in 2005; in fact, the state produced more foster care

30   Politics of Foster Care Administration

legislation than any other case state that year. These laws covered a wide variety of matters related to foster care, including post-adoption issues, social worker loan forgiveness, the courts, kinship care, early intervention, residential treatment, and transition from foster care.[48] This data suggests that New York might have used legislation as a control mechanism for dealing with foster care issues rather using than some of the techniques presented as variables in the next section.

VARIABLE SELECTION

Because foster care caseload size and foster care cases per capita are not related to a state's success with foster care administration (see the previous section "Quantitative Data: State Size"), this case research sets out to understand what is related to a successful foster care system in a given state. In this section, I identify and test four variables that I have hypothesized to be significantly related to the success of foster care administration. In particular, the hypothesis posed is that a stronger case state should have higher levels of a combination of these variables, and this, in turn, would help to explain why the state performed better on the federal outcome measures. Figure 2.10 depicts these four variables: community partners, mentors, leadership from public managers, and federal government relationships.

Following Richard Fenno's "soak and poke" mandate, a flexible research design was created to draw out a deeper understanding of social science variables, rather than using fixed controls that would not allow for variance among interview results.[49] One way to permit flexibility is to allow the strength of a variable to be counted by multiple means. For instance, strong community partners can mean either the state partners with multiple

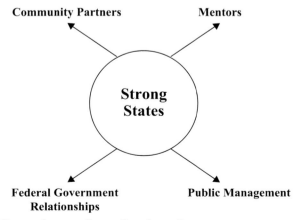

Figure 2.10   Factors Stronger Foster Care States Possess

Data Collection Approach 31

community organizations with weaker relationships to all, or the state partners with only one or two community organizations in a deeper relationship. Likewise, strong mentors can mean either the state partners with multiple mentors with weaker relationships to all, or the state partners with only one or two mentors in a deeper relationship. This method recognizes that a variable is not "one size fits all," but rather that the variable may appear in a plethora of forms in each case.

Variables in this study were measured by incorporating some familiar political science terms. For example, members of Congress are designated by some political scientists as either "show horses," who prioritize publicity at the expense of legislative work, or "workhorses," who prioritize legislative tasks above publicity.[50] Applying this classification to measure community partnerships, I have substituted the word "transactional" for "show horse" to suggest that only minimal paperwork/basic transactions among partners are emphasized as opposed to publicity. Each variable will be classified as a strong partnership (workhorse) or weak partnership (transactional) for each of the case states.

In the following sections, each variable is outlined and some case data is presented that was available *prior to* field research so as to provide additional evidence for the selection of these four variables.

Community Partnerships

This case research will measure whether the role of community partnerships is a variable that leads to higher levels of success in foster care administration. The hypothesis is that a state would have better foster care outcomes when it allows a community partner to identify and help solve foster care problems in the state, as well as when it allows a community partner to take an active role in creating stronger foster care programs and policies. The case will identify any community organizations that have moved into a community partnership with the state.

The hypothesis is that the stronger states will have stronger (defined as more or deeper) community partnerships. *Community partnerships are defined here as state and/or local[51] foster care agency relationships with local nonprofits, faith-based organizations, and community organizations.* The strong presence of community partnerships is reflected by a workhorse relationship in which the state has either a large network of community partners or a rigorous relationship with one community partner. Workhorse relationships are deeper relationships in which community partners discuss ideas with the state, and the state then takes action.

A workhorse relationship might include government and community organizations copromoting a conference with mutual organizational roles, or deciding together to more aggressively pursue homes for older female teens. This variable will be defined as having a stronger presence when community partnerships have significantly shifted the direction of the

32   *Politics of Foster Care Administration*

state's decision-making path regarding the provision of foster care in some area. Basic administrative paperwork or meetings between a community partner and the state do not qualify as a stronger presence of this variable.

As the hypothesis suggests, both Delaware and Michigan have prioritized strong community partnerships when administering foster care. Delaware created and funded a system that would generate community support as an addendum to government services. This system organized foster homes into geographical clusters so that the disruption to children's lives could be minimized, foster homes could be located near birth families, the foster families could become natural support groups, and each cluster could take responsibility for all families within its boundaries.[52] Michigan noted in the early 2000s that building collaboration and community partnerships is an approach that "Michigan human service agencies and their partners have found successful in recent years."[53]

On the other hand, a transactional relationship, signified as a weaker presence of the community partnership variable, occurs when community partners primarily focus on required administrative items with the state, as opposed to participating in strategic decision making. An example might be a community partner roundtable, where suggestions for improvement ultimately fall on deaf ears in the state.

Mentors

This case research will measure whether the role of mentors is a variable that leads to higher levels of success in foster care administration. The hypothesis is that the stronger states will have stronger (defined as more or deeper) mentors who offer strategic advice or training on the issue of foster care. *Mentors are defined here as foundations, issue-expert national nonprofit organizations, or think tanks that focus on foster care.* The strong presence of mentors is reflected by a workhorse relationship in which the state has either a large network of mentors or a rigorous relationship with one mentor organization. Workhorse relationships are deeper relationships in which mentors discuss ideas with the state, and the state then takes action.

This variable will be defined as having a stronger presence when the mentors have significantly shifted the direction of the state's decision-making path regarding the provision of foster care in some nonrequired area.

As the hypothesis suggests, both stronger states have sought to learn from mentors. The Annie Casey Foundation offered $1 million plus strategic assistance and resources to the state of Michigan.[54] The foundation implemented its Family to Family Initiative in Michigan in order to improve foster care programs.

State court and agency leaders from Delaware and Michigan[55] were among representatives from the 15 states that partnered with the Pew

Commission on Children in Foster Care to work on defining and establishing best practices in the courts.[56]

On the other hand, a transactional relationship, identified by a weaker presence of this variable, occurs when there is no recruitment of mentors or when the mentors' ideas are not readily accepted or do not lead to implementation.

Leadership from Public Managers

This case research will measure whether *leadership from public managers* is a variable that leads to higher levels of success in foster care administration. The hypothesis is that the stronger states will have more leadership from public managers.

Ample public administration literature supports the claim that leadership from public managers leads to increased levels of success. Examples of this literature include: Kaufman (1960);[57] Burns (1978);[58] Cohen et al. (2008);[59] DiIulio (1994);[60] Doig and Hargrove (1987);[61] O'Toole and Meier (2011);[62] and Moore (1995).[63]

Similar to previous social science studies, this research measures whether leadership from public managers helps to explain success in foster care. *A public manager is shown to evidence leadership when he or she is operating as a "principled agent" in the state or local government or agency responsible for the area of foster care.*

As a reaction to the principal agent rational choice theory, DiIulio coined the term "principled agent" to describe public employees who "do not shirk, subvert or steal on the job" even when consequences are lacking.[64] By also holding a range of positive characteristics as well, these principled agents "strive [work hard and go 'by the book'], support [put public and organizational goals ahead of private goals], and sacrifice [go 'above and beyond the call of duty'] on the job."[65] The public administration book *The Forest Ranger*[66] offers Gifford Pinchot as an example of a principled agent.

In the context of this study, a principled agent is a government employee (public manager) who goes above and beyond his or her public duty to cultivate successful foster care administration. Harvard Kennedy School professor Mark Moore argued that a successful manager "increase(s) the public value produced by public sector organizations in both the short and the long run."[67] A principled agent performs as a workhorse, rather than as a standard government employee who is focused on routine functions. The strong presence of this variable is reflected by a greater presence of principled agents working in foster care in the case state.

As the hypothesis suggests, both stronger states have demonstrated leadership by public managers in the area of foster care. Delaware's governor and its cabinet secretary of the Department of Services for Children, Youth and their Families recognized a strong need for improvement of the

34 Politics of Foster Care Administration

system and followed this recognition with immediate action, funding, and implementation. The task force created in January 2001 held eight meetings to develop foster care recommendations for Governor Minner. She subsequently approved *all* of them and provided funding for them in July 2001. Three months later, Delaware's foster care system was completely restructured into decentralized cluster support communities.[68] This is a striking example of fast-track implementation of public policy with strong government leadership.

Michigan's Structured Decision Making (SDM) was championed by the Family Independence Agency director, Douglas E. Howard.[69] In the state's 2004–2006 Program Improvement Plan, Logino Gonzales, Michigan's acting deputy for children's services, advocated "increased focus" on the quality provision of child welfare services. He emphasized "changing or moving (their) agency culture in a direction that is synonymous with the CFSR outcomes."[70] Furthermore, his plan was "to garner the commitment of other county directors to utilize these tools or to develop a set that will work well for their local office."[71] The Institute for Government Innovation at Harvard's Kennedy School of Government named Michigan's SDM model as one of their finalists in 2003. Harvard referred to the model as a "widely replicated case management program."[72]

Federal Government Relationships

This case research will assess whether the *federal government relationships* lead to higher levels of success in foster care administration. The hypothesis is that the stronger states will have deeper or better relationships with the federal government.

Federalism, as well as the federal government's increased use of third parties to deliver its services, has created a burgeoning literature on the increased entanglement of federal–state relationships. The following books outline the changing role of the federal government in regard to the states: Kettl (1987);[73] Light (1999);[74] Bane (2000);[75] and Meek and Thurmaier (2011).[76]

This research looks at the relationship between the federal government and the states and assesses the degree to which the federal government assumes more than a transactional role in delivery of foster care services. This research measures whether the greater presence of federal government relationships contributes to higher degrees of success in foster care administration. *Federal government relationships are defined here as: The availability of federal government resources (problem solving, strategic planning, training) to foster care agencies beyond the standard federal–state requirements.* For example, a more active relationship will be reflected in data documents, such as the attendance of extra conferences or additional conference calls beyond the minimal requirements for the federal government.

Data Collection Approach   35

This variable is shown to have a stronger presence when the federal government relationship *has significantly shifted the direction of the state's decision-making path regarding the provision of foster care in some nonrequired area.* A stronger presence of federal government relationships is measured by a workhorse relationship in which the state and federal governments work together on foster care issues in a more rigorous manner than is required of them. Interviews or documents should show a pattern of interaction between the federal government and the state that transcends the required form completion, grant processing, regulation monitoring, and data gathering and moves beyond them into a fruitful discussion of how to fix and transform foster care.

On the other hand, a transactional relationship, signified as a weaker presence of this variable, occurs when only required work between the federal government and the states is completed. In this case, the relationship between the state and the federal government would reflect the required minimalist relationship as opposed to a stronger, creative, and problem-solving relationship.

Some evidence suggests that the federal government may be involved with states on foster care issues beyond the minimal level of interaction that is required. The government agency Senior Corps, which is a division of the Corporation for National and Community Service, has partnered with all the states to improve foster care outcomes by providing 2,000 volunteers that have served 4,200 foster youth with 375,000 hours of donated time.[77] Senior Corps is serving children in foster care in all 50 states.[78] Case research will determine whether federal relationships such as these have strengthened the states' performance on foster care issues.

Furthermore, states also tend to have varying levels of involvement with key players in the federal government on community-serving and faith-based initiatives. I have surmised that the strength of these state–federal relationships can affect the states' success with foster care issues.

To recap, I have hypothesized that *Delaware and Michigan became stronger-performing states in the area of foster care by placing a priority on building community partners, integrating the advice of mentors, providing leadership from public managers, and cultivating relationships with the federal government.* These variables provide an agency-centered hypothesis for the successful administration of foster care programs. Figure 2.11 offers a sample visualization of a possible anticipated outcome, if this hypothesis holds. As this mock chart shows, Delaware and Michigan have a stronger presence of each of these four variables than either Rhode Island or New York.

An alternative political science hypothesis might be that a state's success with foster care administration is based on structural change rather than agency-centered change. For this to be true, there would need to be a relationship between the passage of legislation and program success or a change in government structure, whether federal to state, state to county, or the

36 Politics of Foster Care Administration

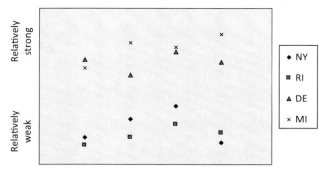

Figure 2.11 Variable Presence in States
Points show a sample pattern of one possible outcome based on four variables of partners, mentor, managers, and federal.

rearrangement of agency units (courts, HHS, etc.) within a government. Yet, this study encountered no evidence that agency realignment or legislation passage affected the overall level of foster care success that was identified either prior to or during field research.

For instance, legislation *does not* always equate to implementation, as Pressman and Wildavsky noted in *Implementation*.[79] If legislation is often not implemented at the authorized levels, then one cannot deduce that legislation automatically leads to program improvement. In the stronger states, there was a pattern of passed legislation and subsequent implementation being responsible for the states' success in foster care.

Additionally, there does not appear to be any strong evidence to support the notion that government structural change theory, championed by the American Political Development school of thought,[80] explains successful foster care administration. No realignment of agencies preceded improved outcomes for the stronger states.

RESEARCH METHODOLOGY

As previous sections of this chapter emphasized, the case states were selected based upon federal performance data, state population data, and preliminary qualitative research, whereas variables were drawn from public administration fundamentals.

This section will now explain the research methods that were employed in conducting the state case research. The primary method of data collection for the four case study states was qualitative interviews with key players (including elite key players), which were conducted primarily during field research. State and federal documents were obtained online and through field research.

Multiple Case Study Method

Political scientists generally utilize two primary methods to test theories: experimentation and observation.[81] Regarding the latter, the two main types of analysis are large-n (or statistical analysis) and case study analysis (one or multicase). This case state research was conducted via observational analysis of multiple cases.

According to political science methodologist Stephen Van Evera, case study analysis posits that "the analyst explores a small number of cases (as few as one) in detail, to see whether events unfold in the manner predicted and (if the subject involves human behavior) whether actors speak and act as the theory predicts."[82]

Case studies can be "strong tools for exploring American politics" that may be utilized for testing and creating theories.[83]

This observational case study analysis utilized field research and interviews, as well as policy and administrative documents.

Field Research and Interviews

Field research that employed a qualitative multiple case study methodology was this study's primary mechanism for exploring the conditions under which state foster care programs succeed. I traveled to each case state (Michigan, Delaware, Rhode Island, and New York) one or more times during the period from June 2007 to May 2008. I visited the state foster care agency and a few foster care programs in each state. Additionally, I met with local foster care and judicial agencies, as well as child and policy advocates. The purpose of these visits was to understand how these state foster care systems operated, to obtain interviews with influential individuals, and to collect foster care documents.

I conducted prearranged interviews with key players across multiple sectors that were knowledgeable about foster care administration. These key player interviewees included federal, state, and local government workers; managers in foster care agencies; and foster care issue experts. The majority of these interviews were elite interviews, such as the director of a state health and human services agency; a state cabinet secretary; a governor; an HHS federal regional director for foster care; and the executive director of a foster care agency.

The traditional model for qualitative interview-based social science research is non-elite key player interviews. In the area of foster care, case research is often built on interviews with foster care case workers, foster parents, and foster children. This study combines that traditional model (interviews with foster care case workers) along with the addition of elite key player interviews.

Because elite key player interviews are significantly harder to obtain and more time consuming, social scientists have relied on less of this type as a

38 Politics of Foster Care Administration

data source. In this study, key player elite interviews required significant preplanning, and typically more than half a dozen phone calls or e-mails were needed to set up one interview.

Interviews were designed to reflect a cross-sector approach because information was obtained across a number of interviews in different agencies or organizations. This approach eliminated sole-source data and bias and allowed for a more accurate understanding of realistic foster care administration.

I obtained over 55 interviews with key players that had some level of connection to foster care administration. This included a representation of more than 12 interviews per case state, as well as interviews that addressed the perspectives of the federal government, mentors, foundations, or community partners. Actual names and titles were utilized for every interviewee.

After I requested an interview with a potential candidate, the individual would voluntarily agree to be interviewed if he or she so desired. Interviewees were made aware that their interviews were being utilized for foster care research.[84] Most interviewees choose to have all or most of their comments on the record. When an interviewee requested that a comment be confidential, a notation indicating this was included in the associated footnote.

I did not personally inform any interviewees in advance regarding the weak/strong classification of a state, so as not to bias interviewees' responses in relation to my specific interview. With that being said, many interviewees would have already had the data regarding his or her state's federal performance reviews. However, I had no additional private information to determine state classification other than what the federal/state governments and foster care agencies would have already had in their possession.

I had no prior contact with interviewees with the exception of the following individuals via my prior role as a grantmaker at The Pew Charitable Trusts: Brent Thompson,[85] Carole Thompson,[86] Muna Walker,[87] Barbara Wilson, and Harry Wilson.[88] Furthermore, the interview with Arkadi Kuhlmann contained data from a talk radio interview I had conducted with him.[89]

Interviews were requested via e-mail and phone. Most interviews were conducted in person and ranged from 15 minutes to 2 hours, with an average interview length of 1 hour. Some telephone interviews were conducted as follow-up conversations related to leads that had been obtained during the field research. According to methodologist Robert Yin, "most commonly, case study interviews are of an *open-ended nature*, in which you can ask key respondents for the facts of a matter as well as for the respondents' opinions about events."[90] These interviews followed that rationale in that each interview was open ended and centered on the interviewee's area of expertise in relation to the foster care administration. Methodologists Anselm Strauss and Juliet Corbin noted that one type of qualitative research posits that "some researchers believe that data **should not be** analyzed, per se" and that "the aim is to give an honest account with little or no interpretation of—interference with—those spoken words or of the observations made by the researcher."[91] In general, I followed this research approach and refrained from inserting my opinion into interviews except for in one instance with HHS employee Christine Craig. After realizing that only one person was responsible for foster care in two states on behalf of the federal government and that person was also responsible for a dozen other federal initiatives for those two states, I stated, "That's a lot for one person" and Christine Craig responded, "Yes, it is."[92] After making that comment, I recognized that I had crossed the line from interviewer to empathizer because I was so taken aback that one federal employee was responsible for so many large HHS programs. I would argue that my crossing of this line was in itself a data point regarding how the federal government spent so much money on foster care while devoting so few staff members to management of foster care.

One criticism of case study research is that "we have little way of screening or testing for an investigator's ability to do good case studies."[93] To alleviate that concern, and more specifically any potential criticism surrounding my ability to conduct interviews, I am offering some evidence regarding expertise in this area. In the last two decades, I have conducted over 3,000 elite interviews for media outlets and/or academic purposes. Because this number is unusually high for a social scientist, my hope is that my expertise dissuades some of the concerns that might be associated with interviews conducted for case research.

Policy and Administrative Documents

In order to understand state performance on foster care administration, I examined documents produced by HHS and other government agencies. External documents related to foster care from nonprofit organizations and policy groups were reviewed as well. At the conclusion of the field research, I examined developments in public administration that concerned government by proxy, leadership, issue networks, program measurement, and policy implementation.

CONCLUSION

The goal of this research is twofold. First, it is intended to discover the conditions, if any, under which foster care outcomes can be improved. Second, it hopes to determine feasible changes that policymakers and practitioners can make to produce such conditions, thereby increasing predictable and desirable consequences for children in foster care.

The next four chapters offer case state research that seeks to answer these propositions. The research conducted in the case states tested whether

40   *Politics of Foster Care Administration*

the following hypothesis was accurate: *Delaware and Michigan became stronger-performing states in the area of foster care by placing a greater priority than the lower-performing states of New York and Rhode Island on building community partners, integrating the advice of mentors, providing leadership from public managers, and cultivating relationships with the federal government.*

The hypothesis posited that Rhode Island and New York placed less of a priority on utilizing these variables where foster care was concerned, and therefore struggled to obtain better results. The next chapter focuses on Delaware's foster care system.

NOTES

1. U.S. Department of Health and Human Services, "Current State of Child Welfare Financing and the Need for Reform," testimony by Wade Horn, Assistant Secretary for Children and Families, U.S. Department of Health and Human Services. Presented to the Committee on Ways and Means Subcommittee on Human Resources, U.S. House of Representatives, June 5, 2005, http://www.hhs.gov/asl/testify/t050609b.html.
2. Rob Green, Shelly Waters Boots, and Karen C. Tumlin, "The Cost of Protecting Vulnerable Children: Understanding Federal, State and Local Child Welfare Spending," *The Urban Institute,* Occasional Paper Number 20 (January 1, 1999), http://www.urban.org/publications/308046.html.
3. Note: There are additional federal funding streams for foster care, but these are nominal. Examples include: John H. Chaffee Foster Care Independence Program, which assists older children in foster care for approximately $200 million per year; Title XX Social Service Block Grant, which in 2003 provided approximately $332 million to 35 states for foster care children not covered under Title IV-E. (Child Welfare League of America, "President's FY2007 Budget and Children," http://www.cwla.org/advocacy/budgetchildren07.htm.)
4. Cynthia Andrews Scarcella et al., "The Cost of Protecting Vulnerable Children V: Understanding State Variation in Child Welfare Financing," *The Urban Institute* (May 24, 2006), http://www.urban.org/publications/311314.html, 2.
5. U.S. Department of Health and Human Services, Administration for Children and Families, Administration on Children, Youth and Families, Children's Bureau, "Adoption and Foster Care Analysis and Reporting System (AFCARS)," http://www.acf.hhs.gov/programs/cb/systems/afcars/fedguid.htm.
6. Note: This remained the latest available comprehensive data until September 3, 2008, when the U.S. Department of Health and Human Services released the "Child Welfare Outcomes 2002–2005: Report to Congress." The most recent published report, "Child Welfare Outcomes 2008–2011: Report to Congress," was released August 16, 2013. There is a significant delay from the year of the data collection to the report release date.
7. U.S. Department of Health and Human Services, Administration for Children and Families, Administration on Children, Youth, and Families, Children's Bureau, "Child Welfare Outcomes 2003: Annual Report. Safety, Permanency, Well-Being," http://www.acf.hhs.gov/programs/cb/pubs/cwo03/cwo03.pdf.
8. Note: Numbers rounded by author.
9. Note: Wade Horn, Assistant Secretary for Children and Families, also testified: "It is unlikely that disparities this large are the result of actual differences in the costs of operating foster care programs or reflect differential needs

Data Collection Approach 41

among foster care children." Further, he added, "Variation in States' claiming practices may be seen most clearly in the relationship between claims for title IV-E maintenance and title IV-E administrative costs. Six states claim less than 50 cents in title IV-E administrative costs for every dollar they claim in title IV-E maintenance, while nine others claim more than two dollars in title IV-E administrative costs per every title IV-E maintenance dollar."

10. Note: Wade Horn, Assistant Secretary for Children and Families, also testified "Wide disparities in Federal claims might be viewed in a favorable light if States were achieving better outcomes with higher spending; however, this argument does not hold up to scrutiny in the face of the CFSR results. Average per-child claims did not differ appreciably between the highest and lowest performing states. In fact, the CFSR [Child and Family Services Reviews] findings were disappointing even for States with relatively high costs."

11. U.S. Department of Health and Human Services, "Current State of Child Welfare."

12. County Welfare Directors Association, "Questions & Answers: Federal Child and Family Service Review," http://www.cwda.org/downloads/child-fam-review/QAs.pdf.

13. U.S. Department of Health and Human Services, "Current State of Child Welfare."

14. Note: Although a full analysis was conducted for 2003 only, according to a quick perusal of the 2002 data, both states were top performers in 2002 as well.

15. Note: Although a full analysis was conducted for 2003 only, according to a quick perusal of the 2002 data, both states were weak performers in year 2002 as well.

16. Note: Further, HHS has some discrepancies among its 2003 data regarding what it terms the "median across states." For consistency, the 2003 median utilized is that offered by HHS in its executive summary of Child Welfare Outcomes 2003: Annual Report.

17. U.S. Department of Health and Human Services, "Child Welfare Outcomes 2003."

18. Ibid.

19. The Pew Commission on Children in Foster Care, "Foster Care Population and States Ranked by Total Number of Children in Foster Care. FY2003," http://pewfostercare.org/research/docs/Data091505.pdf. Note: To be exact, Rhode Island actually represents 0.44% of the foster care population and Delaware actually represents 0.16%.

20. Ibid.

21. U.S. Children's Bureau, "Ranking of Foster Care Population by State (FY2003)," www.pewfostercare.org. Note: Data is from the Adoption and Foster Care Analysis and Reporting System (AFCARS) collected from the U.S. Children's Bureau.

22. Michigan Family Independence Agency, "Michigan's Approach to the Program Improvement Plan. Approved 2004–2006 PIP Report," http://www.michigan.gov/documents/FIA-CFS-PIP-Narrative_106409_7.pdf.

23. Ibid.

24. U.S. Department of Health and Human Services, Administration for Children and Families, Administration on Children, Youth, and Families, Children's Bureau, "Children in the Public Foster Care System Waiting to Be Adopted, Fiscal Years 1999–2006," Rev. March 2008, http://www.acf.hhs.gov/programs/cb/stats_research/afcars/waiting2006.pdf. Note: This 2006 data was revised during the period of Michigan field research.

25. U.S. Department of Health and Human Services, Administration for Children and Families, Administration on Children, Youth, and Families, Children's

42   Politics of Foster Care Administration

Bureau, "Adoptions of Children with Public Child Welfare Agency Involvement by State, Fiscal Years 1995–2004," Rev. June 2006, http://www.hhs-stat.net/scripts/topic.cfm?id=991#.

26. National Conference of State Legislatures, "State Child Welfare Legislation 2005," http://www.ncsl.org/programs/cyf/cwlegislation05.htm.

27. Government Innovators Network, "Structured Decision Making," Harvard Kennedy School Ash Institute for Democratic Governance and Innovation, http://www.innovations.harvard.edu/awards.html?id=53271.

28. State of Delaware, "Governor Minner Endorses Foster Care Task Force Recommendations," Press Release, June 26, 2001, http://www.state.de.us/kids/pdfs/pr_2001.pdf.

29. The Foster Care Task Force commissioned by Governor Ruth Ann Minner, "How Foster Care Can Work for Delaware's Children," http://www.state.de.us/kids/pdfs/fs_fostercare_rpt_2001.pdf.

30. U.S. Department of Health and Human Services, "Children in the Public Foster Care System."

31. U.S. Department of Health and Human Services, "Adoptions of Children with Public Child Welfare Agency Involvement."

32. U.S. Department of Health and Human Services, "Children in the Public Foster Care System."

33. U.S. Department of Health and Human Services, "Adoptions of Children with Public Child Welfare Agency Involvement."

34. Rhode Island Department of Children, Youth and Families. http://www.dcyf.state.ri.us/foster/index.php

35. Eric Tucker, "Second Trial to Begin in RI Toddler's Beating Death in 2004," *The Day*, November 17, 2008.

36. Eric Tucker, "Lawsuit Alleges Abuse, Neglect of Rhode Island Foster Care Kids," *Associated Press*, June 29, 2007, http://www.boston.com/news/local/rhode_island/articles/2007/06/29/lawsuit_alleges_abuse_neglect_of_ri_foster_care_kids.

37. Children's Rights, "Children's Rights Goes to Court to Fight for Children's Fundamental Rights to be Protected from Harm—and to Grow up in Loving, Permanent Homes," http://www.childrensrights.org/reform-campaigns/legal-cases.

38. Tucker, "Lawsuit Alleges Abuse, Neglect."

39. Children's Rights, "Sam and Tony M. v. Carcieri," http://www.childrensrights.org/reform-campaigns/legal-cases/rhode-island-sam-and-tony-m-v-carcieri.

40. New York State, Office of Children and Family Services, http://www.ocfs.state.ny.us/main/fostercare

41. The Pew Commission on Children in Foster Care, "Foster Care Population and States Ranked."

42. U.S. Department of Health and Human Services, "Children in the Public Foster Care System."

43. U.S. Department of Health and Human Services, "Adoptions of Children with Public Child Welfare Agency Involvement."

44. Leslie Kaufman, "Worst Foster Agencies Endure as City Rolls Drop," *New York Times,* November 2, 2004, 1. Note: In 2005, one of these two problem agencies was eventually defunded.

45. Leslie Kaufman, "Foster Care Contracts Canceled After City Finds Files Doctored," *New York Times,* January 15, 2005, 1.

46. Leslie Kaufman, "Manhattan: Child Welfare Official Arrested," *New York Times,* January 28, 2006, 4.

47. Leslie Kaufmann, "Foster Care Director Quits After Purchases of Luxury Items," *New York Times,* November 8, 2006, 1.

48. National Conference of State Legislatures, "State Child Welfare Legislation."

Data Collection Approach   43

49. Richard Fenno, *Home Style: House Members in their Districts* (London: Longman Publishing, 1978).
50. Richard Hall, "Participation and Purpose in Committee Decision Making," *The American Political Science Review*, Vol. 81, No. 1 (1987): 107. Note: Refers to a number of individuals discussing this theory. See Charles L. Clapp, *The Congressman: His Work as He Sees it* (Washington, DC: Brookings Institution, 1963); Donald R. Matthews, "The Folkways of the United States Senate: Conformity to Group Norms and Legislative Effectiveness," *American Political Science Review*, Vol. 53 (1959): 1064–89; James L. Payne, "Show Horses and Work Horses in the U.S. House of Representatives," *Polity*, Vol. 12 (1980): 428–56.
51. Note: Local becomes of particular importance when states have large foster care operations in cities such as Detroit or New York City.
52. The Foster Care Task Force, "How Foster Care Can Work," 7.
53. State of Michigan, "Michigan Partners with the Annie E. Casey Foundation to Join the Family to Family Network," http://www.michigan.gov/documents/FIA-Fam2Fam_9937_7.pdf.
54. Ibid.
55. Note: Rhode Island and New York were not included, although the New York State Supreme Court passed a resolution in support.
56. The Pew Commission on Children in Foster Care, "Pew Commission Progress Report: State Courts, Congress Act on Commission Recommendations; Key Advocacy Groups Endorse Recommendations," Vol. 25 (2006), http://www.pewfostercare.org/newsletter/index.php?NewsletterID=25.
57. Herbert Kaufman, *The Forest Ranger: A Study in Administrative Behavior* (Baltimore: Johns Hopkins University Press, 1960).
58. James MacGregor Burns, *Leadership* (New York: Harper & Row, 1978).
59. Steve Cohen, William Eimicke, and Tanya Heikkila, *The Effective Public Manager* (San Francisco: Jossey-Bass, 2008).
60. John J. DiIulio, Jr., "Principled Agents: The Cultural Bases of Behavior in a Federal Government Bureaucracy," *Journal of Public Administration Research and Theory*, Vol. 4, No. 3 (1994): 277–318.
61. Jameson W. Doig and Erwin C. Hargrove, *Leadership and Innovation: Entrepreneurs in Government, Unabridged Edition* (Baltimore: Johns Hopkins University Press, 1972).
62. Laurence J. O'Toole, Jr., and Kenneth J. Meier, *Public Management Organizations, Governance, and Performance* (Cambridge, UK: Cambridge University Press, 2011).
63. Mark Moore, *Creating Public Value: Strategic Management in Government* (Cambridge, MA: Harvard University Press, 1995).
64. DiIulio, "Principled Agents," 282.[65] Ibid., 277.
66. Kaufman, *The Forest Ranger*.
67. Moore, *Creating Public Value*, 10.
68. Cari DeSantis (Delaware Children's Department Cabinet Secretary), "Foster Care Reform. 2000–2006," Delaware Children's Department, http://www.state.de.us/kids/pdfs/fs_foster_care_reform_2006.pdf.
69. Michigan Human Services Family, "Independence Agency Program is Semi-Finalist for Prestigious National Award," Press Release, November 15, 2002.
70. Michigan Family Independence Agency, "Michigan's Approach to the Program Improvement Plan."
71. Ibid.
72. "Fifteen Finalists Named for KSG Award," *Harvard University Gazette*, March 20, 2003, http://www.news.harvard.edu/gazette/2003/03.20/15-ksg.html.

44 Politics of Foster Care Administration

73. Donald F. Kettl, *Government by Proxy: Mis?Managing Federal Programs* (Washington, DC: CQ Press, 1987).
74. Paul C. Light, *The True Size of Government* (Washington, DC: Brookings Press, 1999).
75. Mary Jo Bane, *Who Will Provide?: The Changing Role of Religion in American Social Welfare* (Boulder, CO: Westview Press, 2000).
76. Jack W. Meek and Kurt Thurmaier, eds., *Networked Governance: The Future of Intergovernmental Management* (Washington, DC: CQ Press, 2011).
77. Barbara Wilson (program officer, Corporation for National and Community Service [CNCS]). Ms. Wilson provided a document, titled "Senior Corps Highlights Foster Care Activities," prepared for the author as requested in October 2006.
78. Ibid.
79. Jeffrey L. Pressman and Aaron Wildavsky, *Implementation: How Great Expectations in Washington Are Dashed in Oakland; Or, Why It's Amazing That Federal Programs Work at All, This Being a Saga of the Economic Development Administration as Told by Two Sympathetic Observers Who Seek to Build Morals on a Foundation of Ruined Hope*, 3rd ed. (Berkeley: University of California Press, 1984).
80. Note: See Stephen Skowronek, *Building a New American State: The Expansion of National Administrative Capacities, 1877–1920* (Cambridge, UK: Cambridge University Press, 1982); Stephen Skowronek, The *Politics Presidents Make: Leadership from John Adams to Bill Clinton*, rev. ed. (Cambridge, MA: Belknap Press, 1997). See Skowronek's concept of a president serving as a "battering ram" against institutional constraints.
81. Stephen Van Evera, *Guide to Methods for Students of Political Science* (Ithaca, NY: Cornell University Press, 1997), 27.
82. Ibid., 29.
83. Ibid., 30, 55.
84. Note: The exception is Arkadi Kuhlmann's interview, which was conducted for radio and publicly broadcast.
85. Note: This interviewee, as well as the author, are both alumni of the Fels Institute of Government.
86. Note: Thompson served as an advisor for a grant.
87. Note: Walker was a grantee.
88. Note: See List of Interviews in Chapters 3–6 for their titles.
89. Note: See List of Interviews in Chapters 3–6 for his title.
90. Robert Yin, *Case Study Research: Design and Methods*, 2nd ed., Applied Social Research Methods Series, Vol. 5 (Thousand Oaks, CA: SAGE Publications, 1994), 84.
91. Anselm Strauss and Juliet Corbin, *Basics of Qualitative Research: Grounded Theory Procedures and Techniques*, (Newbury Park, CA: SAGE Publications, 1990), 21, emphasis in original.
92. Christine Craig, HHS-ACF Region III Program Specialist, federal government, phone interview, June 3, 2008. Note: Craig oversees Delaware in addition to another state. She worked on Title IV-E eligibility review for Delaware from October 2005 to March 2006.
93. Robert Yin, *Case Study Research; Design and Methods*, 11.

3 Delaware
A Small State with Stronger Performance

"Delaware has made huge strides. We *are* the talk."
—Tania Culley, executive director of the Office of the
Child Advocate, in reference to how other states view
Delaware's foster care system

DELAWARE: FOSTER CARE DATA SUMMARY[1]

Agency and Foster Care Funding

Delaware's Division of Family Services (DFS) has responsibility for foster care administration across the state. In 2007, DFS noted they spent approximately $18.4 million a year on foster care from various sources: $15.9 million from the state, $1.8 million from the federal government through Title IV-E, and $600,000 from a trust fund. Delaware decided to maintain the same level of funding for their foster care population through state funds despite a decrease in federal funding.

Foster Care Population

As of 2003, Delaware had a population of 792,494, with 103 foster care cases per 100,000 people. This is a much lower per capita rate of foster care caseloads than for any of the other three case states. Michigan and New York were the two large states studied, and Rhode Island and Delaware were the two smaller states studied.

As of FY2003, with just 814 foster care children, representing 0.2% of the foster care population across the country, Delaware had the smallest foster care caseload across all states. During the 2007 field research year, Delaware children were permitted to remain in foster care until age 18, and a few were permitted to remain in foster care until age 19.

Foster Care Administration

Foster care is a state-run system and the state licenses the homes. The state arranges regions by clusters so that foster care children have an extended foster family through the clusters in Delaware.

This chapter provides case research on foster care in the state of Delaware. The research was designed to test whether the following hypothesis is accurate: *Delaware and Michigan became stronger-performing states in the area of foster care by placing a greater priority than the lower-performing states of New York and Rhode Island on building community partners, integrating the advice of mentors, providing leadership from public managers, and cultivating relationships with the federal government.*

One of the two smaller states in this study, Delaware also falls into the category of a stronger case state according to the 2003 federal performance measures on foster care administration. As of 2003, Delaware had a population of 792,494,[2] with 103 foster care cases per 100,000 people. This is a much lower per capita rate of foster care than any of the other three case states.[3] In fact, with just 814 foster care children, representing 0.2% of the foster care population across the country, Delaware had the smallest foster care caseload of all the states.[4]

The results of this research suggest that four variables studied had differing degrees of influence on the success of Delaware's foster care system. In contributing to Delaware's successful foster care administration, the cultivation of relationships with the federal government was not a major factor, the building of community partners was a strong factor, the integration of advice from mentors was a minimal factor, and the leadership from public managers was a strong factor.

CASE BACKGROUND

Like all other states during the period of field research, Delaware had been undergoing federal government reviews for Title IV-E eligibility as well as for Child and Family Service Reviews. Delaware performed near the top of the states on the Child and Family Service Reviews as shown by the "Child Welfare Outcomes 2003: Annual Report" in Chapter 2. Delaware qualified as a stronger case state because the state performed above the median on every foster care outcome measured in year 2003. At the same time, Delaware demonstrated no improvement when comparing year 2000 with 2003, and it was below the median across all states for improvement during this period.

I conducted field research in Delaware from June through September 2007, with some additional phone interviews occurring outside that period.

During this 2007 field research year, Delaware children were permitted to remain in foster care until age 18, although a few were permitted to remain in foster care until age 19.[5] Delaware's Division of Family Services (DFS) has responsibility for foster care administration across the state. In 2007, DFS noted that the state had been spending approximately $18.4 million a year on foster care from various sources.[6]

Delaware, through DFS, licenses foster care homes and works with private agencies to place foster care children throughout the state. The state operates foster care on a regional system. In 2001, a new gubernatorial initiative launched a cluster system that allowed regional foster families to provide an additional layer of support for foster children in their regions.[7] Delaware is less than a 3-hour drive in length and includes urban areas such as Wilmington, as well as rural areas in the southern part of the state.

Field research in Delaware involved conducting interviews, viewing documents, and visiting state offices and foster care agencies. The purpose of the field research was to begin to identify what, if any, conditions in Delaware tended to produce better foster care outcomes. Interviews were focused on the interviewee's area of expertise in connection with foster care administration. Although most interviews occurred in the field, some follow-up phone interviews were conducted. At times, interviewees requested that all or part of their comments remain off the record.

Fourteen interviews were conducted on the topic of foster care in the state of Delaware. Interviews were requested with all "key players" who were actively involved in the state's foster care decisions. All interviews requested were granted. The majority of the interviews were conducted in person. Delaware was the only case state in which a governor was actively involved in foster care initiatives, so I requested a 30-minute interview with Governor Ruth Ann Minner at her office. This meeting turned out to last nearly an hour. I also interviewed in person two Delaware cabinet secretaries, a Delaware chief judge, and the Delaware director of the Division of Family Services.

In addition, I conducted six interviews that broadly informed my research on foster care and provided background data for Delaware and the other case states. These included three key player interviews in Philadelphia featuring foundation and policy experts on foster care. I interviewed two key players who worked for the federal government overseeing the regions of the District of Columbia, West Virginia, Delaware, Maryland, Pennsylvania, and Virginia. I also spoke to a key player at the federal Corporation for National and Community Service. A complete list of interviews is offered at the end of this chapter.

CASE FINDINGS

This section discusses findings from the Delaware case research. Each of the four variables is analyzed and a summary is offered, noting the estimated significance of each variable based on research results.

48 Politics of Foster Care Administration

Cultivation of Federal Government Relationships: Significance = None

For the variable *cultivation of federal government relationships* to appear strong, the data needed to show a pattern of interaction between the federal government and the state that went *beyond* the required relationship. This factor is shown to have a stronger presence when the federal government has significantly shifted the direction of the state's decision-making path regarding the provision of foster care in some nonrequired area. In other words, the federal–state relationship on foster care needed to transcend the required form completion, grant processing, regulation monitoring, and data gathering and move into how to fix and transform foster care.

In 2007, Carlyse Giddens, director of the Delaware DFS, noted that Delaware foster care costs approximately $18.4 million a year. This sum includes funding from various sources: $15.9 million from the state, $1.8 million from the federal government through Title IV-E, and $600,000 from a trust fund.[8] The Delaware Department of Services for Children, Youth and Their Families (DCYF) cabinet secretary, Cari DeSantis, said: "Federal Title IV-E has been declining. As the 1996 AFDC [Aid to Families with Dependent Children] dollars change in value, there are fewer and fewer people that meet that [requirement to obtain federal funding for foster care]."[9]

Due to the shrinkage of Title IV-E funds, Giddens said that Delaware has provided an infusion of money to offset federal losses. At the time of field research, the state of Delaware was spending more money on foster care ($15.9 million)[10] than they were receiving from the federal government for foster care ($2.5 million).[11] Governor Minner added that the foster care cost "shift from the federal government to the state hurt us."[12] Delaware made the choice to maintain the same level of funding for its foster care population despite the decrease in federal support. Yet, Delaware questions whether it should continue to accept minimal amounts of federal funds that are attached to significant federal government requirements. DeSantis asked, "Should states participate in federal money [programs], for what we're getting any more?"[13] She added emphatically, "Hello folks. Wake up. This is a Big Problem. It keys up a conversation that is worth having on a national level."[14] DeSantis was clearly frustrated with the significant decline in federal funding despite the heavy federal requirements placed on their state.

Although the federal government requires that states comply with a variety of requirements in order to participate in its foster care programs, interviewees did not mention receiving federal government support in the form of mentoring or volunteers. The federal government's Corporation for National and Community Service (CNCS) did not seem to be contributing to foster care success in Delaware.[15] Although CNCS has provided some volunteers, most key players were not even aware of them, and no interviewee suggested that they had a significant impact. Because CNCS is active in policy decision making and providing volunteers for other social welfare policies, such as the much smaller Mentoring Children of Prisoners program, it was noteworthy that CNCS was not as actively involved with foster care issues.

Christine Craig is the U.S. Department of Health and Human Services Administration for Children and Families (HHS-ACF) Region III program specialist for the federal government appointed to oversee Delaware. Due to staff vacancies, Craig is now assigned to two states. For both states, she handles all of the following initiatives: foster care, CASA, child abuse prevention, adoption, independent living, education and training vouchers, family preservation, safe and stable families, and reunification, as well as technical matters relating to the state's financial report, audit, training for staff, and preplacement costs. After realizing that only one person was responsible for foster care in two states on behalf of the federal government, while at the same time responsible for a dozen other federal initiatives for those two states, I stated, "That's a lot for one person," and she responded, "Yes, it is."[16]

However, the federal government does seem to place significant value on the performance measurement area. When I entered the Delaware DFS offices, I noticed multiple piles of paperwork that had to be completed for the federal government. The Delaware foster care program manager's office included a book with a few hundred pages of federal government foster care forms that the state was required to complete. The state case data in Chapter 2 regarding the "Child Welfare Outcomes 2003: Annual Report" provides an example of the data that states are required to provide to the federal government. In addition to measurement of foster care outcomes, the states are also required to fill out extensive financial documents related to case eligibility. These are the types of forms that were sitting on the desk of the foster care program manager.

In addition, it appeared that the federal government's performance audits were consuming significant blocks of time for Delaware's state foster care staff. The state had just completed its 2007 performance review for the federal government, and was in the process of creating a "program improvement plan." The various measures of federal reporting for performance, audits, improvement, and so forth are extremely time consuming. These federal requirements trickle down to foster care providers as well. One foster care provider noted that his job involved "lots of paperwork for [the] federal government."[17]

Nevertheless, the federal government's performance measure requirements have benefitted Delaware. They allowed the state's public managers to measure Delaware's progress against a benchmark. The DFS director stated, "I don't disagree with the federal standards. The standards should be high."[18] Her voice was animated. She expressed a desire to be challenged by federal standards while honestly recognizing that Delaware's performance

50   Politics of Foster Care Administration

on foster care was not where she wanted it to be. She saw the federal measurements as a bar to be met rather than as an annoyance.

In summary, the case of Delaware reflected a transactional federal government relationship with the state rather than a "workhorse" relationship. The federal government required a significant amount of paperwork, including reporting financial outlays and foster care performance measurement outcomes. However, I classify this variable outcome as "cultivation of federal government relationships = none" because the federal paperwork was required of the state, and the federal government never actively worked to significantly shift the direction of the state's decision-making path regarding the provision of foster care in some nonrequired area. Additionally, the case highlighted the changing role of the federal government's financing of foster care. The federal government provided less money overall to Delaware's foster care program, so Delaware decided to appropriate state money to make up the difference. As a result, Delaware was now fronting the majority of foster care costs for the state while at the same time spending significant time attending to federal paperwork.

Integration of Advice from Mentors: Significance = Minimal

The hypothesis is that the stronger states will have stronger (defined as more or deeper) mentors who offer strategic advice or training on the issue of foster care. *Mentors are defined here as foundations, issue-expert national nonprofit organizations, or think tanks that focus on foster care.* The strong presence of mentors is reflected by a workhorse relationship in which the state has either a large network of mentors or a rigorous relationship with one mentor organization. Workhorse relationships are deeper relationships in which mentors discuss ideas with the state, and the state then takes action.

This factor is shown to have a stronger presence when the mentors have significantly shifted the direction of the state's decision-making path regarding the provision of foster care in some nonrequired area.

The collective Casey family foundations are unquestionably the single largest and most active foundation player on the issue of foster care. In its various forms, Casey has served as a direct funder of foster care, a foster care provider,[19] a policy advocate, and an organization that conducts original foster care research itself. My conversation with a senior program officer at the Annie E. Casey Foundation confirmed Casey's vast wealth of knowledge on this issue and its significant monetary commitment to foster care.[20]

Many Delaware case interviews cited both the Annie E. Casey Foundation and Casey Family Services as excellent resources for learning about effective foster care practices. However, the state's relationship with Casey has never gone beyond a typical transactional relationship. Although Delaware utilized Casey materials to learn best practices, the state did not have a workhorse relationship with Casey.

Delaware 51

The Pew Charitable Trusts[21] served as the only potential mentor relationship in the case of Delaware. The Pew Commission on Children in Foster Care involved both the Delaware chief judge and the director of the Division of Family Services. However, the relationship with the Pew Commission appeared to be more about Delaware teaching Pew than about Pew teaching Delaware. Pew was interested in learning how to create a more effective court system, so it utilized the wisdom of a chief judge and other individuals to learn how to create more effective policy. The upcoming section on leadership from managers offers additional details of Pew's impact upon Delaware.

As shown, Delaware did not significantly seek out mentors or integrate advice from mentors on the issue of foster care. The use of advice from mentors was minimal in Delaware, and it was primarily limited to the Pew relationship. Delaware instead relied on peer organizations and other key players to mentor its foster care system.

Building of Community Partners: Significance = Strong

The hypothesis is that the stronger states will have stronger (defined as more or deeper) community partnerships. *Community partnerships are defined here as state and/or local[22] foster care agency relationships with local nonprofits, faith-based organizations, and community organizations.* The strong presence of community partners is reflected by a workhorse relationship in which the state has either a large network of community partners or a rigorous relationship with one community partner. Workhorse relationships are deeper relationships in which community partners discuss ideas with the state, and the state then takes action.

A workhorse relationship might include government and community organizations copromoting a conference with mutual organizational roles, or deciding together to more aggressively pursue homes for older female teens. This factor is shown to have a stronger presence when the community partners have significantly shifted the direction of the state's decision-making path regarding the provision of foster care in some area. Basic administrative paperwork or meetings between a community partner and the state do not qualify as a strong presence of this variable.

In Delaware, there were numerous foster care committees that involved community partners. One foster care provider noted that DFS hosts five or six new committees that relate to foster care.[23] In fact, so many foster care committees were meeting in this small state that it was confusing to track which committee was meeting where about what topic.

Furthermore, the meetings were so frequent that my interviews were often sandwiched in between community partner meetings. I interviewed the director of DFS a few minutes after she had met with the nonprofit Global Youth Help and Bank of America. I met with a grantee provider who

52 Politics of Foster Care Administration

mentioned having attended a community meeting the night before with DFS. I met with the executive director of the Office of the Child Advocate while a committee meeting was occurring in the same office with other partners.

Community partner meetings were common in Delaware, and for the most part, they were about action and not simply administration. This commitment to working with partners seems to come from the top: The director of DFS articulated her belief that success is related to "communication, coordination, and collaboration."[24] Most committee meetings included state officials and community partners in a problem-solving capacity. People generally viewed the committees as effective at pulling together various government and community players and resulting in specific outcomes such as more training, better caseload standards, pro bono lawyers for children, and attention to abuse issues. The state foster care program manager noted that these partners played a significant role in oversight and stated that "I combine them together—oversight and partnership."[25]

One example of how partners work together and also provide oversight is the Child Protection Accountability Commission (CPAC), which works on caseloads, privatization, and training and emphasizes "a commitment to solve these problems," according to CPAC executive director Tania Culley, Esq.[26] The CPAC's meetings are open to the community and have included major activist Janice Mink (who has a track record of foster care progress); Al Snyder of the Delaware Community Foundation; and Dr. Allan DeJong, MD, medical director of the CARE (Children at Risk Evaluation) Program at Alfred I. duPont Hospital for Children.[27] These meetings emphasize honesty, measure accountability, and implement solutions. The executive director of CPAC said, "Most problem solving happens in public forums. [There is] lots of working together. Leaders of organizations come together and force discussion."[28]

CPAC is one of the strongest committees in Delaware. It was created by the legislature and is led by Culley, a solid public manager. "CPAC forces everyone who's busy to take time [a minimum of seven times a year] to come and sit at the table," Culley observed.[29] She sets the agenda and "throws issues on the table" without "many political restraints."[30] Culley has offered additional nonmandatory CPAC meetings that have helped to set agendas and solve problems, and she is working on one of the foremost national foster care issues, which is the "age of kids in family court, extending services to kids 18 to 21 years old."[31] It appears that CPAC's meetings are excelling beyond its original legislative vision because of a strong leader who works aggressively with other public managers and community partners.

Culley also serves as executive director of the Office of the Child Advocate and has recruited hundreds of pro bono lawyers for foster care children by "getting lawyer organizations in Delaware to donate to them."[32] Currently, over 500 foster children are being represented by these lawyers who are offering their services for free in order to stand up for the interests of these foster children before a court.

Delaware's Division of Family Services has also actively embraced community partners. Carlyse Giddens, the director of DFS, worked alongside community partners to advocate for caseload standards before the legislature. Delaware is only one of a few states that has caseload standards; it aims to cap caseloads at 20 for each different caseload measurement.[33] Although Giddens was instrumental in pushing this idea, the partners and state child protective services championed the request to the legislature to incorporate caseload standards.

Community partners also support Delaware's foster care program by providing foster children with necessary items that the state cannot provide. There are "so many needs the state can't meet. The state only provides a nominal clothing allowance."[34] Giddens of DFS believes that "the state has the responsibility to provide for kids what a biological family would provide for kids. If we're going to remove them from their homes, we need to provide piano lessons, sports, prom dresses. That's what the partners do."[35] Both the state and the foster care provider have a staff person who is assigned to work with community partners on obtaining donations and raising awareness of the issue.[36] These community partners provide what the state cannot. Strong public managers, such as Giddens, have created and brokered these partnerships. ING Direct provided a monetary donation for foster care and hosted a fundraising golf tournament.[37] Verizon provided a cash donation for foster care and has converted used cell phones into emergency phones that can be used by victims of domestic violence.[38]

The Delaware nonprofit organization Global Youth Help is one of the partners that helps to meet the needs of foster care children. Global Youth Help founder and student Meghan Pasricha partnered with DFS to create foster care projects such as prom dress drives, financial literacy, leadership programs for girls, Christmas gifts, school supplies, and self-defense classes. While an undergraduate at Harvard University, Pasricha partnered with Bank of America to provide $5,000 worth of backpacks to foster care children to assist them with their frequent moves.[39] Public managers are working outside their job descriptions to work with community partners as well, and "family court judges are coming off the bench and working to support kids. They worked with a community service organization [Global Youth Help] to provide luggage for kids."[40]

The faith-based community is another major community partner for Delaware. Giddens said that one "can't forget the role of FBOs [faith-based organizations]. Several churches allow us to have meetings, provide money,[41] and allow us to recruit foster parents there."[42] She noted, "FBOs have been successful in helping them to find permanency for kids."[43] Several churches assist the foster care provider, People's Place, particularly around the holidays. The director of children's services, Del Failing, states that "churches have been very good to us."[44] Program director Vincent Giampeitro at the foster care provider Children and Families First said "a large percent of families who become foster parents have faith-based connections."[45]

54 *Politics of Foster Care Administration*

Although Delaware had utilized faith-based partners for years, the state started a targeted campaign in 2007 to increase its relationships with faith-based partners. The Delaware foster care program manager, John Bates, created a plan to recruit 360 faith-based organizations in calendar year 2007 to partner with the state on foster care.[46] DFS sought to have staff members speak at churches in order to recruit new foster parents from their congregants and spark interest in donating goods and services to foster care providers. Bates sends his staff members out in teams of two to knock on church doors and then follows up with a letter, hoping to turn many churches into foster care partners. The director of DFS, Carlyse Giddens, shared a story about the time she saw in the bulletin of her own church an advertisement for a young man in foster care, not having known beforehand that her staff had reached out to that church.[47] She was pleasantly surprised at the results of the campaign. As of mid-August 2007, Bates and his team had already made 178 contacts with churches that resulted in 26 partnerships to date.[48]

Vincent Giampeitro, who serves as program director at the second largest foster care provider in Delaware, stated: "The more integrated the kid is into the community [with activities like church], it automatically increases likelihood the kid will be successful."[49] He added that "church is a wonderful thing" and that you can't make a kid go to church, but it is only once in "every blue moon a kid will say no. . . . Churches are big for foster kids." Church and other community activities that integrated foster children into the community helped to increase the success rate of foster care placements.

Clearly, the building of community partners has been a strong factor in the success of Delaware's foster care system. Delaware governor Ruth Ann Minner told me that she "believes community integration is valuable,"[50] and this was showcased in the myriad of community partnerships. These community partners are nonprofit organizations whose members sit on committee meetings to solve the needs of older foster children, provide everything from backpacks to prom dresses, assist with recruiting foster parents, and provide foster children with faith-based services and support.

Leadership from Public Managers: Significance = Strong

The hypothesis is that the stronger states will have more leadership from public managers. *A public manager is shown to evidence leadership when he or she is operating as a "principled agent" in the state or local government or agency responsible for the area of foster care.* In the context of this study, a principled agent is a government employee (public manager) who goes above and beyond his or her public duty to cultivate successful foster care administration. Harvard Kennedy School professor Mark Moore argued that a successful manager "increase(s) the public value produced by public sector organizations in both the short and the long run."[51] A principled agent performs as a workhorse, rather than as a standard government employee who is focused on routine functions. The strong presence

Delaware   55

of leadership from public managers is reflected by a greater presence of principled agents working in foster care in the case state.

Overall, Delaware had significant leadership from public managers in the area of foster care. The number of positive comments about leadership from public managers among both state workers and the courts far outweighed the negative comments. The program director of Children and Families First, Vincent Giampeitro, made numerous positive comments about the state's foster care leaders and agency: "[DFS director] Carlyse Giddens legitimately cares for the kids. . . . DFS has adoptions hold—they prepare people well. . . . DFS works hard at reunification. . . . A lot of people move up [in government] and tend to lose sight of the kids, but that's not true for [program manager] John Bates."[52] There is a high level of trust between the grantee providers and DFS. Del Failing, the director of children's services, People's Place, noted that there is "lots of honesty in the state, honesty because there's debate—the state is pretty up front."[53] Failing suggested that this is a direct result of the efforts of individual public servants: "There is a strong working relationship with the state but that's because of individual workers." "Foster care is a priority in this state."[54]

The public managers led their teams of state workers in managing relationships with foster care providers. Giampeitro said that DFS workers actively work on providing solutions to foster care providers. He noted, "The contract administrator almost never says no, [if I have] a real problem. This is a small enough state so I can get this done."[55] Meghan Pasricha, founder and president of Global Youth H.E.L.P., said: "State workers are like mentors" and that "family services works really hard" by "protecting [foster care] students and making sure they get what they need from families."[56] Pasricha added that the state workers even "helped students with laundry and homework" and "played a huge role in these student's lives . . . by helping them with personal and family problems."[57]

There were off-the-record comments as well that testified to the strength of Delaware's public managers, including the following: "There are extraordinarily dedicated welfare professionals in DFS." "Outstanding, amazing people. We now have a child advocate."[58] "Delaware is doing a pretty good job. It's small. Change takes forever."[59]

Although leadership from public managers may be defined as the presence of principled agents in agencies, legislatures, or courts, in Delaware, leadership was demonstrated even at the highest levels of the executive branch. Delaware governor Ruth Ann Minner made the choice to be actively involved in foster care issues and she was the most active governor across all four case states.

Governor Minner encouraged the creation of the Foster Care Task Force in January 2001. This task force met eight times to issue recommendations, and the governor approved every recommendation along with issuing half a million dollars in appropriation in July 2001. Three months later, the entire

56 Politics of Foster Care Administration

foster care system was completely changed to support decentralization in communities, including the creation of cluster groups.[60] In under a year, the governor was able to find out what did not work, lead a task force to issue improvements, find $500,000 to fund the recommendations, and fully implement the new system.

Currently, two of the most prominent nationwide topics that relate to children in foster care are "aging out," which refers to foster care children leaving the system between the ages of 17 and 21, and foster children in "kinship care." The former topic, aging out, has been a hot topic for a few decades because as kids age out, they leave the safety net of the resources provided by the foster care system. Many former foster children struggle to transition to adulthood without the financial support and mental health resources provided by the foster care system. The Foster Care Independence Act of 1999 was a national policy created to attempt to address this problem:

> States would promote the self-sufficiency of these young people by providing assistance in obtaining a high school diploma, post-secondary education, career exploration, housing,[61] vocational training, job placement and retention, training in budgeting, substance abuse prevention education, and education in preventive health measures including smoking avoidance, nutrition education, and pregnancy prevention.[62]

Despite policy advances such as these, the foster care field has struggled to solve the issue of aging out and it therefore still garners national debate.

The second nationwide foster care topic is kinship care, which as it relates to foster care is the full-time care of foster children by relatives. This has affected roughly a quarter of the children in foster care in recent years. In a 2013 report, the Annie E. Casey Foundation estimated that approximately 104,000 foster care children nationwide were living with relatives in 2010.[63] In recent years, the field has recognized the significant role kinship caregivers play in both preventing a potential foster care child from entering the foster care system and in supporting foster children in the foster care system. Over time, foster care practitioners and social scientists have begun to recognize that matching foster children with relatives and providing support for the match is of substantial value to the children in many cases.

Governor Minner became involved with this latter issue of kinship care.[64] Governor Minner said, "Why shouldn't these kids be able to go to their family?"[65] Knowing that many grandparents became the primary caretakers of their grandchildren but never enroll them in foster care, Governor Minner encouraged the grandparents to "go through [state foster care] training to at least take care of the kids [appropriately, including learning safety procedures and available resources]."[66] This method does have some costs for the state, but it encourages better treatment for at-risk youth by their relatives.

Delaware 57

Additionally, the governor focused on improving training for foster care. Governor Minner emphasized, "We needed to give more training and we knew we could do that."[67] Program director John Bates noted that the state provided "mandatory supervisor training, which is excellent."[68] Bates added that "training is very valuable, stabilizing kids, and supporting foster kids."[69] Many foster care providers saw this training as a major improvement in Delaware foster care. In fact, the training was so effective that Delaware shared its manual with other states and Bates is frequently asked to speak about Delaware as a model foster care state.[70]

Foster care providers noticed the governor and her team's efforts in support of training. Giampeitro reflected, "The governor helps in this area of looking at the process and the impact it's had. Better training to improve education, more money, more programs that before didn't have additional funding in foster care. Training is a benefit that filters down to kids."[71] Even with these improvements, in 2007, Governor Minner recognized that Delaware's foster care system still had needs. Minner stated, "There's still more we can do: expanding more homes [for children]."[72]

The governors' public management leadership from the top trickled down to her agency leadership. Carlyse Giddens celebrated 10 years as DFS director in September 2007, which made her the longest serving DFS director ever in any agency in any state.[73] Giddens beamed as she announced her milestone, reflecting her passion in a wide smile. Although she was proud of her "public manager first," she was still able to rattle off a list of things for the agency to do in the future.

One area that Giddens and Secretary DeSantis focused on was reducing agency staff turnover. Now the "turnover ratio is a national standard"[74] as a result of their mutual efforts. When Giddens was new to her position in 1998, there was a turnover rate for caseworkers of 48%; by 2007, that number had been reduced to 17%. Giddens said, "We retain staff in this area."[75] The improvement in staff retention did not go unnoticed, and many interviewees mentioned DFS's accomplishment of reducing turnover among foster care caseworkers.

As previously mentioned, DFS public managers also worked alongside community partners to implement caseload standards. Delaware even created a "safety valve" mechanism to manage caseload levels. The state hired 15 extra sideline staff members [over hires] who are caseworkers, but who will only be utilized if the caseload becomes too high. DFS program director John Bates said, "Other states are jealous [of this]."[76] At least five key player interviews noted this success in their interviews.

The governor, the cabinet secretary, and the director of DFS were also involved in creating and implementing the model "Think of the Child First." This foster care philosophy revamped previous modes of thought in the field. It encourages both government and nongovernment partners to make every decision from the foster child's perspective. According to Governor Minner, the single variable is: "What works for the child? Think of

58   Politics of Foster Care Administration

the child first." Minner said DFS transitioned from "trying to keep a state worker's caseload in one region, to shifting to not worrying about whether a state child welfare's caseload is all in the same area, [to now asking instead] what's best for the child?"[77] The second piece of DFS's new child-focused model is the "no reject, no eject" policy. The new policy states that children can never be turned away from foster care, which is in stark contrast to previous practices.

Both policies—"think of the child first" and "no reject, no eject"—were not only implemented within the agency, but they were also communicated to all partners by public managers. It was evident from my interviews that these policies were not merely words, but were practiced among foster care providers and DFS staff. It was clear that foster care providers and other partners were aware of these policies.

Furthermore, both the executive branch and the judicial branch launched nongovernment websites that addressed the issue of foster care, in order to bring in multiple partners in the search for solutions. In other words, these public managers launched websites that were not required by their job description; they wanted to "go above and beyond," as principled agents do. These websites, such as www.delawaregirlsinitiative.org, were developed in addition to the current state government foster care website, www. kids.delaware.gov/fs/fostercare.shtml.

For the most part, Delaware had significant leadership from public managers. However, there were a handful of negative comments about public managers in Delaware. For instance, Children and Families First program director Vincent Giampeitro noted, "DFS is not doing a bad job, but they've been lax on certain things such as a system of care approach where they thought it was a new idea to have wrap around services."[78] One anonymous comment noted, "The administration is treating foster care as [if it has been] fixed."[79] Giampeitro stated, "Even DYFS in New Jersey [a bottom-performing state] operates better than DFS."[80]

There were also questions about the effectiveness of the court system, since foster care leading to adoption is often a one to two year process, whereas private adoption can be completed in weeks. Giampeitro commented that "judges think they're social workers" and "judges get too involved."[81] Although Giampeitro offered his comments on the record, there were other foster care providers who shared similar anonymous complaints. In other words, there were some negative comments that described problematic judges as poor public managers. However, the positive comments significantly outweighed the handful of negatives, and the negative comments still came from individuals who had great respect for most of the public managers.

At the same time, there was evidence that many of the public managers worked to correct some of their internal problems. There was an effort by the judiciary and the executive to have a "very improved" relationship with "natural tension [over cases]—and to agree to disagree."[82] This tension stemmed from the question of who, be it the courts or DFS, has the ultimate decision-making authority over the future of the child. Foster care is one of the many issues that can get caught in the gears of a federalist system; two branches of government are wrestling to define the best interest of the child. The executive branch focused on its self-created motto "Think of the Child First," and the judicial philosophy regarding cases was determined by a mixture of "the best interest of public safety along with the best interest of the child."[83]

At first, there was minimal trust between these branches of government regarding foster care issues, but during Governor Minner's administration the two branches decided to work together despite their natural disagreement over how to handle cases. A key moment of agreement came during a trip to draft legislation, funded by the Pew Charitable Trusts, when significant officials from both branches began to trust one another. Prior to this trip, DFS would make decisions about placements unilaterally and disregard the court's viewpoint. At the same time, the court embraced an activist role, with individual judges taking activist positions on the bench. Some estimated that "approximately half the judges [would] push the envelope."[84] Although judicial activism is controversial, in this case, it created a heightened level of interest that centered on the question of what was a better outcome for the child. As the relationship between the judicial and executive branches improved, one employee of one of the branches noted, "I trust [the other] with my life."[85] The court is now viewed as "better than it was 25 years ago."[86]

Overall, the numerous positive examples of leadership from public managers far outweighed the negative comments. Not only were public managers in the judicial and executive branches making changes, but they also were revising their philosophies about the best approach to foster care. There were public managers in high-level positions who focused on "thinking of the child first" and "no reject, no eject;" public managers who were committed to process improvements such as training and caseload management; and public managers who were focused on relationships with community partners and a desire to improve state performance on the federal requirements. These public managers, making and correcting mistakes along the way, moved beyond simply performing their required functions to making the processes better, creating stronger partnerships, and solving problems. Public managers showed extraordinary leadership by "going above and beyond their duty" as principled agents do. This was consistent across every interview I conducted with public managers in Delaware's foster care system.

AUXILIARY FINDINGS

This research was designed to find out how to improve foster care administration by looking at what variables have led to success in states with better-performing foster care systems. This case research was not designed

60 Politics of Foster Care Administration

to track how former foster care children fared in the long term under the current foster care system. Although the case of Delaware explains some of the factors that contribute to their classification as a top-performing state, the case can also provide a glimpse into the limits of long-term outcomes for former foster children.

This top-performing foster care state still has difficulty in setting foster care children up for success in their adult lives. The interviews uncovered a disconnect between effective public administration, which produced successful outputs as defined by the federal performance measures, and long-term outcomes for former foster care children. Michael Kersteter, executive director of the foster care provider People's Place, stated: "Only 50% of my kids will make it. Not homeless, not in jail. The rest is really a crapshoot."[87] When I asked other interviewees about the long-term prospects of foster children, they were hesitant to conclude that former foster children would have reasonable rates of success in their adult lives.

In response to a question about how these children would succeed in life once they left foster care, Vincent Giampeitro, program director of Children and Families First asked, "When you were 18, were you able to make it on your own without the support of your parents?"[88] He went on to talk about how foster children leave the foster system at the age of 18, have no support network, and struggle to make it on their own.

If the stronger states are struggling to produce long-term foster care success results, this suggests that national foster care and national foster care policy have serious limitations. If Delaware is a top-performing state, possibly *the* top-performing state on foster care issues depending on how you measure the data, and struggles to set up its foster care population for long-term success, then the foster care system is limited.

It could be argued that federal performance measures are too high, and is thus the reason for poor state performance even at the top. The federal government sets its foster care outcome indicators intentionally high, and no states are performing at the expected levels.[89] Wade Horn, Assistant Secretary for Children and Families, noted that of the 14 outcomes measured (this includes suboutcomes), the states reviewed have ranged from meeting only one to nine of the outcomes. Commenting on this, he stated before the U.S. House of Representatives Committee on Ways and Means that "significant weaknesses are evident in programs across the nation."[90] The federal government has raised the state performance bar even higher, from demonstrating successful performance at 90% in 2001, to demonstrating successful performance at 95% in 2007.[91] DFS foster care program manager John Bates said that he felt Delaware was "pressed to meet high standards" when the federal government raised the bar from 90% to 95%. Delaware is struggling to meet its federal performance goals. This research suggests that the foster care system should consider focusing on long-term success rates for foster youth in addition to short-term performance measurements.

CONCLUSION

The hypothesis was that *Delaware became a stronger-performing state in the area of foster care by placing a greater priority on building community partners, integrating the advice of mentors, providing leadership from public managers, and cultivating relationships with the federal government.* This Delaware case research showed that the cultivation of relationships with the federal government was not a major factor, the building of community partners was a strong factor, the integration of advice from mentors was a minimal factor, and the leadership from public managers was a strong factor in contributing to the state's success on foster care issues. In other words, some of the variables were significant and some were not. The strongest factors were the presence of community partners and public managers, particularly the way that public managers brokered relationships across the branches of government and among internal units, as well as with community partners.

Newer public administration literature[92] generally posits that strong public management helps to promote the success of government programs. This Delaware case research builds on the thesis that strong public management matters and helps to explain *what* strong public managers do to create success. In other words, how do strong public managers who act as principled agents "strive, support and sacrifice"? Years ago, I asked the former mayor of Philadelphia what an individual could accomplish in the role of mayor. Mayor W. Wilson Goode, Sr., responded that the mayor has the ability to make everyone sit around a table and solve a problem. In Delaware, public managers are gathering community partners and conducting cross-branch collaboration in order to problem-solve at the foster care table.

At the same time that Delaware was entertaining the thought of not taking federal money for foster care programs in the future, Delaware public managers were still focused on improving the state's federal performance measurements. These federal performance measurements would not be necessary if the state rejected federal money. This suggests that the state's interest in improving foster care for children was not tied to money, but rather to a real desire to improve the lives of foster children.

List of Interviews

Interviewees listed here may have been utilized for quotes, off-the-record data, and/or background data only. Some interviews were conducted specifically for this Delaware case and others served to inform more broadly across many states or across issue areas addressed in this study.

62 Politics of Foster Care Administration

John Bates, Foster Care Program Manager, Division of Family Services, Delaware, interview, Wilmington, Delaware, August 15, 2007. Bates was Delaware's foster care program manager for over five years. Additional foster care data was provided on August 15, 2007, by DFS worker Mike.

Elizabeth Bouchelle, Director of Grants and Donor Services, Delaware Community Foundation, phone interview, August 7, 2007. Delaware Community Foundation makes grants to foster care.

Christine Craig, HHS-ACF Region III Program Specialist, federal government, phone interview, June 3, 2008. Craig oversees Delaware in addition to another state. Craig worked on the Title IV-E eligibility review for Delaware from October 2005 to March 2006.

Tania Culley, Executive Director of the Office of the Child Advocate; Executive Director of Child Protection Accountability Commission (CPAC), interview, Wilmington, Delaware, September 6, 2007.

Cari DeSantis, Cabinet Secretary, Department of Services for Children, Youth and Their Families, Delaware; Chair, National Council State Human Service Administrators, phone interview, December 19, 2007.

Del Failing, Director of Children's Services, People's Place, interview, Milford, Delaware, August 24, 2007. Failing also serves as a member of the Delaware Foster Care Advisory and Advocacy Council. People's Place is a foster care provider in Delaware.

Vincent Giampeitro, Program Director, Children and Families First, interview, Wilmington, Delaware, August 24, 2007. Giampeitro served as the foster care program director for five years for the second largest provider of foster care in Delaware. He also worked on youth issues/foster care for the Division of Family and Youth Services in New Jersey for 25 years.

Carlyse Giddens, Director, Division of Family Services, Delaware, interview, Wilmington, Delaware, August 15, 2007. Giddens, who reports directly to the Delaware Cabinet Secretary of the Department of Services for Children, Youth and Their Families, is the nation's longest serving DFS director. She celebrated 10 years in September 2007 with DFS.

Sandy Johnson, Director, Delaware State Housing Authority, interview, Philadelphia, Pennsylvania, date not recorded. Johnson provided an overview of Delaware's government structure.

Michael Kersteter, Executive Director, People's Place, interview, Milford, Delaware, August 24, 2007. People's Place is a Delaware foster care provider that handles the most challenging foster care cases.

Arkadi Kuhlmann, Chairman, President, and CEO, ING Direct, author-conducted interview on WWDB, Philadelphia Business Talk

Radio, November 3, 2006. Kuhlmann has a personal interest in foster care issues and funds Delaware foster care programs through the ING Direct Kids Foundation.

Chandlee Johnson Kuhn, Chief Judge, Family Court of the State of Delaware, interview, Wilmington, Delaware, August 30, 2007. Kuhn served as chief judge for 4 years and served 10 years as a judge with jurisdiction over foster care.

Ruth Ann Minner, Governor of Delaware, interview, Wilmington, Delaware, October 1, 2007. Minner had served as governor since 2001.

Leslie Newman, Executive Director, Children and Families First, interview, Wilmington, Delaware, August 24, 2007. Children and Families First is the second largest provider of foster care in Delaware. Newman also previously served as a development director at Children and Families First.

Meghan Pasricha, Founder and President, Global Youth H.E.L.P., phone interview, October 19, 2007. Pasricha is a Harvard undergraduate and received the 2007 World of Children Founder's Youth Award. Global Youth H.E.L.P. partnered with Bank of America to serve foster children.

Lisa Pearson, HHS-ACF Region III Program Manager, federal government, phone interview, June 3, 2008. Pearson reports directly to the HHS-ACF Commissioner. She is responsible for management of Delaware, the District of Columbia, Maryland, Pennsylvania, Virginia, and West Virginia.

Brent Thompson, Director of Communications, William Penn Foundation, informal interview, Philadelphia, Pennsylvania, August 7, 2007. Thompson reported directly to the Penn Foundation's former president and served as a primary contact in the president's absence.

Carole Thompson, Senior Program Officer, Annie E. Casey Foundation, interview, Philadelphia, Pennsylvania, August 16, 2007. The collective Casey family foundations make it the single largest foundation to conduct work in the area of foster care.

Muna Walker, Senior Program Officer, Amachi, Public/Private Ventures, interview, Philadelphia, Pennsylvania, fall 2006. Walker has responsibility for the Mentoring Children of Prisoners program, which has significant client overlap with the foster care system.

Barbara Wilson, Program Officer, Senior Corps, Corporation for National and Community Service (CNCS) federal program, phone and written correspondence with author, fall 2006. Senior Corps provides volunteers in states for foster care.

64   *Politics of Foster Care Administration*

NOTES

1. Note: All references in the summary are cited in this chapter. Data refers to the period of research.
2. U.S. Census Bureau, "2003 American Community Survey," http://www.census.gov.
3. The Pew Commission on Children in Foster Care, "Foster Care Population and States Ranked by Total Number of Children in Foster Care. FY2003," http://pewfostercare.org/research/docs/Data091505.pdf.
4. Ibid.
5. John Bates, Foster Care Program Manager, Division of Family Services, Delaware, foster care general statistics letter to author, August 2007.
6. Carlyse Giddens, Director, Division of Family Services, Delaware, interview, Wilmington, Delaware, August 15, 2007.
7. State of Delaware, "Governor Minner Endorses Foster Care Task Force Recommendations," Press Release, June 26, 2001, http://www.state.de.us/kids/pdfs/pr_2001.pdf.
8. Carlyse Giddens, interview.
9. Cari DeSantis, Cabinet Secretary, Department of Services for Children, Youth and Their Families, Delaware; Chair, National Council State Human Service Administrators, phone interview, December 19, 2007.
10. Carlyse Giddens, interview.
11. Ibid.
12. Ruth Ann Minner, Governor of Delaware, interview, Wilmington, Delaware, October 1, 2007.
13. Carlyse DeSantis, interview.
14. Ibid.
15. Barbara Wilson, Program Officer, Senior Corps, Corporation for National and Community Service (CNCS) federal program, phone and written correspondence with author, fall 2006; Barbara Wilson, 16-page paper prepared for author, "Senior Corps Highlights Foster Care Activities," October 2006. Note: This conclusion was based on the above information plus other interviews.
16. Christine Craig, HHS-ACF Region III Program Specialist, federal government, phone interview, June 3, 2008.
17. Del Failing, Director of Children's Services, People's Place, interview, Milford, Delaware, August 24, 2007.
18. Carlyse Giddens, interview.
19. Note: This work is conducted through Casey Family Services.
20. Carole Thompson, Senior Program Officer, Annie E. Casey Foundation, interview, Philadelphia, Pennsylvania, August 16, 2007.
21. Note: Padot worked for a different unit of the Pew Charitable Trusts and, therefore, had no involvement on the project cited.
22. Note: Local becomes of particular importance when states have large foster care operations in cities such as Detroit or New York City.
23. Vincent Giampeitro, Program Director, Children and Families First, interview, Wilmington, Delaware, August 24, 2007.
24. Carlyse Giddens, interview.
25. John Bates, interview.
26. Tania Culley, Executive Director of the Office of the Child Advocate; Executive Director of Child Protection Accountability Commission, interview, Wilmington, Delaware, September 6, 2007.

Delaware 65

27. "Delaware State Courts: The Official Website of the Delaware Judiciary," http://courts.state.de.us/childadvocate/html/cpac.htm#membership.
28. Tania Culley, interview.
29. Ibid.
30. Ibid.
31. Ibid.
32. Ibid.
33. Carlyse Giddens, interview; John Bates, interview; Tania Culley, interview; Vince Giampeitro, interview; Del Failing, interview.
34. Michael Kersteter, Executive Director, People's Place, interview, Milford, Delaware, August 24, 2007; Del Failing, interview.
35. Carlyse Giddens, interview.
36. John Bates, interview; Del Failing, interview.
37. Arkadi Kuhlmann, Chairman, President, and CEO, ING Direct, author-conducted interview on WWDB, Philadelphia Business Talk Radio, November 3, 2006; Del Failing, interview.
38. Del Failing, interview.
39. Meghan Pasricha, Founder and President, Global Youth H.E.L.P., phone interview, October 19, 2007.
40. Carlyse Giddens, interview.
41. Note: Churches have provided direct donations to foster care organizations.
42. Carlyse Giddens, interview.
43. Ibid.
44. Del Failing, interview.
45. Vincent Giampeitro, interview.
46. John Bates, interview.
47. Carlyse Giddens, interview.
48. John Bates, interview.
49. Vincent Giampeitro, interview.
50. Ruth Ann Minner, interview.
51. Mark Moore, *Creating Public Value: Strategic Management in Government* (Cambridge, MA: Harvard University Press, 1995), 10.
52. Vincent Giampeitro, interview.
53. Del Failing, interview.
54. Ibid.
55. Vincent Giampeitro, interview.
56. Meghan Pasricha, interview.
57. Ibid.
58. Confidential remarks.
59. Ibid.
60. Cari DeSantis (Delaware Children's Department Cabinet Secretary), "Think of the Child First. Foster Care Reform 2000–2006," Delaware Children's Department, http://www.state.de.us/kids/pdfs/fs_foster_care_reform_2006.pdf.
61. Note: This legislation changed the name of the Independent Living program to the Chafee Foster Care Independence Program.
62. U.S. Social Security Administration, "The Foster Care Independence Act of 1999," *Social Security Legislative Bulletin*, November 24, 1999, pp. 106–12. http://www.ssa.gov/legislation/legis_bulletin_112499.html.
63. Kids Count Data Center, a Project of the Annie E. Casey Foundation, "Children in Foster Care by Placement Type," http://datacenter.kidscount.org/data/tables/6247-children-in-foster-care-by-placement-type?loc=1&loct=2#ranking/2/any/true/133/2621/12994.

66 Politics of Foster Care Administration

64. Note: The Delaware Kinship Care Program is a multi-agency partnership that does not provide a fixed amount to all kinship caregivers. Financial eligibility is instead determined by the caregiver's family income and financial assistance is authorized for clothing, school supplies, bedroom supplies, and so forth. Effective January 6, 2014. http://dhss.delaware.gov/dhss/dsaapd/relative.html.
65. Ruth Ann Minner, interview.
66. Ibid.
67. Ibid.
68. John Bates, interview.
69. Ibid.
70. Ibid.
71. Vincent Giampeitro, interview.
72. Ruth Ann Minner, interview.
73. Carlyse Giddens, interview.
74. John Bates, interview.
75. Carlyse Giddens, interview.
76. John Bates, interview.
77. Ruth Ann Minner, interview.
78. Vincent Giampeitro, interview.
79. Confidential remarks.
80. Vincent Giampeitro, interview.
81. Ibid.
82. Confidential remarks.
83. Confidential remarks.
84. Confidential remarks.
85. Confidential remarks.
86. Vincent Giampeitro, interview.
87. Michael Kersteter, interview.
88. Vincent Giampeitro, interview.
89. County Welfare Directors Association of California, "Questions & Answers: Federal Child and Family Service Review," http://www.cwda.org/downloads/child-fam-review/QAs.pdf.
90. U.S. Department of Health and Human Services, "Current State of Child Welfare Financing and the Need for Reform," testimony by Wade Horn, Assistant Secretary for Children and Families, U.S. Department of Health and Human Services. Presented to the Committee on Ways and Means Subcommittee on Human Resources. U.S. House of Representatives, June 5, 2005, http://www.hhs.gov/asl/testify/t050609b.html.
91. Beth Miller, "Delaware Child Welfare Gets B-Minus, Official Says," *The News Journal*, August 8, 2007.
92. John J. DiIulio, Jr., *Governing Prisons: A Comparative Study of Correctional Management* (New York: The Free Press, 1987); Jameson W. Doig and Erwin C. Hargrove, *Leadership and Innovation: Entrepreneurs in Government*, Abridged (Baltimore, MD: The Johns Hopkins University Press, 1990).

4 New York
A Larger State with Weaker Performance

There is "very little involvement by the state" on foster care.

—Nicholas Pirro, former president of the New York State Association of Counties and former president of the County Executive Association for New York

---

NEW YORK: FOSTER CARE DATA SUMMARY[1]

Agency and Foster Care Funding

The New York State Office of Children and Family Services handles foster care administration for the state of New York. New York City's Administration for Children's Services (ACS) serves as the major hub of foster care in New York State. New York State estimates that it spends an average of $18,552 per foster child. The director of the Office of Strategic Planning for the New York State Office of Children and Family Services (the top foster care official in the state) stated that in 1996, 80% of foster care cases were federal government Title IV-E eligible, and in 2007, only 40% of foster care cases were Title IV-E eligible.

Foster Care Population

As of 2003, New York had a population of 18,600,527 with 199 foster care cases per 100,000 people. New York was the second-largest foster care state in 2003. Michigan and New York were the two large states studied, and Rhode Island and Delaware were the two smaller states studied.

As of FY 2003, New York had 37,067 foster care children representing 7.1% of the foster care population across the country. Although New York had 37,067 children in the foster care system in 2003, by 2007

68 Politics of Foster Care Administration

there were only 27,300 children in foster care. More foster care children were from New York City than the rest of the state combined. The Highbridge region in the Bronx was the number one largest foster care district in New York City. Foster children are permitted to stay in care until age 21, although they are not permitted to enter foster care after age 18 unless they were previously in foster care. Approximately 50% of the children in New York State's foster care system are aged 13 to 21.

Foster Care Administration

New York foster care is state administered and county implemented. New York State is responsible for setting overall policy, foster care provider rates, and federal/state spending decisions. Shelters are utilized minimally in the state and there is a current emphasis to shift children out of residential placements into families. New York State incorporates a county-run system, with New York City being the largest segment. New York City's ACS reports to New York State's Office of Children and Family Services, although this seems to be primarily for administrative purposes. New York City manages its own foster care administration and handles approximately two-thirds of the foster care caseload for the state. New York City is divided into 5 boroughs and 59 service districts for foster care and other community services.

This chapter provides case research on foster care in the state of New York. The research was designed to test whether the following hypothesis is accurate: *Delaware and Michigan became stronger-performing states in the area of foster care by placing a greater priority than the lower-performing states of New York and Rhode Island on building community partners, integrating the advice of mentors, providing leadership from public managers, and cultivating relationships with the federal government.* The hypothesis posed is that Rhode Island and New York relied less on these strategies and therefore struggled to obtain better results.

New York is one of the two larger states in this study, and it falls into the category of a weaker case state according to the 2003 federal performance measures. As of 2003, New York had a population of 18,600,527[2] with 199 foster care cases per 100,000 people.[3] New York was the second-largest foster care state in 2003. As of FY 2003, New York had 37,067 foster care children, representing 7.1% of the foster care population across the country.[4] Although New York had 37,067 children in the foster care system in 2003, by 2007 there were only 27,300 children in foster care.[5]

The results of this research suggest that the four variables studied had differing degrees of influence upon the success of New York's foster care system. The cultivation of relationships with the federal government was not a major factor, whereas the building of community partners, the integration of advice from mentors, and the leadership from public managers only showed a stronger presence over time. I also found that when these variables were shown to have a greater significance, this was at the city level rather than the state level.

CASE BACKGROUND

Like all other states during the period of field research, New York had been undergoing federal government reviews for Title IV-E eligibility as well as for Child and Family Service Reviews. New York performed near the bottom of the states on the Child and Family Service Reviews as shown by the "Child Welfare Outcomes 2003: Annual Report" in Chapter 2. New York was designated as a weaker case state because the state performed below the median on six out of seven foster care outcomes measured in 2003. The state barely improved its score on these outcome measures between the years 2000 and 2003; its improvement was less than the median improvement of all states during that period.

In the area of foster care, New York is "state administered and county implemented."[6] New York State is responsible for setting the overall policy, foster care provider rates, and federal/state spending allocations. The state uses a county-run system, with New York City carrying the bulk of the foster care caseload. The larger New York counties "mix contract and direct provider, such as Suffolk and Erie Counties."[7] The counties license and determine subsidy rates for foster parents.[8] New York City's ACS officially reports to New York State's Office of Children and Family Services, but in practice it operates as a peer to the state because the city serves more foster care children than the rest of the state combined. According to the New York State Citizens' Coalition for Children, approximately two-thirds of foster care children in the state come from New York City.[9] New York City is divided into 5 boroughs and 59 service districts, which provide foster care and other community services. The city is "all contract out,"[10] meaning that it does not maintain any of its own foster care programs but rather pays external nonprofit organizations to maintain them.

Across New York State, shelters are utilized minimally for foster care programs. There is a current emphasis to shift children out of residential placements and into families, according to the New York State Citizens' Coalition for Children.[11] Foster children are permitted to stay in care until age 21, although they are not permitted to enter foster care after age 18 unless they were previously in foster care.[12] Approximately 50% of the children in New York State foster care are aged 13 to 21.[13]

70 *Politics of Foster Care Administration*

Field research was completed in New York between October and December 2007, and it involved conducting interviews, viewing documents, and visiting state offices and foster care agencies. The purpose of field research was to begin to identify what conditions produce better foster care outcomes. Interview topics focused on the interviewee's areas of expertise in relation to foster care administration. Although the majority of interviews occurred in the field, some follow-up telephone interviews in 2007 and 2008 were conducted. At times, interviewees requested that all or part of their comments remain off the record.

Ten interviews were conducted on foster care in the state of New York specifically. Interviews were requested with "key players" who were actively involved with New York's foster care decisions. All interviews pursued in the state were granted. I interviewed the New York State foster care manager and individuals who held upper-level positions at New York City's Administration for Children's Services. I also interviewed the co-director of the New York City Partnership for Family Supports and Justice; the executive director of the New York State Citizens' Coalition for Children; the program director of Foster Family Services for the Jewish Child Care Association; the reunification supervisor of Foster Family Services for the Jewish Child Care Association; the director of the Child Welfare Organizing Project; and the former president of the New York State Association of Counties who also served as the president of the County Executive Association of New York.

Similar to the interviewees from the case state of Delaware, the New York interviewees were fairly honest about the effectiveness of their foster care system, and accounts were fairly consistent across interviews. The average New York interviewee had an extensive history with New York foster care and a career path that reflected various stops at city agencies and private sector positions. Of the four case states, New York had the most interviewees who had been involved with foster care over a long time period in many different public/private positions. This long-term, multi-agency perspective gave the New York interviewees, in particular, a deeper understanding of the intricacies of foster care in their state. As a result, I was able to capture the New York story in a condensed time frame.

Most of the New York interviews took place in person and were completed during field research in upstate New York, lower Manhattan, Harlem, and the Bronx. I traveled to upstate New York to visit the New York State Office of Children and Family Services and to interview the New York State foster care program manager.

Some of the areas of New York City with dense foster care population also posed a danger for me as a researcher. In Harlem, a firecracker was intentionally thrown in my direction as I was walking to an interview. Another time, after a cab driver dropped me off at the wrong address in Harlem, several residents would not assist me because, I suspect, they feared I was with the government and was there to "bust someone." While walking through the largest foster care district in New York City, I was the only

Caucasian among thousands of people in the Highbridge area of the Bronx. I was both hollered at and followed while walking dozens of blocks.

The dangerous situations that I encountered while conducting interviews in New York City far exceeded the number of similar experiences in any other case state, including Michigan and its heavy foster care caseload in Detroit. With the exception of a handful of sites in New York City, I never feared for my safety in any other case state interview. I share these observations to illuminate one of the key challenges that New York faces in its drive to improve foster care. For instance, potential foster care parents in Manhattan may not be willing to foster a child in Highbridge if they must travel to areas that may pose danger.

The New York case was much more complicated than that of Delaware because of the complex relationship between the cities/counties and the state. While the state is ultimately responsible for foster care outcomes, the bulk of foster care work takes place in New York City. Thus, in this state, I conducted more interviews with local officials, such as those from New York City's ACS. On the other hand, I did not request interviews with chief executives, such as the governor and mayor, because they were not consistently involved with foster care issues. Unlike my experience in Delaware, not one interviewee in New York referred to the governor's role on the issue of foster care.

In addition, I conducted seven interviews that broadly informed my research on foster care and provided background for New York and the other case states. These interviews were referred to in the Delaware chapter as well, with the exception of the associate commissioner of the Family Youth and Services Bureau at the U.S. Department of Health and Human Services. A complete list of interviews is offered at the end of this chapter.

CASE FINDINGS

This section presents the findings from the New York case research. Each of the four variables is analyzed, and a summary is offered noting their estimated significance based on research results. New York is considered a bottom-performing state with very little improvement from 2000 to 2003. Yet, this section will illustrate that New York is in a transitional period of improvement that corresponds with the 2007–2008 research period.

New York City has its own distinct pattern of performance. The city has employed three different commissioners at the Administration for Children's Services over the last 15 years. Commissioner Nicholas Scoppetta served from 1996 to 2001, Commissioner William C. Bell served from 2001 to 2004, and Commissioner John B. Mattingly served from 2004 through the period of this research. This case study demonstrates that there have been signs of foster care administration improvement in New York City with each new commissioner. These improvements had a positive influence on some of the variables in the study.

72 Politics of Foster Care Administration

Cultivation of Federal Government Relationships:
Significance = None

For the variable *cultivation of federal government relationships* to appear strong, the data needed to show a pattern of interaction between the federal government and the state that went *beyond* the required relationship. This factor is shown to have a stronger presence when the federal government has significantly shifted the direction of the state's decision-making path regarding the provision of foster care in some nonrequired area. In other words, the federal–state relationship on foster care needed to transcend the required form completion, grant processing, regulation monitoring, and data gathering and move into how to fix and transform foster care.

New York, like the other case states, has experienced a rapid decrease in the federal funds that helped to cover the expenses of its foster care caseload. Nancy Martinez, director of strategic planning and policy development for the New York State Office of Children and Family Services, stated: "In 1996, 80% of [New York] foster care cases were federal government Title IV-E eligible, and in 2007 only 40% of [New York] foster care cases are IV-E eligible."[14] Like Delaware, New York has increased its level of foster care funding to make up for the decline in federal foster care funds. At the time of this field research, New York spent an average of $18,552 per foster care child; this total includes funds from the federal government, New York State, and the counties.[15]

In what is best described as a domino effect, New York State has also chosen to shift some of the foster care funding burden to its counties. According to Nicholas Pirro, who was the former president of the New York State Association of Counties as well as the former president of the County Executive Associations, "The state of New York has consistently tried to push off their responsibility for funding to county and local governments [for foster care, as well as in other areas]."[16] Pirro, who also served as the Onondaga County executive and as the chairman of the Onondaga County Legislature (Syracuse area) added, "When the state budget comes out, there's always some attempt to shift some of the cost to the local programs. This is a constant battle."[17] In 2004, Pirro fought New York State when the state attempted to change the foster care funding formula and retroactively reduced the amount of funding that the counties would receive for their previous 10 months of expenses. His county would have lost $727,000, although it only carries an average caseload of 250 to 300 foster care children.[18] Pirro eventually had some success in fighting New York State after going public with his battle and spending some money on advertising. In New York, the federal state funding tug-of-war turned into a funding tug-of-war between the state and the counties.

The other area of potential interaction between the states and the federal government on foster care issues is technical assistance to the state foster care program. Christine Craig, a program specialist with the federal government, said: "We provide technical assistance [to the states]. We can provide on-site technical assistance as well. [The states] may only use a couple of resource centers during the years. [The states] may go for practice, legal, or judicial issues."[19] However, the New York State foster care program manager, Nancy Martinez, did not even reference this assistance by the federal government when she was asked about the role of the federal government's relationship with New York State. Although the question was specifically asked, there was very little mention of the federal government's role in New York's foster care system throughout most interviews.

Additionally, it seemed clear that the federal government did not cultivate a relationship with the state beyond the level of normal required paperwork. As in Delaware, the New York State foster care program manager, Nancy Martinez, actually showed me a copy of the heavy report in her office that was to be completed for the federal government. There were references throughout New York interviews to the piles of paperwork and onerous form completion requested by the federal government. As is the case for all states, the federal government required New York to report on financial outlays and foster care performance measurement outcomes. The federal government has also begun to require significant paperwork from the states on Title IV-E. The federal government audits the individual case paperwork, and now it "won't even allow cases [for federal funding] that are potentially eligible. This reduced funding [to the state]."[20]

In summary, the New York case shows a transactional relationship between the federal government and the state instead of a "workhorse" relationship. The federal government required a significant amount of paperwork despite its reduced role in funding foster care in the state. In this study, New York is considered a weaker state; therefore, one would expect a lower significance level for this variable. The case highlighted the changing role of the federal government because of its reduced financing of foster care. New York State's response to this was to pass off some of these costs to its counties.

The Integration of Advice from Mentors: Significance = None in the Past, Stronger Presence over Time

The hypothesis is that the stronger states will have stronger (defined as more or deeper) mentors who offer strategic advice or training on the issue of foster care. *Mentors are defined here as foundations, issue-expert national nonprofit organizations, or think tanks that focus on foster care.* The strong presence of mentors is reflected by a workhorse relationship in which the state has either a large network of mentors or a rigorous relationship with one mentor organization. Workhorse relationships are deeper relationships in which mentors discuss ideas with the state, and the state then takes action.

74 Politics of Foster Care Administration

This factor is shown to have a stronger presence when the mentors have significantly shifted the direction of the state's decision-making path regarding the provision of foster care in some nonrequired area.

Previous Utilization of Mentors
The organizations that conduct work in the field of foster care nationally are the Annie E. Casey Foundation, Casey Family Services, the Pew Charitable Trusts, and other child welfare organizations and policy advocates. Interviewees could not identify any influential organization that had promoted successful foster care administration during the earlier NYC ACS Scoppetta and Bell terms. Interviewees were not aware of model foster care states to mimic or best practices.

New York State interviewees also did not reference any mentoring from organizations during any time period. The state foster care program manager noted simply that "there are occasions when we reach out to foundations and nonprofits."[21] Because so many interviewees had a decade or more of employment in the area of New York child welfare and were easily able to cite key players and key organizations, these interviews confirmed that New York State and City were not utilizing mentors in their administration of foster care programs.

The Mattingly Era 2004–2008
As I suggested earlier, the stronger significance of certain variables has corresponded with an increase in foster care success in New York State because of developments in the New York City region. Following terms of Commissioners Scoppetta and Bell, New York City ACS Commissioner John B. Mattingly was appointed in July 2004 and has served in this position throughout the period of this research. His administration marked a change in the utilization of mentors in New York City and this was partially because he had previously worked for the Casey foundations. While at the Annie E. Casey Foundation, Mattingly served as the director of human service reforms. During his tenure at Casey, Mattingly "designed and for twelve years managed the Family to Family foster care initiative."[22] Most interviewees were aware of the fact that Mattingly was "from Casey" and recognized that he had brought best practices from Casey with him.

Mattingly filled many current NYC ACS positions with former Casey staff members, and he also relied upon current Casey staff for advice on best practices. Many interviewees were aware of this influx of Casey influence and thought it led to improvements in foster care. Richard Hucke, program director of foster family services at the Jewish Child Care Association, noted that "half of the staff at ACS are people [Mattingly has] pulled in from Casey."[23] This new era also brought more emphasis on training and coordination. Hucke had just attended a Casey seminar the week before our conversation; the seminar had been arranged by one of Mattingly's Casey contacts. Hucke concluded, "Casey has been involved in a lot of the work groups and has helped agencies collaborate."[24]

New York   75

Because Casey had such an influence during the Mattingly era at ACS, this also brought clashes of culture from the two organizations. One interviewee noted:

> I don't find [Casey] to be very helpful. Here in New York [they don't have a lot of impact]. They don't even know how the whole system works and they're giving info on family visiting. Most of them come from Cleveland, Ohio. There, you're not dealing with a lot of voluntary agencies.[25]

However, it appears that a heightened presence of best practices was connected with the foundation and has led to some systematic change. Casey was the only mentor mentioned in the New York case.

In summary, the New York case reflects a lack of integration of advice from mentors on the state level, but a stronger presence of mentors in New York City during the Mattingly administration specifically. The perception of improvement in New York by interviewees has paralleled the stronger incorporation of recent mentoring by Casey.

Building of Community Partners: Significance = None in the Past, Stronger Presence over Time

The hypothesis is that the stronger states will have stronger (defined as more or deeper) community partnerships. *Community partnerships are defined here as state and/or local[26] foster care agency relationships with local nonprofits, faith-based organizations, and community organizations.* The strong presence of community partners is reflected by a workhorse relationship in which the state has either a large network of community partners or a rigorous relationship with one community partner. Workhorse relationships are deeper relationships in which community partners discuss ideas with the state, and the state then takes action.

A workhorse relationship might include government and community organizations copromoting a conference with mutual organizational roles, or deciding together to more aggressively pursue homes for older female teens. This factor is shown to have a stronger presence when the community partners have significantly shifted the direction of the state's decision-making path regarding the provision of foster care in some area. Basic administrative paperwork or meetings between a community partner and the state do not qualify as a strong presence of this variable.

Previous Utilization of Community Partners

New York has always had many community partners in the area of foster care, particularly in New York City. However, no interviewee made reference to community partners having a significant influence on the state's decision-making path regarding the provision of foster care in some area. Prior to the Mattingly administration, although community partners served

76 Politics of Foster Care Administration

the community, the government was not utilizing the expertise of the community partners to help the state solve problems or create effective policy.

2004–2008

The integration of community partners by New York City government has become more noticeable over time. Further, NYC ACS commissioner Mattingly (post 2004) has integrated community partnerships into the process more so than earlier administrations.

There are multiple examples of a clear shift in New York City administrative policy toward working with community partners. Highbridge, New York, was the region with the largest number of foster care children in New York City as of 2002–2003; therefore, it had developed a reputation as the "number one worst."[27] So, in 2003, a group of community partners, foundations, and nonprofits convened to create an organization called "Bridge Builders." The meeting resulted in 10 foundation partners committing to a 4-year initiative and conceptualizing a desire to involve neighborhoods by creating six seats for residents who would have a voice on foster care issues. Today, Bridge Builders works with 4,000 families in the area, with the goal of providing help before the children end up in foster care. One example included a 23-year-old with five children who had no running water or food and a landlord threatening to evict the family. Bridge Builders went to her landlord and said "we'll expose you [to folks]."[28] Then, Bridge Builders worked with the family to secure care for the children and keep them out of the foster care system. This type of preventative work is in addition to the work Bridge Builders provides to foster care families on the back end by assisting with placements, length of stay, and reunification.

Bridge Builders was funded entirely by $1 million in donations by community partners in its first year; NYC ACS did not provide any support. ACS said, "We have no money [for Bridge Builders], but we want a voice." However, after seeing the organizations' success, ACS offered to provide an in-kind donation of a one person full-time equivalent to Bridge Builders. This person was Francis Ayuso, who was at the time responsible for all 12 foster care service districts in the Bronx as the ACS borough coordinator. Initially, Ayuso served as the liaison for ACS between the Bridge Builders and the government. Then ACS took over the project, and he became an ACS employee serving as project director of Bridge Builders. Ayuso's love for his job was evident. He remarked, "There are 6,000 employees in ACS and I'm the luckiest employee. This is my passion to shape a program. I love community organizing with dollars."[29]

Operating as an employee of NYC ACS, Ayuso set out to repair the government's scarred relationship with the community. He said, "We know there's baggage [from the government] and we want you to be part of the solution."[30] Ayuso attempted to repair the government's tarnished reputation by reaching out to the community. Ayuso's ability to broker partners, the government, and the community is an example of strong leadership by a public manager.

Because of the success of Bridge Builders, the donors' collaborative decided to extend the project through 2009 and then transition the program back over to the neighborhood. Ayuso believes that as a result of their preventative work, they have stabilized the number of children entering foster care. From the absolute worst foster care area in New York City, Highbridge had become the second-worst foster care area within the first few years of Bridge Builders' work.

The Bridge Builders community partnership has changed foster care in the Bronx so much so that Commissioner Mattingly has noticed and visited. Ayuso believes that a visit from previous Commissioners Scoppetta and Bell to the Bronx would not have occurred.[31] Ayuso recalled Mattingly's public comments during his on-site visit: "We have a lot of meetings around complaints. We are here, and we want to help with this project. Include us in the solution."[32]

Bridge Builders' work in this neighborhood community was so influential that Mattingly returned to visit Highbridge a second time, and as a result created and seeded the Community Partnership Initiative (CPI) with $150,000. In 2007, Mattingly decided to initiate a CPI pilot in 11 neighborhoods, including Highbridge, Bronx; Jamaica, Queens; and Bedford, Brooklyn.[33] In the *New York Nonprofit Press* in January 2005, Mattingly said, "I think [Bridge Builders] is a perfect example of how a commitment to neighborhood-based services can lead to better services and outcomes."[34] This Bridge Builders project shows how a community partnership with positive results can affect government policy.

The Agenda for Children Tomorrow (ACT), located in lower New York City, provides a second example of a community partnership that has had an impact on public policy in New York. ACT, a public–private collaborative, involves funding from two foundations and has space in the mayor's office. ACT initially brought together 100 leaders from different service sectors in New York City and lobbied for neighborhood and public–private involvement. ACT builds upon and convenes coalitions of organizations and individuals in child welfare to plan strategically and assists public and nonprofit agencies to be more responsive to the needs and strengths of local communities.[35]

The Agenda for Children Tomorrow was influential in shaping a reform plan to divide New York City into service planning areas (SPAs). According to the co-executive directors of ACT, "ACS harvested neighborhood networks [SPAs] in 59 neighborhoods, and ACT had a role in this."[36] The entire New York City foster care system was divided into 59 neighborhoods, with an emphasis on neighborhood networks for better service delivery. This reorganization eliminated the need for caseworkers to sometimes travel more than an hour to reach their cases.

The Child Welfare Organizing Project (CWOP) is a third example of a community partnership that has an impact on public policy in New York. CWOP, located in East Harlem, was created to identify ways that clients of the public child welfare system could become involved in the design, practice,

78 *Politics of Foster Care Administration*

and evaluation of programs and policies that impact their families. CWOP offers parent advisory groups, serves as a contractor lead agency for preventative services, and does research and evaluation of the performance agencies.

Michael Arsham, the director of the Child Welfare Organizing Project, felt that Commissioner Scoppetta was not receptive to invitations to the town hall meetings, nor did he listen to parents. Social worker Arsham noted that Bell was receptive to CWOP's overtures and began to attend town hall meetings. CWOP began work on the parent advisory group with Scoppetta, but it was "more dormant," whereas "Bell took it to the next level" and "even more so with Mattingly."[37]

With the assistance of CWOP, 70% of parents who have lost their children to foster care have had their children returned within 6 months, compared to the New York City average stay of 4 years for foster children.[38] CWOP works with parents to identify tasks that are necessary to improve parenting and acts as a mentor to parents who are working on reunification with their children. Not only is CWOP affecting foster care reunification rates in New York City, but they are also being recognized for their impact on the city. Arsham states, "Both Commissioner Bell and Mattingly would say CWOP had influence on them."[39]

In summary, in the New York case, there was no integration of community partners at the state level, however there was a stronger integration of community partners in New York City over time. The interviewees' perceptions of improvement in the city's foster care situation paralleled the stronger involvement of community partners.

All three examples—Bridge Builders, ACT, and CWOP—showed how community partners increased both their presence and impact over time as they navigated relationships with changing NYC administrations. The community partners had the most impact on the Mattingly administration, which was most receptive to their ideas. Historically, the state has not had a deep relationship with community partners in the areas discussed.

Leadership from Public Managers: Significance = Stronger over Time

The hypothesis is that the stronger states will have more leadership from public managers. *A public manager is shown to evidence leadership when he or she is operating as a "principled agent" in the state or local government or agency responsible for the area of foster care.* In the context of this study, a principled agent is a government employee (public manager) who goes above and beyond his or her public duty to cultivate successful foster care administration. Harvard Kennedy School professor Mark Moore argued that a successful manager "increase(s) the public value produced by public sector organizations in both the short and the long run."[40] A principled agent performs as a workhorse, rather than as a standard government employee who is focused on routine functions. The strong presence

New York   79

of leadership from public managers is reflected by a greater presence of principled agents working in foster care in the case state.

The leadership shown by public managers in New York's foster care system appears to have grown stronger with the changing administrations in New York City. There was nearly universal consensus among the interviewees that NYC ACS commissioner Mattingly represented the strongest administration. This corresponded with the perception among key players reflected in the interviews that New York City has recently emphasized improvement in foster care. The first glimpse of stronger leadership from public managers over time was highlighted in the aforementioned section on community partnerships.

New York City, 1996–2004
During the late 1980s, New York City suffered from a widespread crack epidemic; one costly side effect was a spike in foster care levels to highs of over 40,000 cases as recently as FY 1998.[41] Then, from FY 1998 to FY 2006, New York City experienced a significant and consistent decline in its foster care caseload, from approximately 40,000 foster children in 1998 to 16,700 in 2006.[42]

In addition to the decreasing effect of the crack epidemic, the fluctuation in New York City's foster care caseload can best be attributed to changing foster care administration philosophies. Michael Arsham, the director of the Child Welfare Organizing Project, noted that the initial philosophy of ACS at its 1996 inception was that if there was any ambiguity regarding a child's safety, the safest thing to do was to remove the child from the home. When Scoppetta was commissioner of NYC ACS (1996–2001), he came into the system at

> one of its lowest ebbs; it had been neglected by New York City Mayor Giuliani during the first few years of his administration and he was forced to pay attention to it. Giuliani came down on the side of "remove the kids" (as opposed to family reunification) and then realized the wrong-headedness of that and so changed direction.[43]

This was the opinion expressed by John Courtney, former director of program planning with New York's Child Welfare Administration. Courtney added:

> [Scoppetta operated as if] I'd rather make the mistake of removing the child than run the risk of ever having that child being seriously abused. He painted [with] a much too easy brush. Scoppetta, of anyone, should have realized that a young child being separated from their families for 6 months is not acceptable public policy. We shouldn't just say let's cover our ass and let's sort it out afterwards.[44]

This "remove the child" philosophy helps to partially explain the high number of children in NYC foster care during Commissioner Scoppetta's

80   *Politics of Foster Care Administration*

years (1996–2001). However, Scoppetta did receive praise for "spearheading moving citywide foster care to community-based [care] . . . [so that] reunifying families was a whole lot easier."[45]

Mayor Giuliani had also made cuts in child preventative services, which in New York City comprised a major piece of child welfare policy.[46] These child preventative services were designed to prevent a turbulent family situation from reaching the point where foster care became necessary. The director of the Child Welfare Organizing Project, Michael Arsham, painted a picture of how the Giuliani administration did not like criticism or special interest groups and therefore created a closed organization. In Arsham's opinion, Giuliani treated people as if they were either his cheerleaders or his enemies, but nothing in between.[47] As a result, the Giuliani administration did not promote communication with neighborhoods or the foster care community.

In 2001, Commissioner William C. Bell took over the leadership role for NYC ACS. During his term of service, which continued through 2004, Bell helped to shift the role of parents in the child welfare system and "began to use parents in a more meaningful capacity."[48] The co-executive directors for the public agency Agenda for Children for Tomorrow believed that Commissioner Bell understood how to make changes.[49] Michael Arsham said, "[Prior to Bell] there was a mutually antagonistic relationship with ACS. Now there is more work with collaboration [with Bell's administration]."[50] CWOP approached Bell and Bell was receptive to its overtures, which had not been the case with the previous administration. As the aforementioned community partners section mentioned, Bell began coming to town hall meetings and listening to parents.

The Bell administration also corresponded chronologically with an increase in repeat abuse, well above the 2007 federal standard of 5.4% or less.[51] According to a report funded by the Robert Sterling Clark Foundation and the Edward and Ellen Roche Relief Foundation, the proportion of New York City children whose families were investigated by ACS for repeat maltreatment within 1 year jumped from 9.3% in 2000 to 14.8% in 2005, a 59% increase.[52] As the "remove the child" philosophy was replaced with the more lenient Bell administration philosophy of allowing children to remain with their parents, the rate of repeat maltreatment of children increased. This high repeat maltreatment rate was present during the first 2 years (2004–2005) of the Mattingly administration as well.

Although the ACS has had difficulties with its performance, key players have recognized that improvements in foster care corresponded to changing administrations and a trend of overall progress from Commissioners Scoppetta to Bell to Mattingly. The general consensus was that there have been improvements in foster care over the last decade in New York City, and that while it still has its faults, the system is in better shape today than it was a decade ago. Arsham noted that "the shift to neighborhood-based services began with Scoppetta, then Bell, and now under this commissioner [Mattingly]."[53] He added that there was a "dramatic shift" in regard to relationships that ACS had with neighborhoods over time.[54]

New York City, 2004–2008

The child welfare philosophy regarding the removal of children for placement into foster care shifted again under ACS Commissioner Mattingly, who took office in 2004 and still held the position at the time of field research. During the first 3 years of the Scoppetta administration, 12,000 children a year were removed from their homes, whereas during the first full year of the Mattingly administration in 2004, only 4,800 were removed.[55] These numbers reflect a clear shift in approach, including decisions that ACS would not remove children from their parents because of a potential for future abuse. This marked shift in philosophy, spearheaded by Mattingly, was partially responsible for the significant drop in the number of children in foster care.

At the same time, ACS under Mattingly struggled with its failure to follow up on a pattern of abuse that led to a child's death. New York has had a handful of child deaths under the watch of ACS, including the death of Nixzmary Brown. Brown was a 7-year-old child who was literally beaten to death by her stepfather on January 11, 2006, while her mother watched.[56] Her death occurred after ACS had failed to take action on two abuse complaints, one of which involved Brown showing up to school with a black eye. This story brought additional attention to the issue of child abuse and brought an influx of children into the foster care system. In response, New York City mayor Michael Bloomberg issued a series of foster care reforms, including the creation of a city panel and the decision to create liaison positions between the police department and ACS, with the intent of enabling a more rapid response to abuse claims.[57] In both Delaware and New York, child death cases have prompted officials to implement foster care reforms.

The relationship between Bloomberg and Mattingly has been perceived as close, and as a result, this perception aids Mattingly's ability to implement changes at ACS. According to the former director of program planning with New York City's Child Welfare Administration, John Courtney, "[Bloomberg] sees commissioners as being supported. He expects commissioners to do the job and give them resources."[58] The director of the Child Welfare Organizing Project, Michael Arsham, added: "the mayoral role is tremendous" and acknowledges that Mattingly and Bloomberg have a "tight relationship."[59] Courtney believed that Mattingly was able to convince the mayor to increase resources when needed.[60] Both co-executive directors of the Agenda for Children Tomorrow felt that Bloomberg listens to Mattingly and follows his lead on certain issues.[61] For instance, Mattingly prevailed on the mayor to reinvest in services to hold the foster care population down, and the mayor was supportive.[62] The perception has been that Mattingly also has a good relationship with his ACS deputy, Linda Gibbs.

There are a number of ways in which Mattingly has helped to improve foster care. Mattingly has taken a more active role with the neighborhoods by launching the aforementioned Community Partnership Initiative. Mattingly mandated ACS to become more responsive to neighborhood concerns,[63] and his field offices improved. Mattingly micromanaged the foster care providers less and encouraged foster care providers to use more of their

82 Politics of Foster Care Administration

own judgment. He issued these relaxed policies so that foster care providers could regain some power as managers.[64]

Mattingly also realigned the payment structure in order to motivate agencies to perform. Foster care reimbursement had previously been structured in such a way that foster care providers were financially rewarded for keeping foster children in care longer, so there was no incentive to achieve permanency for a child or to reunify the children with their parents. Foster care providers were previously paid for every day that they had a foster child in their care. When children were moved out of care, the providers stopped getting paid. In essence, foster care providers had a financial disincentive to help these children achieve permanency. The *New York Times* reported that at least three times "reformers have proposed and even won experimental changes in payment, but each experiment has foundered under legal challenges, changes in administration and swelling foster care populations."[65] In 2007, Mattingly was able to eliminate the previous payment structure. His reforms, phased in between 2007 and 2009, instead mandated that foster care agencies "would be paid an amount based on the number of children they serve annually."[66]

Mattingly also increased the number of staff members that were involved with child protection and made improvements in training. "There is a focus now on exiting the system, in addition to entering the system," said John Courtney, former director of program planning with New York City's Child Welfare Administration.[67] He added, "The current administration has been able to hold the number to 17,000 for over a year now."[68]

In March 2007, as part of his reform efforts, Mattingly launched the Improved Outcomes for Children Initiative (IOC). The IOC is a series of reforms that are intended to improve the results of ACS's performance with foster care and preventative services.[69] The IOC was designed to reduce caseloads and incorporate a shared parenting philosophy that fosters communication among all parties involved in the child's life. Another IOC goal was to identify multiple potential caretakers for a child, such as a foster family, original parents, or relatives, and to understand when the child should be moved among caretakers.

The Jewish Child Care Association (JCCA), which receives IOC funding, played a major role in the pilot for this program. The reunification supervisor at JCCA, Kelly Garvey, said that the IOC was expected to move from a pilot program to full implementation throughout the city beginning in July 2008.

Although the shared parenting philosophy was a new concept for Mattingly, JCCA had been implementing this concept for years. Garvey said, "We work with the relationship with the foster parent and parent together . . . feeling the child has split loyalties but helping the child feel more comfortable."[70] Richard Hucke, the program director for Foster Family Services at JCCA, stated: "The Commissioner's new plan—IOC—in theory seems like a good thing."[71]

New York 83

In general, interviewees were aware of the many changes at ACS and were pleased with the improvements that the Mattingly administration was attempting to implement. John Courtney said, "John Mattingly brings experience and knowledge [from] working for Annie Casey. We have a good commissioner . . . barring some unfortunate fatalities that have occurred."[72] The co-executive directors of Agenda for Children Tomorrow added, "Mattingly has conceptual knowledge, and he's getting ACS to be more responsive to the neighborhood."[73]

The perception in New York City that ACS had improved was correlated with the presence of stronger public management over time. Mattingly, a public manager who operated as a "principled agent" by going above and beyond his job requirements, was the first public manager who had been able to reform the 150-year-old foster care provider payment system.[74] Mattingly reached out to foster care providers in the field and brokered relationships with the neighborhoods, as well as with the mayor. He started partnering with community organizations like Bridge Builders and testing new ideas such as IOC. He championed ideas, tested them, and then saw to it that they were implemented.

The presence of other NYC ACS public managers was also noteworthy, such as Francis Ayuso, who was able to institute the Bridge Builders pilot program that improved the foster care situation in Highbridge after Ayuso and community partners together implemented better foster care and preventative services.

Although the New York City system is far from perfect, the presence of stronger public management in the face of changing administrations has corresponded with an increased perception of improvement among interviewees.

New York State

New York State operates independently of New York City's ACS, as do the counties throughout the state. The former Bronx borough coordinator for New York City commented, "The state is very removed, [although there is] some partnership work."[75] The former president of the New York State Association of Counties and the former president of the County Executives Association, Nick Pirro, said there was "very little involvement by the state" on foster care.[76]

The New York State Citizens' Coalition for Children is the longest running and only active statewide foster care parent organization, representing 140 volunteer adoptive and foster parent groups in every region of the state. Executive director Sarah Gerstenzang commented, "There are good efforts by lots of people in New York to improve things."[77] However, there was minimal discussion about how the state helped solve these problems. Gerstenzang stated, "One of our biggest issues in New York State is that there are not enough family court judges. There is a request for 39 judges. Caseworkers are overwhelmed because they're going to court."[78]

84   Politics of Foster Care Administration

The New York State foster care program overseer, Nancy Martinez, splits her time between financial paperwork, the federal government, and a few targeted policies. In her role at the New York State Office of Children and Family Services, she designed a Medicaid waiver that serves 3,000 children in foster care in the state.[79] New York was the first state in the nation to have a Medicaid-funded home with a mental health component for foster care children. In addition to this Medicaid project, which was completed at the state level, the state also handles a few other tasks that are related to foster care. The state sets rates for foster care providers and manages the shifting role of federal government spending versus state spending on this issue.

In general, New York State allows the local service districts to manage their own foster care programs. New York permits the 58 local social service districts in the state to set their own foster care board rates. The state only determines the maximum amount that it will reimburse to the local districts; there is no minimum.[80]

In sum, New York State does not have many public managers assigned to the foster care issue, nor does it have a large organizational structure for foster care. Foster care administration in New York State is largely being implemented in New York City, where approximately two-thirds of the state's foster care population resides.

CONCLUSION

The hypothesis was that New York, defined as one of the two weaker case states, *would have less of an emphasis on building community partners, integrating the advice of mentors, providing leadership from public managers, and cultivating relationships with the federal government.* The findings from this chapter on foster care in New York suggest that the cultivation of federal government relationships was not a major factor, whereas the building of community partners, the integration of mentors, and the leadership from public managers only showed a stronger presence over time. When the variables were shown to have a greater significance, this was found only at the city level, rather than at the state level.

The federal performance data showed New York to be a weaker state in the area of foster care administration. However, there has been a trend toward improvement in New York City, which is the major foster care hub in New York. A stronger community partnership relationship with the government, increased mentoring by the Casey foundations, and stronger leadership from public managers has corresponded with an increase in perception among key players that New York City is having increased success with the foster care issue.

The changing administrations in NYC ACS led to stronger public management, and as the public managers became stronger, they reached out. Mattingly reached out to the foster care agencies in the community, he built

New York 85

partnerships with community organizations, and he was able to get the mayor's ear. Even in this weak case state, the increased role of the public management factor led to significant positive changes.

List of Interviews

Interviewees listed here may have been utilized for quotes, off-the-record data, and/or background data only. Some interviews were conducted specifically for this New York case, and others served to inform more broadly across many states or across issue areas addressed in this study.

Michael Arsham, Director of the Child Welfare Organizing Project (CWOP), interview, East Harlem, New York, November 8, 2007. Arsham previously served as the Director of Social Service Policy for the New York State Council of Family and Child-Caring Agencies. Arsham also served at the Rheedlen Centers for Children and Families (now known as the Harlem Children's Zone) for 13 years, staffing, developing, and directing preventive service programs in Central Harlem, Manhattan Valley, and Hell's Kitchen.

Francis Ayuso, New York City Administration for Children's Services (ACS) Neighborhood-Based Services Coordinator; Project Director of Bridge Builders, interview, Highbridge section of Bronx, New York, November 2, 2007. Highbridge has the highest number of foster care placement rates in New York City. Ayuso also served as the Borough Coordinator for the entire Bronx bureau for ACS.

John Courtney, Co-Director of the New York City Partnership for Family Supports and Justice; Senior Advisor to both the Child Welfare Fund and FAR Fund, phone interview, November 20, 2007. Courtney was formerly the Director of Program Planning with New York City's Child Welfare Administration.

Christine Craig, HHS-ACF Region III Program Specialist, federal government, phone interview, June 3, 2008. Craig oversees Delaware in addition to another state. Craig worked on the Title IV-E eligibility review for Delaware from October 2005 to March 2006.

Kelly Garvey, Reunification Supervisor of Foster Family Resources, Jewish Child Care Association, Bronx, New York, phone interview, February 5, 2008.

Sarah Gerstenzang, Executive Director, New York State Citizens' Coalition for Children, phone interview, October 2, 2008.

Richard Hucke, Program Director of Foster Family Services, Jewish Child Care Association, Bronx, New York, phone interviews, December 6, 2007, and December 14, 2007. The author visited the Jewish

Child Care Association in the Highbridge section of the Bronx, but both interviews were phone interviews.

Nancy Martinez, Director, Strategic Planning and Policy Development, New York State Office of Children and Family Services, interview, Rensselaer, New York, November 30, 2007. Martinez is responsible for foster care policy decisions for New York State Commissioner Gladys Carrion, Esq. Martinez is referred to as the state foster care manager.

Lisa Pearson, HHS-ACF Region III Program Manager, federal government, phone interview, June 3, 2008. Pearson reports directly to the HHS-ACF Commissioner. She is responsible for management of the following six states: Delaware, District of Columbia, Maryland, Pennsylvania, Virginia, and West Virginia.

LaTrella R. Penny, Interim Co-Executive Director, Agenda for Children Tomorrow (ACT), interview, Manhattan, New York, October 26, 2007. ACT is a public agency housed in the offices of ACS that also receives private funding. Penny spent 17 years in child welfare in New York City.

Nicholas Pirro, Former Onondaga County Executive (Syracuse, New York, area); Former President of the New York State Association of Counties; Former President of the County Executive Association for New York; Former Chairman of the Onondaga Legislature, phone interview, October 14, 2008.

Deborah Rubien, Interim Co-Executive Director, Agenda for Children Tomorrow (ACT), interview, Manhattan, New York, October 26, 2007. Rubien previously served as a policy analyst with New York City's Mayor's Office for Children and Families and the Citizen's Committee for Children.

Brent Thompson, Director of Communications, William Penn Foundation, informal interview, Philadelphia, Pennsylvania, August 7, 2007. Thompson reported directly to the Penn Foundation's former president and served as a primary contact in the president's absence.

Carole Thompson, Senior Program Officer, Annie E. Casey Foundation, interview, Philadelphia, Pennsylvania, August 16, 2007. The collective Casey family foundations make it the single largest foundation conducting work on foster care.

Muna Walker, Senior Program Officer, Amachi, Public/Private Ventures, interview, Philadelphia, Pennsylvania, fall 2006. Walker has responsibility for the Mentoring Children of Prisoners program, which has significant client overlap with foster care.

Barbara Wilson, Program Officer, Senior Corps, Corporation for National and Community Service (CNCS) federal program, phone and written correspondence with author, fall 2006. Senior Corps provides volunteers in states for foster care.

> Harry Wilson, Associate Commissioner, Family Youth and Services Bureau, U.S. Department of Health and Human Services, Administration for Children and Families, Family Youth and Services Bureau, informal background information, dozens of meetings in 2003–2006, Washington, DC.

NOTES

1. Note: All references in the summary are cited in this chapter. Data refers to the period of research.
2. U.S. Census Bureau, "2003 American Community Survey," http://www.census.gov.
3. The Pew Commission on Children in Foster Care, "Foster Care Population and States Ranked by Total Number of Children in Foster Care. FY2003," http://pewfostercare.org/research/docs/Data091505.pdf.
4. Ibid.
5. New York State Office of Children and Family Services, "Agency Priorities and Budget Request," testimony of Gladys Carrion, Esq., Commissioner, October 25, 2007, http://www.ocfs.state.ny.us/main/news/2007/2007_10_25_CarrionBudgetTestimony.pdf
6. Nicholas Pirro, Former Onondaga County Executive (Syracuse, New York, area); Former President of New York State Association of Counties; Former President of County Executive Association for New York; Former Chairman of the Onondaga Legislature, phone interview, October 14, 2008.
7. Nancy Martinez, Director, Strategic Planning and Policy Development, New York State Office of Children and Family Services, interview, Rensselaer, New York, November 30, 2007.
8. Sarah Gerstenzang, Executive Director, New York State Citizens' Coalition for Children, phone interview, October 2, 2008.
9. Ibid.
10. Nancy Martinez, interview.
11. Sarah Gerstenzang, interview.
12. Nancy Martinez, interview.
13. Kids Are Waiting: A Project of the Pew Charitable Trusts, "New York State Fact Sheet," http://www.kidsarewaiting.org.
14. Nancy Martinez, interview.
15. New York City Administration for Children's Services, "Table 19. Title IVE Foster Care, State Ward Board and Care: Children and Payments, Entire State, Fiscal Years 2005, 2006, 2007," http://www.nyc.gov/html/acs/html/home/home.shtml.
16. Nicholas Pirro, interview.
17. Ibid.
18. Ibid.
19. Christine Craig, HHS-ACF Region III Program Specialist, federal government, phone interview, June 3, 2008.
20. Nancy Martinez, interview.
21. Ibid.
22. New York City Administration for Children's Services, "Commissioner John B. Mattingly Biography," http://www.nyc.gov/html/acs/html/about/commissioner_bio.shtml.

88 *Politics of Foster Care Administration*

23. Richard Hucke, Program Director of Foster Family Services, Jewish Child Care Association, phone interviews, December 6, 2007, and December 14, 2007.
24. Ibid.
25. Confidential remarks.
26. Note: Local becomes of particular importance when states have large foster care operations in cities such as Detroit or New York City.
27. Francis Ayuso, New York City Administration for Children's Services (ACS) Neighborhood-Based Services Coordinator; Project Director of Bridge Builders, interview, Highbridge section of Bronx, New York, November 2, 2007.
28. Ibid.
29. Ibid.
30. Ibid.
31. Ibid.
32. Ibid.
33. New York City Administration for Children's Services, "Safeguarding Our Children: Safety Reforms Update," http://www.nyc.gov/html/acs/downloads/pdf/pub_safety_reform_sept07.pdf.
34. Quoted in Fund for Social Change, "The Partnership for Family Supports and Justice (Bridge Builders)," The New York Nonprofit Press.
35. Agenda for Children Tomorrow, http://www.actnyc.org/index.php.
36. LaTrella R. Penny, Interim Co-Executive Director, Agenda for Children Tomorrow (ACT), interview, Manhattan, New York, October 26, 2007; Deborah Rubien, Interim Co-Executive Director, Agenda for Children Tomorrow (ACT), interview, Manhattan, New York, October 26, 2007.
37. Michael Arsham, Director of the Child Welfare Organizing Project (CWOP), interview, East Harlem, New York, November 8, 2007.
38. Ibid.
39. Ibid.
40. Mark Moore, *Creating Public Value: Strategic Management in Government* (Cambridge, MA: Harvard University Press, 1995), 10.
41. Children's Rights, "At the Crossroads: Better Infrastructure, Too Few Results—A Decade of Child Reform in New York City, July 2007," http://www.childrensrights.org/wp-content/uploads/2008/06/at_the_crossroads_full_report.pdf, 74; John Courtney, Co-Director of the New York City Partnership for Family Supports and Justice; Senior Advisor to both the Child Welfare Fund and FAR Fund, phone interview, November 20, 2007.
42. Children's Rights, "At the Crossroads," 74.
43. John Courtney, interview.
44. Ibid.
45. Richard Hucke, interview.
46. Michael Arsham, interview.
47. Ibid.
48. Ibid.
49. LaTrella R. Penny, interview; Deborah Rubien, interview.
50. Michael Arsham, interview.
51. Children's Rights, "At the Crossroads," 35.
52. Ibid., 35.
53. Michael Arsham, interview.
54. Ibid.
55. John Courtney, interview.
56. Scott Shifrel and Tracy Connor, "Nixzmary Brown's Mother, Nixaliz Santiago, Found Guilty of Manslaughter in 7 Year Old's Death," *New York*

New York 89

Daily News, October 17, 2008, http://www.nydailynews.com/news/ny_crime/2008/10/17/2008–10–17_nixzmary_browns_mother_nixaliz_santiago_.html.
57. Sewell Chan, "City to Adopt Changes in Handling of Abuse Cases," *New York Times,* March 30, 2006, http://www.nytimes.com/2006/03/30/nyregion/30abuse.html?_r=1&n=Top/Reference/Times%20Topics/Organizations/A/Administration%20for%20Children's%20Services&oref=slogin.
58. John Courtney, interview.
59. Michael Arsham, interview.
60. John Courtney, interview.
61. LaTrella R. Penny, interview; Deborah Rubien, interview.
62. Michael Arsham, interview.
63. LaTrella R. Penny, interview; Deborah Rubien, interview.
64. Ibid.
65. Leslie Kaufman, "Foster Care Plan Faces a History of Failure," *New York Times,* February 6, 2005, http://query.nytimes.com/gst/fullpage.html?res=9D06E6DE1E3BF935A35751C0A9639C8B63.
66. Leslie Kaufman, "New York Acts to Ease Process in Foster Care," *New York Times,* March 22, 2007, http://query.nytimes.com/gst/fullpage.html?res=9D05E6DA1430F931A15750C0A9619C8B63.
67. John Courtney, interview.
68. Ibid.
69. New York City Administration for Children's Services, "Improved Outcomes for Children (IOC)," http://www.nyc.gov/html/acs/html/about/about.shtml.
70. Kelley Garvey, Reunification Supervisor of Foster Family Resources, Jewish Child Care Association, Bronx, New York, phone interview, February 5, 2008.
71. Richard Hucke, interview.
72. John Courtney, interview.
73. LaTrella R. Penny, interview; Deborah Rubien, interview.
74. Kaufman, "Foster Care Plan Faces a History of Failure."
75. Francis Ayuso, interview.
76. Nicholas Pirro, interview.
77. Sarah Gerstenzang, interview.
78. Ibid.
79. Nancy Martinez, interview.
80. Sarah Gerstenzang, interview.

5 Rhode Island
A Smaller State with Weaker Performance

"A CASA attorney may have 300 kids on a caseload. They couldn't pick my CASA child out of a line-up."

—Lisa Guillette, executive director, Rhode Island Foster Parents Association

"The DCYF foster care workers sold their right to reduce caseloads. DCYF offered to give each caseworker a $4,000 bonus per year in return for no limits on caseloads."

—Maureen Robbins, chief casework supervisor, Adoption and Foster Care Preparation and Support Unit, Rhode Island Department of Children, Youth and Families

---

RHODE ISLAND: FOSTER CARE DATA SUMMARY[1]

Agency and Foster Care Funding

Rhode Island's Department of Children, Youth and Families (DCYF) is responsible for foster care administration. Rhode Island does not estimate its average cost per foster care child or agency cost for foster care.

Foster Care Population

As of 2003, Rhode Island had a population of 1,037,196, with 225 foster care cases per 100,000 people. Michigan and New York were the two large states studied, and Rhode Island and Delaware were the two smaller states studied.

As of FY 2003, Rhode Island had 2,334 children in foster care representing 0.4% of the overall U.S. foster care caseload. As of October 31, 2007, Rhode Island had a caseload of 1,618 children, which represented a significant drop. In 2007, the Rhode Island state legislature reduced the foster care age from 21 to 18 as a "cost-saving measure."

Foster Care Administration

Since 1997, Rhode Island has used a "four region" system. The system is centralized and DCYF creates policy and licenses foster care.

The senior casework supervisor at DCYF has "five staff for 1,000 foster care homes for licensing." DCYF requires a face-to-face meeting with a DCYF caseworker and the foster care parent/child every 30 days, but this is "most likely not occurring for most children." Unlike most states, which object to the widespread use of shelters and group homes, Rhode Island foster care utilizes shelters as well as group homes for children. One estimate suggests that the state has 40% of its foster care children in institutional care, while in other states the number is approximately 20%. This large institutional care bill is a major financial burden on the state.

This chapter provides case research on foster care in the state of Rhode Island. The research was designed to test whether the following hypothesis is accurate: *Delaware and Michigan became stronger-performing states in the area of foster care by placing a greater priority than the lower-performing states of New York and Rhode Island on building community partners, integrating the advice of mentors, providing leadership from public managers, and cultivating relationships with the federal government.* The hypothesis posed that Rhode Island and New York relied less upon these strategies and therefore struggled to obtain better results.

Rhode Island is one of the two smaller states in this study and also falls into the category of a weaker case state, according to the 2003 federal performance measures. As of 2003, Rhode Island had a population of 1,037,196,[2] with 225 foster care cases per 100,000 people.[3] In 2003, the state had 2,334 foster care children, representing 0.4% of the foster care population across the country.[4]

The findings from this chapter on Rhode Island foster care suggest that none of the following factors contributed to the successful administration of the state's foster care system: the cultivation of federal government relationships, the building of community partners, the integration of advice from mentors, and the leadership from public managers. As anticipated from the hypothesis, Rhode Island did not possess higher levels of any of these four variables that could potentially lead to greater success in its foster care system.

92 *Politics of Foster Care Administration*

CASE BACKGROUND

Like all other states during the period of field research, Rhode Island had been undergoing federal government reviews for Title IV-E eligibility as well as for Child and Family Service Reviews. Rhode Island performed near the bottom of the states on the Child and Family Service Reviews, as shown by the "Child Welfare Outcomes 2003: Annual Report" in Chapter 2. Rhode Island was designated as a weaker case state because the state performed below the median on six of seven foster care outcomes measured in 2003. Rhode Island did improve between 2000 and 2003 by showing gains above the median across all states. But, even with this progress, Rhode Island still performed near the bottom of the states in 2003.

Since 1997, Rhode Island foster care has been based on a "four region" system.[5] The Rhode Island Department of Children, Youth and Families (DCYF) creates policy and licenses foster care in the centralized Rhode Island foster care program.

As of October 31, 2007, Rhode Island had a caseload of only 1,618,[6] which represented a significant drop from approximately 2,334 in 2003. This decrease was due to a concentrated state effort to release children from the rolls, mostly because the state could not afford the foster children anymore.[7] In 2007, the Rhode Island legislature reduced the foster care age from 21 to 18 as a "cost-saving measure."[8]

Field research was completed in Rhode Island in January 2008, and it involved conducting interviews, viewing documents, and visiting state offices and foster care agencies. The purpose of this field research was to identify conditions that produced better foster care outcomes. Interview topics were centered on the interviewee's area of expertise in connection with foster care administration. Although the majority of interviews occurred in the field, some follow-up telephone interviews were conducted in 2008. At times, interviewees requested that all or part of their comments remain off the record.

Thirteen interviews were conducted in the state of Rhode Island. Interviews were requested with "key players" who were actively involved with Rhode Island's foster care decisions. All interviews pursued in the state were granted, with the exception of one foster care agency that turned down the request for an interview for unspecified reasons. I also pursued an interview with officials in the Rhode Island court system in order to understand the court's role in state foster care matters. However, court administrative staff members repeatedly lost the interview request and failed to follow up on their stated commitments multiple times. I stopped pursuing this interview because the request process itself had been enough to provide me with some insight into Rhode Island's judicial system.

A small state, Rhode Island is comparable to Delaware in some ways. For instance, it takes less than an hour to travel across Rhode Island. Neither state's urban areas had evidence of the higher levels of danger I experienced while visiting New York City's foster care areas.

Rhode Island 93

Providence, located in Rhode Island Region 1, is the largest city in Rhode Island and houses the majority of its foster care caseload. I traveled to foster care agencies in Providence and to those across the state in Pascoag. I also visited East Providence to meet with an advocacy group, the Rhode Island Foster Parents Association. In addition, I conducted a phone interview with another agency in North Providence.

I visited the Providence site of the Department of Children, Youth and Families, which is situated across the street from its partner in gridlock, the family court. I spoke with the director of DCYF, as well as the state liaison to the federal government, Kevin Savage. I did not request an interview with the governor or state legislators because they were mostly inactive on the issue of foster care.

Similar to my experiences in Delaware and New York, the Rhode Island interviewees were fairly honest about the level of effectiveness of the foster care system, and their accounts were fairly consistent across interviews. For instance, there was a universal consensus regarding an ongoing tension between the family court and DCYF that was, in turn, creating problems for the implementation of foster care programs across the state.

As in the other case states, Rhode Island interviewees were very generous with their interview time. For instance, some interviews prescheduled for 30 minutes turned into an hour, and two interviews turned into 2-hour conversations. Interviewees appreciated the research that had been conducted in advance of each interview that was designed to understand and respect their particular roles in the foster care system.

In addition, I conducted seven interviews that broadly informed my research on foster care and provided background for Rhode Island and other case states, as well as the implications across all states. These interviews were referred to in the New York chapter as well. A complete list of interviews is offered at the end of this chapter.

CASE FINDINGS

This section offers findings from the Rhode Island case research. Each of the four variables is analyzed and a summary is offered, noting their significance levels based on the research results.

Cultivation of Federal Government Relationships: Significance = None

For the variable *cultivation of federal government relationships* to appear strong, the data needed to show a pattern of interaction between the federal government and the state that went *beyond* the required relationship. This factor is shown to have a stronger presence when the federal government has significantly shifted the direction of the state's decision-making path regarding the provision of foster care in some nonrequired area. In other words, the federal–state relationship on foster care needed to transcend the

94 *Politics of Foster Care Administration*

required form completion, grant processing, regulation monitoring, and data gathering and move into how to fix and transform foster care.

In the majority of Rhode Island interviews, there was very little mention of the role that the federal government played in regard to foster care. When there was a discussion about the federal government's role, it centered on the reduction of federal funding and onerous reporting and paperwork requirements.

Like other states, Rhode Island has experienced a rapid decrease in federal funds that partially cover the expenses of its foster care caseload. The Rhode Island DCYF director, Patricia Martinez,[9] said: "What has been reduced is the federal match, our total agency budget across IV-E [foster care], Medicaid, everything else."[10] Kevin Savage, the state administrator appointed as the liaison to the federal government, said: "There certainly has been a reduction in Federal IV-E. It dropped rather dramatically. We're working to bring that back up. When there are kids in care, we [the state] have to pay for it."[11]

Additionally, there were references in the interviews to the extensive form-filing required by the federal government. Dorothy Hultine, the chief policy creator for DCYF, said: "There's so much paperwork regarding the Title IV-E."[12] Hultine, who first served as a social caseworker for DCYF before moving on to policy, showed me copies of the report on her desk that needed to be completed for the federal government.[13] Similar to my experiences in Delaware and New York, the Rhode Island interviewees also wanted to visibly display the paperwork burden the federal government placed on their state.

As in Delaware, interviewees in Rhode Island suggested that the federal government's Program Improvement Plan had encouraged positive changes in foster care. Hultine stated, "The Program Improvement Plan has driven activity in a lot of different areas."[14] DCYF director Patricia Martinez said, "Any framework that you have to improve your services is good."[15] While recognizing that Rhode Island has struggled with its federal performance measures, Martinez added, "Every single state is very different. It's hard to have a very different set of standards to deal with."[16]

In other words, the data collection of the performance measurement is encouraging states to *think* about how to improve foster care. Lisa Pearson, a regional program manager for the federal government, said: "When states look at the CFSR process as a way to improve, reviews can be an opportunity to improve systems."[17] Christine Craig, a program specialist for the federal government, stated: "When states look at Title IV-E and CFSRs as not a [positive], I don't know if it impacts much."[18]

In summary, this Rhode Island case demonstrates a transactional federal government relationship with the state and no "workhorse" relationship between Rhode Island and the federal government. The federal government required a significant amount of paperwork, while simultaneously playing a reduced role in funding foster care in the state. In this study, Rhode Island is considered a weaker state based on the federal performance measures; therefore, one would expect a weaker presence of this variable.

The Integration of Advice of Mentors: Significance = None

The hypothesis is that the stronger states will have stronger (defined as more or deeper) mentors who offer strategic advice or training on the issue of foster care. *Mentors are defined here as foundations, issue-expert national nonprofit organizations, or think tanks that focus on foster care.* The strong presence of mentors is reflected by a workhorse relationship in which the state has either a large network of mentors or a rigorous relationship with one mentor organization. Workhorse relationships are deeper relationships in which mentors discuss ideas with the state, and the state then takes action.

This factor is shown to have a stronger presence when the mentors have significantly shifted the direction of the state's decision-making path regarding the provision of foster care in some nonrequired area.

Organizations that consistently do work in the field of foster care include the Annie E. Casey Foundation, Casey Family Services, the Pew Charitable Trusts, and other child welfare organizations and policy advocates. However, there was no evidence from Rhode Island's interviewees that the state learned from any of these or from other mentors. Furthermore, there was no mention in any interview of the state's utilization of mentors.

Although Rhode Island has not actively integrated the advice of mentors into its foster care system, a major community organization, the Foster Parents Association, chose to utilize Casey as a mentor. This organization obtained guidance and funding from the Casey Youth Opportunities Initiative in order to design the program Real Connections for foster care youth between the ages of 14 and 24 who were aging out of the system.[19] Executive director Lisa Guillette noted that one of the major Casey key leaders was local, and therefore they "realized a lot more opportunities to work together."[20] Only after the money started flowing in for Real Connections and a pattern of success had been demonstrated did DCYF decide to partner with the Foster Parents Association. The Foster Parents Association added, "Finally the department [DCYF] came to the realization [that this was a good program] and found community funding to make it happen."[21]

In summary, the case of Rhode Island does not demonstrate any integration of advice from mentors into the foster care system at the state level. The sole example cited described a community partner that reached out to Casey as a mentor, followed by state involvement at a later stage.

Building of Community Partners: Significance = Weak

The hypothesis is that the stronger states will have stronger (defined as more or deeper) community partnerships. *Community partnerships are defined here as: state and/or local[22] foster care agency relationships with local nonprofits, faith-based organizations, and community organizations.* The strong presence of community partners is reflected by a workhorse relationship in

96   Politics of Foster Care Administration

which the state has either a large network of community partners or a rigorous relationship with one community partner. Workhorse relationships are deeper relationships in which community partners discuss ideas with the state, and the state then takes action.

A workhorse relationship might include government and community organizations copromoting a conference with mutual organizational roles, or deciding together to more aggressively pursue homes for older female teens. This factor is shown to have a stronger presence when the community partners have significantly shifted the direction of the state's decision-making path regarding the provision of foster care in some area. Basic administrative paperwork or meetings between a community partner and the state do not qualify as a strong presence of this variable.

In Delaware, community partners met repeatedly with the state in order to create and implement action plans related to foster care administration. In Rhode Island, the opposite occurred. When interviewees in Rhode Island were asked to name community partners that the state utilized on foster care matters, the question consistently drew pauses. When the state interacted with community partners around foster care issues, the relationship was primarily transactional and often contentious. For example, Rhode Island hosted a monthly foster care planning task force meeting, but there was little evidence that it fostered collaboration among all agencies in attendance. One attendee stated, "once the issues are presented to DCYF [in that meeting], they are slow to change. I've been very shocked about how DCYF handles things. It makes you laugh—Are you serious?"[23]

Rhode Island's primary community partner on foster care issues is the Foster Parents Association. This organization is an active community partner and advocacy organization that has been working on behalf of 800 to 1,000 Rhode Island foster parent families for 20 years. At the time of this field research, the 501(c)3 Foster Parents Association budget was substantially dependent on state money—70% was funding from state contracts (with the majority of that money passed down from the federal government to the states) and the remaining 30% was from private donations. One foster care agency noted that the new Foster Parents Association executive director Lisa Guillette "has turned around the [Foster Parents Association]. That agency wasn't well-respected before."[24] Active in the state, the Foster Parents Association shows up at court hearings for child rights, sits on foster care associations, and lobbies the state to make changes to foster care.

Although the state has had a contentious relationship with the Foster Parents Association, they were able to work together on the Real Connections program. The Foster Parents Association stated, "We have a strong relationship with the department [DCYF]"[25] due to the Real Connections program. Yet, the association and the state publicly battle frequently. The Foster Parents Association battles with the state government on a wide range of issues, such as rates to parents for boarding foster children, the court system, the application process by caseworkers, and the change in

Rhode Island   97

eligibility from age 21 to 18. In general, the Foster Parents Association also challenges the state legislature and the governor on their lack of support for the foster care community.

I interviewed the Foster Parents Association executive director on the same day that an intrastate court battle was brewing over poor state foster care performance. She had come directly from an all-day court session, in which she said that the state child advocate had "courageously"[26] sued both Governor Carcieri and DCYF director Martinez on behalf of 10 plaintiffs who represented a class action lawsuit for 3,000 children in care. The lawsuit alleged that Rhode Island children in foster care have been neglected, molested, beaten, and in one case, killed. Guillette said she cried when she learned about these kids' stories[27] and referred to the litigation as "long overdue."[28]

Julie DiBari, the assistant director of the Foster Parents Association, believed one issue that has fallen on deaf ears at DCYF is the unacceptable number of kids who live in group homes in Rhode Island.[29] A number of interviews suggested that Rhode Island DCYF could easily shift this high number of group home residents into foster family homes. This would better align Rhode Island with the national trend of placing foster children into permanency with a family.

The Foster Parents Association was also frustrated that the state legislature and the governor tended to forget about foster care in times of a budget crisis. In January 2008, Rhode Island was facing a fiscal crisis. As Governor Carcieri stated in his 2008 State of the State Address, "We are staring at a combined 550 million dollar deficit this year and next. . . . We are in the process of reducing the state workforce by 1,000 people."[30] In that context, the Foster Parents Association did not believe there was much support for foster care improvement from the governor or the state legislature. DiBari noted, "Dialogue is budget-motivated. Politics about kids and families are not a priority."[31] When transitioning out of foster care, the "youth are at the bottom of the list [of all individuals waiting to get public housing] to get youth housing."[32]

Guillette has taken these issues before the legislature, as well as to DCYF. She shared a story in which members of the legislature heard testimony about foster care children sitting outside DCYF with their black plastic garbage bags. She recalled that some legislators wept listening to these children speak about night-to-night placement and the uncertainty associated with not knowing where they would sleep each night. In response, the state eliminated the concept of night-to-night placement and sent children to shelters for 45-day placements. Yet, rather than attempting to achieve permanency, the state simply rolls over the placements for another 45-days after one placement period ends. The state ran out of potential foster care parents, and the children now sit in these shelters. St. Mary's Home for Children, a North Providence foster care agency, even noted that while it has openings in its therapeutic foster care program, DCYF is sending children to shelters

98   Politics of Foster Care Administration

instead.[33] As a result, there are children in shelters at age 5.[34] Guillette cannot understand how some legislators who previously reacted emotionally in support of these children's concerns are now turning their backs on the foster care issues presented by the community and the Foster Parents Association.

The Foster Parents Association is also concerned about the state legislature's decision to remove foster care children from the caseload due to the state's grave fiscal situation. For budgetary reasons, the state legislature has reduced the age of children permitted on the foster care rolls from 21 to age 18. Accordingly, the state's rolls declined from 2,334 children in foster care in FY 2003 to 1,618 as of October 31, 2007, which could be considered a positive development if the reductions were the result of more children achieving permanency.[35] However, in 2007, the state reduction was partially due to the purging of older children from the program. Maureen Robbins, chief casework supervisor for DCYF, stated that the decision to close children at 18 was a "cost-saving measure."[36] She noted that 200 children were closed out in 2007 for this reason alone. The Foster Parents Association noted that the state even started closing out kids *before* their 18th birthdays, and 17-year-olds were closed out prior to the July 1, 2007, purge.[37] Although the Foster Parents Association made its position known regarding the damage this policy would do to foster children, the state proceeded to delete foster children from their rolls.

These examples demonstrate a pattern in which a major community partner has had to fight the state on issues of foster care. Rather than utilizing the Foster Parents Association as a community partner to help solve problems on a wide range of foster care issues, the state of Rhode Island has chosen not to utilize the Foster Parents Association beyond the level of minimal interaction. An exception to this was the Real Connections program; however, the state only partnered with the Foster Parents Association after the organization had developed and implemented the program without the state's involvement.

Unlike Delaware, which has partnered with community organizations to bring about foster care success, in Rhode Island the main community organization has had to fight the state in order to encourage success. Not only was the main community advocacy group in combat with the state, but there also were no other major community partnerships identified in Rhode Island. Clearly Rhode Island does not have a workhorse relationship with community partners in the area of foster care.

Leadership from Public Managers: Significance = None

The hypothesis is that the stronger states will have more leadership from public managers. *A public manager is shown to evidence leadership when he or she is operating as a "principled agent" in the state or local government or agency responsible for the area of foster care.* In the context of this study, a principled agent is a government employee (public manager) who goes above and beyond his or her public duty to cultivate successful foster care administration. Harvard Kennedy School professor Mark Moore argued that a successful manager "increase(s) the public value produced by public sector organizations in both the short and the long run."[38] A principled agent performs as a workhorse, rather than as a standard government employee who is focused on routine functions. The strong presence of leadership from public managers is reflected by a greater presence of principled agents working in foster care in the case state.

Rhode Island had very few "principled agents" overseeing foster care in state management positions. There were employees with good intentions, but in general they did not have the skills and/or the desire and means to implement change. In the comparably small state of Delaware, there was leadership on this issue from the governor, to the cabinet secretary, down to the foster care program manager. In Rhode Island, however, the majority of public managers did not create and/or implement foster care improvement.

Related to Rhode Island foster care, almost every interview suggested a public management disaster. The state lost foster care parent records, took months to process potential foster care parent forms for children waiting in shelters, did not license kinship foster care parents while children were under their care, and maintained an atmosphere of in-fighting between administrative branches. As stated previously, these problems did not correspond to the fiscal crisis timeline. Rather, the problems were largely related to poor public management. The foster care public management failure implicated every branch of government in Rhode Island—the legislature, the courts, and DCYF. To summarize, the state of Rhode Island operated in public management chaos.

State Legislature

The role of Rhode Island's legislature was almost nonexistent where foster care improvement was concerned. In many interviews with key players, I asked about state legislators who were active on foster care issues, but found no leads. DCYF chief casework supervisor Maureen Robbins stated, "No legislators are really active on this issue [of foster care]."[39] The executive director of the Foster Parents Association added that the General Assembly "is not really active" on foster care, with "everything being dictated by a dollar."[40] Another key player commented, "There's not an active role from anyone in the state legislature."[41] A foster care provider said, "The legislature doesn't care that much. They're looking at the bottom line."[42]

The legislature appeared to make decisions with the publicly stated goal of "cost savings," but this sometimes served as a mask for poor management decisions. For instance, the state legislature made a decision to try 17-year-old offenders as adults. This put these youths with "the hardest of the hardened criminals" in Supermax for $104,000 a year.[43] This decision was made as a cost-saving measure, but it is now ridiculed by key players because it ended up costing the state more money. The state legislature ultimately had to reverse its decision.

100 *Politics of Foster Care Administration*

The Courts

If the Rhode Island legislature is apathetic about foster care, the state's court system is virtually incapable of acting on behalf of foster care children. A prime example of the court's administrative chaos concerned the court's response to my interview requests. The court contact stated that telephone calls would be returned and they repeatedly were not. Then the court contact would phone and apologize, but not fulfill the next agreed-to obligation. This mismanagement of interview requests by e-mail and telephone transpired over several months, and easily was the worst interview request process I experienced out of more than 50 interview requests. This process confirmed the statements made by Rhode Island's key players regarding the mismanagement of the courts.

First, the Court Appointed Special Advocate (CASA) Program at the Rhode Island Family Court is overwhelmed. Although the program is staffed by government employees and supported by volunteers that they recruit, the foster children do not have appropriate representation. The executive director of the Foster Parents Association said, "A CASA attorney may have 300 kids on a caseload. They couldn't pick my CASA child out of a line-up."[44]

Second, the court's processes related to foster care issues are complex, and by comparison to other case states, very inefficient. In Rhode Island, the same foster care case can be dragged through many different courts. For instance, DCYF senior casework supervisor Philip Steiner stated, "There's a huge amount of court involvement—mental health court, truancy court, drug court—so you'll be three or four days on the same case. There's a special court for everything instead of [a system that's] all-encompassing."[45]

Another problematic issue that child welfare advocates have identified is a lack of accountability on the part of the courts. Both Steiner and the chief casework supervisor believe that the courts should be opened up to the public so the courts can be held accountable.[46] Robbins stated, "We need to open up the cases to hold the judges accountable. Child deaths are sometimes the court's fault. Judges order certain kids into certain foster care placements over the heads of the agency."[47] The chief judge of the family court is referred to as "Judge Jeremiah for life" because judges are appointed for life and don't have to answer to anybody.[48]

Finally, interbranch conflict over the control of foster care policy further undermines any progress in this area generally, and the well-being of specific children in particular. In Delaware, the judicial and executive branches are in natural tension and work in tandem to determine the best action plan for the foster child. In Rhode Island, the courts and the agency work against each other by wrestling over control of case outcomes. According to the Rhode Island DCYF policy officer in central management, there is a "lot of animosity between the family courts and the state. There is a fight going on."[49] When I asked Dana Mullen, the permanency program manager for Children's Friend and Service about the relationship between the family court and the state, she said, "or the lack . . . of a relationship?"[50] In her opinion, the one major area that needed improvement in the state was the court system. She said, "We need to have a more collaborative relationship, better communication with [the court system]. They need to [better] understand what we're up against."[51]

In Rhode Island, the courts and DCYF disregard each other's decisions. For instance, they cannot agree on whether children who are 19 are under the jurisdiction of DCYF or the courts. At the time of field research, the legislature had recently changed a rule to end state jurisdiction of children at age 18 to save money, but they determined that DCYF is responsible for providing services to existing children in care until age 21. The DCYF public policy officer stated, "The court is upset they no longer have jurisdiction, so they're saying it's prescriptive, which only applies to kids going forward, not 19-year-olds currently under their jurisdiction."[52] Over objections of the legislature, the court decided that it wanted jurisdiction over these older children who were already in state care. As of January 2008, it was still unclear who had jurisdiction over children aged 18 to 21 who were wards of the state, and the tug-of-war continued.

The current DCYF director, Patricia Martinez, has attempted to make reconciliatory efforts with the family court. Director Martinez said, "We have a better relationship with the family courts. I meet with the chief judge once a month. I also pick up the phone and say, 'Your Honor, I don't think that's the best placement for that particular child.'"[53] Yet, tension still exists between the agency and the court.

The DCYF senior casework supervisor said, "The family court still orders things that it thinks kids will need, regardless of whether they can be provided to them."[54] The permanency program manager for Children's Friend and Service said, "One of the things we're trying to do is get buy-in from the court system. You can be advocating for one permanency plan and the judge out of nowhere rules otherwise and there's no debating it once that's made."[55] Lisa Guillette of the Foster Parents Association stated, "We can't count on Rhode Island family court to make appropriate decisions. Foster parents have a right to be heard in court, but [they] can't be. There's no oversight by family court."[56]

The Agency

Like the legislature, DCYF also appeared to make decisions with the publicly stated goal of "cost savings," but this served as a mask for poor management decisions.

Some DCYF foster care staff have been characterized as possessing a "lack of work ethic."[57] A story from one DCYF caseworker exemplified this point:

> When I was training I went out with a couple of my co-workers and there was a lot of sitting around that I didn't understand. It's hard with unions and with management, they should be holding these

102　*Politics of Foster Care Administration*

[caseworkers] accountable. When I see one of my coworkers get disciplined and they file a grievance, it's such a huge issue. I definitely see why unions started. At least where I work now it seems to protect people who don't want to work.[58]

She believes her 10-person foster care unit is "really bad and embarrassing and I can only chalk it up to the union." Elaborating further, she shared:

When I first started out, I went out shadowing one of our co-workers to do a home visit. We went to Dunkin Donuts for 45 minutes in the morning to kill time, and then we did one home visit in the morning, then lunch, then another home visit in the afternoon, and then went home. It was embarrassing. That was our day and then the same person bitches and complained about how overworked he is.[59]

This laziness can be partially attributed to the public management's inability to hold workers to high standards. A DCYF internal worker noted, "We're allowed a half hour lunch and two 15-minute breaks, or you can take an hour lunch. Many co-workers take an hour lunch *and* two 15-minute breaks."[60] The same interviewee shared a story about one DCYF caseworker who "barely comes to work. She comes in late, we all sort of joke about it. They only give her menial things. They'll talk to her and maybe she'll start crying. If you give her too many [cases], she gets upset."[61]

A new manager, Kevin Savage, came in to DCYF and he came on really strong in a positive way. Staff members started to be on time, but then everyone reverted to their old ways when he did not hold them accountable with consequences. This suggests that management had the ability to change this organizational culture of "lack of work ethic," but did not do so.

Another key player noted, "Government workers being unionized contributes to it. They're unwilling to place a child on Saturday. The workers will state 'I don't work on a Saturday.'"[62] So, as a result, children sit in shelters over weekends.

By far one of the most problematic public management decisions in Rhode Island was the decision regarding caseloads. In essence, DCYF foster care workers *sold their right* to reduce the number of caseloads, which would have put them more into line with national standards. According to the chief casework supervisor for DCYF, Maureen Robbins, said the DCYF leadership offered to give each caseworker a "$4,000 bonus per year in return for no limits on caseloads."[63] Robbins referred to this deal as "no limits on caseloads. They've [caseworkers] sold it." Another DCYF foster care worker referred to it as an option to reduce caseloads and "they [caseworkers] wanted money instead."[64] The Foster Parents Association said "unions negotiated away caseload caps. Caseworkers will have 21 families with 60 to 65 kids."[65] Weak public managers negotiated this trade with foster care workers, despite the fact that the outcome is against the interest

Rhode Island 103

of foster children. The result has been very high caseloads. The DCYF senior casework supervisor, Philip Steiner, stated: "I have five staff for 1,000 foster homes for licensing, which means 200 homes per caseworker."[66] As the national wave of kinship care has gained momentum, along with Rhode Island's no limit caseloads, Steiner lamented, "There's an increase in referrals for 60 to 70 kinship providers. Seventy new referrals per month. I can't even return all the phone calls."[67] Children sit in shelters awaiting foster care placements, while relatives who want to house these foster children await return phone calls from DCYF.

Furthermore, Steiner observed that caseworkers are unable to meet state-mandated standards, such as an in-person meeting between the DCYF caseworker and the foster care parent and child. He said, "There's a required face to face every 30 days, I'm not sure *anybody* is able to do it."[68] In other words, caseworkers are *not* monitoring their caseload children on a monthly basis. The state is having foster children placed with their relatives without having the relative undergo the required licensing. In the judgment of one key player, "I don't know if it's really placing children without that due diligence."[69] And, as the caseloads previously mentioned suggest, the placements are receiving minimal monitoring. When relicensing occurs, the foster parents are often not cleared in time to continue their care of the child. Sarah St. Jacques, junior human services and policy systems specialist for DCYF, stated: "That's my goal, to complete the relicense before the kid in care period is up. That's my goal and it doesn't happen."[70] Ironically, this is another way that a state so supposedly concerned with cost savings is losing money. Although the child continues to be in care, if the foster parent's license has expired, the state is losing federal reimbursement dollars.[71]

The heavy caseloads are creating other management challenges. A foster care agency recounted, "There are astronomical caseloads of 25 families and it's getting worse. We hear more jobs are getting cut at DCYF."[72] As a result, the turnover of DCYF employees is a major problem. Steiner, who has been working in foster care at DCYF since 1980, has seen "turnover more so now" than previously.[73] Caseworkers feel like they "just can't do this any longer. [They] worry about kids they haven't seen."[74] He recalled that in the past, he and other caseworkers had relationships with the parents on their caseloads. Now this does not regularly occur. The program director of Tannerhill Specialized Foster Care stated, "A lot of the stress comes from DCYF social workers not having the time to return phone calls, and get documentation done. The best of them try to make the effort but don't have the time."[75]

Another area of public management failure involves licensing. One person stated:

> A foster care agency can do all of the licensing preparation for DCYF including reference checks, child abuse and tracking system, all results and the foster parents are trained, and then from the date of

104   *Politics of Foster Care Administration*

the application it can take 6 to 8 months for DCYF to approve the placement.[76]

Foster parents also often wait for their placements for 8 to 12 months at the same time that children are sitting in shelters. A typical example is that two fire inspections of a potential foster parent home have been sitting at the state level waiting for state approval for 6 months.[77] The program director of a foster care agency noted:

> On the licensing front, we have a lot of problems with DCYF. It's been difficult to get the paperwork done and have DCYF license the family. Foster parents are very frustrated. The paperwork is sitting there. There are all these kids waiting for homes. Kids could be placed in foster care families sooner.[78]

Public managers have also failed to implement fair and consistent stipend rates across foster care agencies. The DCYF directors can favor one agency over another without regard to performance measurement and can vary the pay across agencies. According to Heidi Mulligan, recruiter at St. Mary's Home for Children Foster Care:

> There are extremely low and extremely different daily stipends. There was no set standard to what a state would pay an agency. If I was friends with Director A and they like me, then I get more money. Another DCYF director goes to the agency and then they negotiate a different rate. We have some agencies that have the ability to pay their parents $100 a day while others pay $50 a day. It is hard to compete. It's tough when you train people and they bring up the price differences. The variation could be as much as $100.[79]

When I asked Mulligan if she had brought this up to DCYF, she said, "I have gotten nowhere on legitimate issues."[80]

During their interviews, both DCYF director Martinez and Kevin Savage, the federal benefits overseer, did not know the state's average cost per foster care child. This differs from other case state interviews, in that Delaware's DFS director quickly rattled off various foster care costs, as did some of the NYC ACS interviewees. The Rhode Island interviewees were able to cite the daily stipend that the state pays to foster care homes and for institutional care, but during the interviews they could not identify what the state spends on average per child on foster care.

Rhode Island is also spending extra money on group home placements, rather than saving money by increasing the number of matches between foster children and home placements. Rhode Island had disregarded the pervasive national foster care philosophy that a state should use shelters and group homes minimally. Anne Fortier, director of clinical services at the

Urban League of Rhode Island, noted that the state believes it is acceptable to place children in an institutional setting. She said, "Rhode Island has a higher rate of kids in institutional care than with foster care parents."[81] She noted that nearly 40% of Rhode Island's foster children are in institutional care, compared with around 20% in other states. As a result, Fortier said that the state was paying significantly more than they would if children were in foster homes.[82] DCYF director Martinez said that the cost of foster care per child for the state is $16 to $80 per day, whereas the cost to the state for residential treatment for children is $150 to $500 per day.[83] In the state, residential treatment often pertains to medically fragile foster children. Director Martinez then said, "The state is looking . . . to find ways to bring residential program care into foster homes."[84] However, the state still continues to spend more money on higher rates at institutional care despite the stated goal of cutting costs.

Rhode Island's decisions to pay more for residential care have occurred at the same time DCYF is being pressured by the state to reduce its costs. DCYF was told that it has quarterly allotments for foster care, and that it must be conservative about removing children and placing them into foster care.[85]

In addition to the state's problems with foster care cost mismanagement, foster parents are frustrated about DCYF's administrative mismanagement. One example cited was frustration with how frequently DCYF repeatedly loses records. Lisa Guillette from the Foster Parents Association recounted that DCYF "will lose fingerprinting; they'll lose an original full exam and the foster parent has to take another day off work to do fingerprinting again."[86] Also, foster parents believe that their interactions with the CASA office and DCYF are a "very rude process."[87]

One foster care agency referred to the problems as "the mystery of DCYF and who does what."[88] Another foster care provider noted:

> There are some people [at DCYF] that go way and above and then there's others that go way below what they need to be. I've never seen anything like it—their excuses and their lack of organization—and a lot of it is territorial. I've been shocked at the [low] level of compassion and common sense. I can't even put into words the shock.[89]

Leadership Challenges at the Agency
A class action lawsuit, *Sam and Tony M. v. Carcieri*, was filed on January 23, 2007, by the Child Advocate of Rhode Island and the child advocacy group Children's Rights. It seems to have summarized the problems Rhode Island faces due to poor public management. This lawsuit cited "pervasive and ongoing harm to children in foster care resulting from systemic problems, including mismanagement and lack of oversight within (DCYF)"[90] and was filed against Governor Carcieri; Jane A. Hayward, the secretary of the Executive Office of Health and Human Services; and Patricia Martinez, the director of the Department of Children, Youth and Families. The Foster

106 _Politics of Foster Care Administration_

Parents Association believed this lawsuit was long overdue. Even the chief casework supervisor at DCYF stated, "She [the state child advocate] was brave to do it—to get people to pay attention. Kids are getting abused and neglected in foster care. She had to send a message."[91]

Amidst the hundreds of negative comments about poor public management, there were only a few positive comments about public management leadership. The Urban League of Rhode Island noted, "I have a good relationship with Maureen Robbins at DCYF. Patricia Martinez has come to community events. I do think the director seems headed in some positive direction. I think the leadership is good—it's budget driving everything."[92] However, these few positive comments were overshadowed by comments such as, "I think there's definitely a lack of support from our administration and particularly our governor."[93]

The poor leadership from public managers on foster care has a long history in Rhode Island. A previous director of DCYF cut the policy position for foster care, and consequently no one was creating or updating foster care policy in the agency from 1983 to 1991. Dorothy Hultine, the current head of foster care policy at DCYF, noted the significant backlog as a result. Policies were not updated, and there was no new policy manual. The state was still behind in 2008 in updating policy manuals concerning foster care.[94]

Every DCYF director has the authority to fill vacant job positions. This includes hiring more foster care caseworkers, which would then reduce caseloads. In response to how different DCYF directors have approached foster care, one DCYF worker said, "They have gotten vacancies filled. In order to get vacancies filled, they can get hires [authorized]."[95] In other words, every director has the power to reduce caseloads by filling foster care caseworker positions. Yet, DCYF director Martinez did not make caseload reduction a priority.

DCYF director Martinez did not think the poor results on the state's performance measures were all that bad. When referring to Rhode Island's program improvement plan that was required by the federal government, she said, "Keep in mind that the program improvement plan was during my transition [to the position of director] in 2005, and I just completed the improvement in August 2007."[96] She only referred to two areas as being very challenging: "the technical assistance and reoccurrence of maltreatment, [those are] the only areas we're looking at improving."[97]

Overall, both Director Martinez and her top official, Kevin Savage, did not seem to be aware of the state's poor foster care performance. Instead, Martinez itemized the number of improvements the state was making, such as meeting with residential providers twice a month in order to ask them to create networks and manage the kids differently, and increasing opportunities for wrap-around communities 24–7.[98] The Foster Parents Association believed that its relationship with the DCYF director was getting better, but also felt that the director still has not been able to make many of the necessary improvements for foster care success.[99]

Rhode Island's foster care program also did not receive much leadership from Governor Carcieri. Unlike Delaware's Governor Minner, Governor Carcieri was not actively involved in foster care policy. DCYF is the Governor's Agency for Children, Youth and Families, yet Governor Carcieri is perceived to be disengaged from the foster care work in his own agency. Most key players who were interviewed suggested that Governor Carcieri was not particularly interested in foster care. The Foster Parents Association does not perceive that the issue receives any support from the governor. Sarah St. Jacques, a DCYF worker, stated: "I don't feel [Governor Carcieri] really knows too much about it. I don't see him doing anything specifically."[100] Maureen Robbins, chief casework supervisor, stated: "The governor has farmed out my work in favor of privatizing," criticizing his overall management method.[101] Another key player noted, "People are not happy with the governor."[102] The foster care recruiter for St. Mary's Home for the Children, founded in 1877, stated: "We're really in a bad way in the state of Rhode Island. There wasn't a lot of thought into how this [fiscal crisis] would affect different populations [such as foster care]."[103]

When discussing the way that foster care is administered in the state of Rhode Island, the Foster Parents Association said, "This is the absolute worst that we've ever seen it."[104] Referring to the Rhode Island's 2008 report, "State of the State," Guillette said: "Governor Carcieri is going to completely decimate our social services safety net. . . . The governor proposed horrific cuts to kids in care."[105]

Overall, Rhode Island's public managers have demonstrated a consistent lack of leadership in the area of foster care administration. From nearly every perspective, including those of government workers, foster care agencies, and foster care advocates, Rhode Island's public managers were viewed as lacking the passion to achieve success in foster care.

CONCLUSION

The hypothesis was that Rhode Island, defined as one of the two weaker case states, *would have less of an emphasis on building community partners, integrating the advice of mentors, providing leadership from public managers, and cultivating relationships with the federal government.* The case research has demonstrated that Rhode Island does not exhibit any higher levels of these factors that could lead to foster care success. There is virtually no mentoring, cultivation of federal government relationships, or leadership from public managers, and there is only minimal building of community partnerships. This scenario is closely aligned with Rhode Island's poor performance on the federal performance reviews, which is the basis of why they were classified as a weaker state.

An alternative thesis might posit that poor performance on foster care in Rhode Island is tied to the poor fiscal climate of this state, since budget

108　*Politics of Foster Care Administration*

reductions have played a role in the state's foster care decisions. Key foster care players said that saving money is a key criterion in many legislative, agency, and gubernatorial foster care decisions. Yet, the poor performance of the state does *not* line up with the fiscal crisis time line. Rhode Island Governor Carcieri's 2008 State of the State Address acknowledged a $550 million deficit for 2008 and 2009.[106] However, the state did not face a severe fiscal problem until roughly around the year 2004, which was *after* Rhode Island was rated as a poor-performing state in 2000 and 2003. The weak 2008–2009 fiscal climate does not explain the poor-performing status of the Rhode Island foster care system for the years 2000 and 2003.

Although Delaware and Rhode Island are roughly the same size and have similar foster care caseloads, the two states have taken very different approaches to foster care. Rhode Island's approach has been characterized by conflict among internal and external partners, whereas Delaware's approach involved building strong partnerships that have created a harmonious checks and balances system. In Rhode Island, the governor does not support foster care improvements, the courts and state are dueling, foster care agencies have little respect for the state, and the largest foster care community partner continuously fights with the state in order to initiate improvements. In Delaware, the branches of state government, agencies, and community partners have worked together to solve foster care problems. The various pieces of the broken foster care system in Rhode Island have led to systemic delays in foster care licensing and increased operating costs in a state that claimed to be concerned with reducing them. To use a term that is often associated with the U.S. Congress, this state is in foster care "gridlock."

Rhode Island did not possess any high levels of the factors that I hypothesized could lead to more successful foster care administration. The public managers were fighting internally; public managers did not have strong relationships with the agencies; the community partners fought against the state foster care managers; the state child advocate has been suing DCYF and the governor (the same governor who appointed her);[107] and the state's public managers believe that the governor is unsupportive of foster care. The contentious climate in Rhode Island has turned community partners into community opponents. During the period of research, Rhode Island foster care operated in chaos and was not effective at caring for foster care children.

It is not at all surprising that the U.S. Department of Health and Human services stated that Rhode Island had the "single highest rate of substantiated child abuse or neglect occurring to children in foster care among all states that reported data," with those rates "far exceeding benchmarks set by the federal government."[108] One foster care provider summed up foster care in Rhode Island best: "If they [DCYF] were a business, they would [have been] out of business 20 years ago."[109]

List of Interviews

Interviewees listed here may have been utilized for quotes, off-the-record data, and/or background data only. Some interviews were conducted specifically for this Rhode Island case, and others served to inform more broadly across many states or across issue areas addressed in this study.

Christine Craig, HHS-ACF Region III Program Specialist, federal government, phone interview, June 3, 2008. Craig oversees Delaware in addition to another state. Craig worked on Title IV-E eligibility review for Delaware from October 2005 to March 2006.

Julie DiBari, Deputy Director, Rhode Island Foster Parents Association, interview, East Providence, Rhode Island, January 23, 2008. DiBari previously worked for the United Way in Boston, Massachusetts.

Anne Fortier, Director of Clinical Services, Urban League of Rhode Island, interview, Providence, Rhode Island, January 24, 2008. The Urban League of Rhode Island, an affiliate of the National Urban League, is a foster care agency that also provides advocacy and research.

Lisa Guillette, Executive Director, Rhode Island Foster Parents Association, interview, East Providence, Rhode Island, January 23, 2008.

Dorothy Hultine, Policy, Central Management, Department of Children, Youth and Families, interview, Providence, Rhode Island, January 23, 2008. Hultine worked for DCYF for 27 years.

Patricia Martinez, Director, Department of Children, Youth and Families, Rhode Island, phone interview, February 5, 2008. Martinez oversees all child welfare programs for Rhode Island, including foster care.

Dana Mullen, Permanency Program Manager, Children's Friend and Service, Providence, Rhode Island, phone interview, February 5, 2008. Children's Friend and Service is a foster care agency that was founded in 1834.

Heidi Mulligan, Foster Care Recruiter, St. Mary's Home for Children, North Providence, Rhode Island, phone interview, February 11, 2008. St. Mary's Home for Children is a foster care agency.

Dr. Maureen O'Shea, Clinical Director, Tannerhill Specialized Foster Care, interview, Pascoag, Rhode Island, January 24, 2008. Tannerhill is a therapeutic foster care provider.

Lisa Pearson, HHS-ACF Region III Program Manager, federal government, phone interview, June 3, 2008. Pearson reports directly to the HHS-ACF commissioner. She is responsible for management of the following six states: Delaware, District of Columbia, Maryland, Pennsylvania, Virginia, and West Virginia.

Maureen Robbins, Chief Casework Supervisor, Adoption and Foster Care Preparation and Support Unit, Department of Children, Youth and Families, interview, Providence, Rhode Island, January 24, 2008. Robbins is referred to as the state foster care program manager.

Kevin Savage, Licensing Administrator and Federal Benefits, Department of Children, Youth and Families, Rhode Island, phone interview, February 5, 2008. Savage serves as liaison to the federal government for foster care.

Jennifer Silva, Program Director and Recruiter, Tannerhill Specialized Foster Care, interview, Pascoag, Rhode Island, January 24, 2008.

Sarah St. Jacques, Junior Human Services and Policy Systems Specialist, Department of Children, Youth and Families, Rhode Island, phone interview, February 11, 2008.

Philip Steiner, Senior Casework Supervisor, Adoption and Foster Care Preparation and Support Unit, Department of Children, Youth and Families, interview, Providence, Rhode Island, January 24, 2008.

Brent Thompson, Director of Communications, William Penn Foundation, informal interview, Philadelphia, Pennsylvania, August 7, 2007. Thompson reported directly to the former president and served as a primary contact in the president's absence.

Carole Thompson, Senior Program Officer, Annie E. Casey Foundation, interview, Philadelphia, Pennsylvania, August 16, 2007. The collective Casey family foundations make it the single largest foundation to conduct work in the area of foster care.

Muna Walker, Senior Program Officer, Amachi, Public/Private Ventures, Philadelphia, Pennsylvania, interview, fall 2006. Walker has responsibility for the Mentoring Children of Prisoners program, which has significant client overlap with foster care.

Barbara Wilson, Program Officer, Senior Corps, Corporation for National and Community Service (CNCS) federal program, phone and written correspondence with author, fall 2006. Senior Corps provides volunteers in states for foster care.

Harry Wilson, Associate Commissioner, Family Youth and Services Bureau, U.S. Department of Health and Human Services, Administration for Children and Families, Family Youth and Services Bureau, informal background information, dozens of meetings in 2003–2006, Washington, DC.

NOTES

1. All references in the summary are cited in this chapter. Data refers to the period of research.
2. U.S. Census Bureau, "2003 American Community Survey," http://www.census.gov.
3. The Pew Commission on Children in Foster Care, "Foster Care Population and States Ranked by Total Number of Children in Foster Care. FY2003," http://pewfostercare.org/research/docs/Data091505.pdf. Note: To be exact, Rhode Island actually represents .44% of the foster care population and Delaware actually represents .16%.
4. Ibid.
5. Philip Steiner, Senior Casework Supervisor, Adoption and Foster Care Preparation and Support Unit, Department of Children, Youth and Families, interview, Providence, Rhode Island, January 24, 2008.
6. State of Rhode Island, "Department of Children, Youth and Families Fact Sheet: Children Served Month Ending 10/31/2007," internal document provided to author from DCYF in January 2008.
7. Ibid.
8. Philip Steiner, interview.
9. Note: Martinez holds a bachelor of social work from Rhode Island College and a master of management, health and human services from Springfield College. http://www.dcyf.ri.gov/director.php
10. Patricia Martinez, Director, Department of Children, Youth and Families, Rhode Island, phone interview, February 5, 2008.
11. Kevin Savage, Licensing Administrator and Federal Benefits, Department of Children, Youth and Families, Rhode Island, phone interview, February 5, 2008.
12. Dorothy Hultine, Policy, Central Management, Department of Children, Youth and Families, interview, Providence, Rhode Island, January 23, 2008.
13. Ibid.
14. Ibid.
15. Patricia Martinez, interview.
16. Ibid.
17. Lisa Pearson, HHS-ACF Region III Program Manager, federal government, phone interview, June 3, 2008.
18. Christine Craig, HHS-ACF Region III Program Specialist, federal government, phone interview, June 3, 2008.
19. Lisa Guillette, Executive Director, Rhode Island Foster Parents Association, interview, East Providence, Rhode Island, January 23, 2008. Note: After field research was completed, the Rhode Island Foster Parents Association was renamed Foster Forward.
20. Ibid.
21. Ibid.
22. Note: Local becomes of particular importance when states have large foster care operations in cities such as Detroit or New York City.
23. Confidential remarks.
24. Jennifer Silva, Program Director and Recruiter, Tannerhill Specialized Foster Care, interview, Pascoag, Rhode Island, January 24, 2008.
25. Lisa Guillette, interview.
26. Edward Fitzpatrick, "Litigation Long Overdue, Says Head of Foster Parents Group," *The Providence Journal*, July 1, 2007, http://www.projo.com/news/

content/dcyf_lawsuit1_07–01–07_45676LM.35eb8c5.html. Note: Guillette used the term "courageously" in this newspaper interview.

27. Ibid.
28. Ibid.
29. Julie DiBari, Deputy Director, Rhode Island Foster Care Association, interview, East Providence, Rhode Island, January 23, 2008.
30. Governor Donald L. Carcieri, "2008 State of the State Address," delivered January 22, 2008, http://www.governor.ri.gov/documents/statemessage08.pdf.
31. Julie DiBari, interview.
32. Ibid.
33. Heidi Mulligan, Foster Care Recruiter, St. Mary's Home for Children, North Providence, Rhode Island, phone interview, February 11, 2008.
34. Ibid.
35. State of Rhode Island, "Department of Children, Youth and Families Fact Sheet."
36. Maureen Robbins, Chief Casework Supervisor, Adoption and Foster Care Preparation and Support Unit, Department of Children, Youth and Families, interview, Providence, Rhode Island, January 24, 2008.
37. Lisa Guillette, interview.
38. Mark Moore, *Creating Public Value: Strategic Management in Government* (Cambridge, MA: Harvard University Press, 1995), 10.
39. Maureen Robbins, interview.
40. Lisa Guillette, interview. Note: Although the Rhode Island Foster Parents Association had trouble gaining traction in foster care improvement via the legislature, the organization gained significant national attention after this field research, including being recognized by the 2010 Bright Idea program at Harvard University. They were also awarded a $2 million Children's Bureau federal grant in 2009 as well as federal funding via ACF beginning in 2011.
41. Confidential remarks.
42. Jennifer Silva, interview.
43. Lisa Guillette, interview.
44. Ibid.
45. Philip Steiner, interview.
46. Maureen Robbins, interview; Philip Steiner, interview.
47. Maureen Robbins, interview.
48. Ibid.
49. Dorothy Hultine, interview.
50. Dana Mullen, Permanency Program Manager, Children's Friend and Service, Providence, Rhode Island, phone interview, February 5, 2008.
51. Ibid.
52. Dorothy Hultine, interview.
53. Patricia Martinez, interview.
54. Philip Steiner, interview.
55. Dana Mullen, interview.
56. Lisa Guillette, interview.
57. Sarah St. Jacques, Junior Human Services and Policy Systems Specialist, Department of Children Youth, and Families, Rhode Island, phone interview, February 11, 2008.
58. Ibid.
59. Ibid.
60. Confidential remarks.

Rhode Island 113

61. Confidential remarks.
62. Confidential remarks.
63. Maureen Robbins, interview.
64. Sarah St. Jacques, interview.
65. Lisa Guillette, interview.
66. Philip Steiner, interview.
67. Ibid.
68. Ibid.
69. Confidential remarks.
70. Sarah St. Jacques, interview.
71. Ibid.
72. Dana Mullen, interview.
73. Philip Steiner, interview.
74. Ibid.
75. Jennifer Silva, interview.
76. Confidential remarks.
77. Confidential remarks.
78. Jennifer Silva, interview.
79. Heidi Mulligan, interview.
80. Ibid.
81. Anne Fortier, Director of Clinical Services, Urban League of Rhode Island, interview, Providence, Rhode Island, January 24, 2008.
82. Ibid.
83. Patricia Martinez, interview.
84. Ibid.
85. Lisa Guillette, interview.
86. Ibid.
87. Ibid.
88. Anne Fortier, interview.
89. Confidential remarks.
90. Children's Rights, "Children's Rights and Rhode Island Child Advocate Sue to Protect Rhode Island Foster Children," http://www.childrensrights.org/news-events/press/childrens-rights-and-rhode-island-child-advocate-sue-to-protect-rhode-island-foster-children.
91. Maureen Robbins, interview.
92. Anne Fortier, interview.
93. Dana Mullen, interview.
94. Dorothy Hultine, interview.
95. Maureen Robbins, interview.
96. Patricia Martinez, interview.
97. Ibid.
98. Ibid. Note: Wrap-around refers to individualized and comprehensive support.
99. Lisa Guillette, interview.
100. Sarah St. Jacques, interview.
101. Maureen Robbins, interview.
102. Confidential remarks.
103. Heidi Mulligan, interview.
104. Lisa Guillette, interview.
105. Ibid.
106. Carcieri, "2008 State of the State Address."
107. Children's Rights, www.childrensrights.org. Note: Since the period of research, this class action lawsuit has faced various appeals and delays over the years. Rhode Island state officials resubmitted a motion to dismiss in November

114 *Politics of Foster Care Administration*

2010—resulting in a July 2011 decision denying that motion in part and ultimately allowing the case to once again proceed. Children's Rights filed the Second Amended Complaint in February 2012, and discovery is currently ongoing.

108. Fitzpatrick, "Litigation Long Overdue."
109. Confidential remarks.

6 Michigan
A Larger State with Stronger Performance

"I'm praying that Jim Casey and Annie Casey will continue their commitment."

—Justice Maura D. Corrigan, former Michigan chief justice, referring to the impact that these mentors have had on the foster care system in Michigan

"I frankly don't want judges to jeopardize IV-E dollars. Don't touch a placement, that's DHS's call."

—Justice Maura D. Corrigan, former Michigan chief justice, in stark contrast to the judicial and executive branch disputes over case placement in Rhode Island

---

MICHIGAN: FOSTER CARE DATA SUMMARY[1]

Agency and Foster Care Funding

Michigan's Department of Human Services (DHS) has responsibility for foster care administration across the state. DHS is Michigan's second-largest state agency, with approximately 10,000 employees and an annual budget of over $4 billion. In FY 2003, Michigan spent approximately $400 million on foster care and had 1,233 staff members overseeing foster care programs.

In most cases, Title IV-E federal funding provided approximately 50% of the money for foster care board and care payments, with administrative costs and training with the state providing the remainder. For services and foster care placements, the county and the state split the cost evenly. There were a number of other federal and state sources of funding for foster care as well, such as the Chafee Foster Care Independence Program for Youth in Transition.

116 *Politics of Foster Care Administration*

Foster Care Population

As of 2003, Michigan had a population of 10,095,643 with 211.7 foster care cases per 100,000 people. Michigan and New York were the two large states studied, and Rhode Island and Delaware were the two smaller states studied.

As of FY 2003, Michigan had 21,376 foster care children representing 4.3% of the foster care population across the country. As of March 2008, there were 18,452 foster care children with 6,786 in relative care and approximately 1,200 in residential care placements. Approximately two-thirds of foster children were in the Detroit metropolitan area. During this research period, Michigan foster children were permitted to remain in foster care until age 19, and when the court permits may stay until age 20.

Foster Care Administration

Foster care is a state-run system, and the state licenses the foster care homes and works with private agencies to place foster children throughout the state. At the time of the field research, approximately 60% of the caseload was completed by private agencies and 40% was completed by public agencies. Due to Michigan's fiscal crisis, there has been a legislative impetus for a major shift toward higher levels of privatization in foster care and other services. The legislators passed a budget that would shift half of the public cases to the private sector so that they would attain the goal of ultimately having 75% of cases being serviced by the private sector.

This chapter provides case research on foster care in the state of Michigan. The research was designed to test whether the following hypothesis is accurate: *Delaware and Michigan became stronger-performing states in the area of foster care by placing a greater priority than the lower-performing states of New York and Rhode Island on building community partners, integrating the advice of mentors, providing leadership from public managers, and cultivating relationships with the federal government.*

Michigan is one of the two larger states in this study and also falls into the category of a stronger case state, according to the 2003 federal performance measures. As of 2003, Michigan had a population of 9,825,840,[2] with 218 foster care cases per 100,000 people.[3] Michigan had the seventh-largest foster care caseload of all states, with 21,376 foster care children, representing 4.1% of the nation's total foster care population.[4]

The findings from this chapter on Michigan suggest that the four variables studied contributed in various ways to the successful administration of

Michigan 117

the state's foster care system: cultivation of federal government relationships was not a major factor, the building of community partners was a strong factor, the integration of advice from mentors was a strong factor, and the leadership from public managers was a strong factor that led to success.

CASE BACKGROUND

Like all other states during the period of field research, Michigan had been undergoing federal government reviews for Title IV-E eligibility as well as for Child and Family Service Reviews. Michigan performed near the top of the states on the Child and Family Service Reviews as shown by the "Child Welfare Outcomes 2003: Annual Report" in Chapter 2. Michigan qualified as a stronger case state because the state performed above the median on six out of seven foster care outcomes measured in 2003. At the same time, Michigan had a major decrease in improvement when comparing 2000 with 2003, and was below the median across all states for improvement over this period.

I conducted field research in Michigan in March 2008, with some additional phone interviews occurring outside that period. Michigan's Department of Human Services (DHS) has responsibility for foster care administration across the state. During this research period, Michigan foster children were permitted to remain in foster care until age 19, and when the court permits they may stay until age 20.[5]

DHS is Michigan's second-largest state agency with approximately 10,000 employees and an annual budget of over $4 billion. In FY 2003, Michigan spent approximately $400 million on foster care, with 1,233 staff members overseeing the programs.[6]

Michigan is a "state-run system" in which the state licenses foster care homes and works with private agencies to place foster children throughout the state.[7] Approximately 60% of the caseload is completed by private agencies and 40% is completed by public agencies. Due to Michigan's fiscal crisis, there has been a legislative impetus for a major shift toward higher levels of privatization in foster care and other services. The legislators passed a budget that would shift half of the public cases to the private sector, with the goal being to service 75% of cases within the private sector.[8]

In most cases, Title IV-E federal funding provides approximately 50% of the money for foster children's board and care payments, administrative costs, and training, with the state providing the remainder. For services and foster care placements, the county and the state split the cost evenly. There are a number of other federal and state sources of funding for foster care as well, such as the Chafee Foster Care Independence Program for Youth in Transition.[9]

As of March 2008, the number of foster care children currently in care in Michigan was 18,452, with 6,786 of those in relative care and approximately

118 *Politics of Foster Care Administration*

1,200 in residential care. The state foster care manager reported that the number of children in care has always been around 18,000 to 19,000, with a recent spike above 20,000.[10] Wayne County (which includes Detroit) has a higher number of children in foster care than any other county in the state.[11] Approximately two-thirds of Michigan's foster children are in the Detroit metro area.[12]

Field research in Michigan involved conducting interviews, viewing documents, and visiting state offices and foster care agencies. The purpose of the field research was to begin to identify which conditions, if any, produce better foster care outcomes. Interview topics focused on the interviewee's area of expertise in connection with foster care administration. Although the majority of interviews occurred in the field, some follow-up telephone interviews were conducted. At times, interviewees requested that all or part of their comments remain off the record.

Thirteen interviews were conducted on foster care in the state of Michigan specifically. Interviews were requested with "key players" who were actively involved in Michigan's foster care decisions. All interviews pursued within the state of Michigan were granted. The majority of interviews took place in-person. One key player interview never occurred, due to many delayed and rescheduled interview appointments that ultimately extended beyond the case research period.

Field research was conducted primarily in areas surrounding these three Michigan cities: Lansing, Detroit, and Ann Arbor. I interviewed the director of DHS, the state foster care manager, and the state foster care policy creator at DHS headquarters located in downtown Lansing. I also traveled to Ann Arbor to interview the former DHS director, who stepped down in 2007. The pattern continued that interviewees were generous with their time. Most prescheduled interviews for 30 minutes turned into hour-long interviews. The former director allowed me to speak with her for one hour, and the current director allowed the 30-minute scheduled interview to exceed the scheduled time as well.

Because Detroit (Wayne County) has a large foster care caseload, many of the private foster care agencies are located in the Detroit region. I traveled to Detroit to conduct interviews at some of these private agencies, as well as to conduct an interview with the Foster Care Review Board.

In addition, the recent chief justice of the Michigan State Supreme Court, now a current justice, permitted me to interview her for an hour by telephone. Unlike Delaware, I did not put in a gubernatorial interview request because Governor Granholm did not appear to take a personal interest in this issue. The highest ranking Michigan key player to be interviewed on foster care was the director of DHS.

I also conducted seven interviews that broadly informed my research on foster care and provided background for Michigan and other case states, as well as the implications across all states. These interviews were referred to in earlier chapters as well. A complete list of interviews is offered at the end of this chapter.

CASE FINDINGS

This section offers findings from the Michigan case research. Each of the four variables is analyzed and a summary is offered, noting their estimated significance based on research results.

Cultivation of Federal Government Relationships: Significance = None

For the variable *cultivation of federal government relationships* to appear strong, the data needed to show a pattern of interaction between the federal government and the state that went *beyond* the required relationship. This factor is shown to have a stronger presence when the federal government has significantly shifted the direction of the state's decision-making path regarding the provision of foster care in some nonrequired area. In other words, the federal–state relationship on foster care needed to transcend the required form completion, grant processing, regulation monitoring, and data gathering and move into how to fix and transform foster care.

Like other states, Michigan is monitored by the federal government through the Child and Family Service Reviews (CFSR), which includes Program Improvement Plans (PIPs) and financial audits.

The first round of state performance reviews by the federal government (HHS), Child and Family Service Reviews, occurred between October 2000 and early 2004.[13] Although they performed near the top of all states, Michigan performed poorly according to federal standards. All states subsequently underwent a Performance Improvement Plan. Michigan's PIP began in 2004 and was completed in May 2006. On March 26, 2008, DHS director Ishmael Ahmed stated, "Michigan does not yet have results as to whether the Federal Department of Health and Human Services considers Michigan's performance on the PIP to have met all applicable standards."[14]

Michigan went through its next round of the Child and Family Service Review in 2009 and the state formed a committee around meeting the required benchmarks.[15]

I asked Marianne Udow, former Michigan DHS director, whether the federal performance measures were too high. She responded, "No, I would never say the bar is too high because we have to do better by our children."[16] Mary Chaliman, Michigan's foster care program manager said, "I think the CFSR has been referenced more and more as an impetus for change."[17] She went on to say, "Permanency [getting kids into permanent placements] has improved as a result of the CFSR."[18] Like Delaware, Michigan viewed these performance measures as an impetus for change.

Yet, when states do not meet federal benchmarks they are frequently penalized. Chief Supreme Court Justice Corrigan said, "The federal government audits you. They try to take money away from you. The penalty environment I find difficult. 'We're going to assess penalties if you haven't accomplished the impossible.'"[19]

120 *Politics of Foster Care Administration*

Although the federal government requires significant paperwork from the states, none of Michigan's interviewees mentioned receiving federal support in the form of mentoring or volunteers.

Like every other case state, Michigan had to contend with the federal government shifting costs to the state level. As the Title IV-E levels became outdated, fewer Michigan foster care cases were eligible for federal funding. Former Michigan DHS director Marianne Udow referred to this shift as "a huge issue: how arcane Title IV-E is."[20]

The state was facing decreased federal funding for overall foster care costs, while at the same time facing a financial crisis in the state. The state budget was in fairly good shape in 1999 and 2000. By the fall of 2000, Michigan saw the first signs of the financial crisis that began to escalate in 2001. According to Jane Zehnder-Merrell, senior research associate at the Michigan League for Human Services, 2008 was the first state budget in many years that did not start out with a deficit.[21]

One of Michigan's budgetary challenges is that the state has been heavily reliant on the auto industry for a large portion of its revenue, while most other states have a broader revenue base from many industries. Zehnder-Merrell noted that the state experienced a financial crisis largely due to the auto industry losses. She pointed out that auto workers are now making $14 an hour for jobs that used to pay $28 an hour at the same company.[22] She went on to explain that this reduction in wages, as well as job loss, has a ripple effect and is driving more folks into poverty and onto the child welfare rolls. This simultaneously puts more pressure on the foster care program.

These observations led me to two conclusions. First, I did not find that the relationship between the federal government and Michigan went beyond the normal required relationship. Like all other case states, Michigan was experiencing increased performance reporting requirements from the federal government, along with decreased federal funding for the overall costs of foster care.

Furthermore, I dismissed the alternative hypothesis that increased state or federal funding for foster care leads to higher levels of success. Michigan was a top-performing state on the federal performance measurement data in 2003. During the 2000–2003 period, Michigan was experiencing a state financial crisis and saw declining federal dollars for overall foster care program costs. The state did not infuse significant additional funding during that period. Instead, Michigan was able to perform near the top of all states on foster care in spite of depleted financial resources. The next three sections explain why Michigan was still able to perform well under these circumstances.

The Integration of Advice from Mentors: Significance = Strong

The hypothesis is that the stronger states will have stronger (defined as more or deeper) mentors who offer strategic advice or training on the issue of foster care. *Mentors are defined here as foundations, issue-expert national nonprofit organizations, or think tanks that focus on foster care.*

The strong presence of mentors is reflected by a workhorse relationship in which the state has either a large network of mentors or a rigorous relationship with one mentor organization. Workhorse relationships are deeper relationships in which mentors discuss ideas with the state, and the state then takes action.

This factor is shown to have a stronger presence when the mentors have significantly shifted the direction of the state's decision-making path regarding the provision of foster care in some nonrequired area.

One key mentoring relationship is between the foundation community and the state. Michigan sought out and utilized members of the foundation community as mentors for training and policy initiatives. Marianne Udow stated, "Pew and Annie Casey here in Michigan really were mentors, partially because here in Michigan I didn't see leaders in child welfare. Governor Engler's interest was on cash assistance, not on child welfare."[23] DHS director Ishmael Ahmed referred to the relationships with the foundation community, such as Jim Casey, Annie E. Casey, Kellogg, Skillman, and community foundations, and shared the same sentiment: "Generally speaking the foundation community has been really good—they've given us the ability to try new things, to draw on a wealth of knowledge from across the country with best practices."[24] He referred to community foundations as "a tremendous support."[25]

Annie E. Casey's "Family to Family Initiative" emphasizes "the need to bring birth families and children to the table during case planning."[26] The implementation of Casey's model shifted foster care placements away from strangers as a first option and, in Michigan, redirected thousands of placements toward the extended family of the foster child. Chaliman said, "We now have 7,000 kids with relatives—most of those are going to move to adoption; most of them don't go to termination."[27] The shift was so significant that Michigan is now considering dual licensing. This would license foster care families as adoptive families congruently instead of the existing process, which pursues two separate licensing routes.[28]

Many interviewees credited the foundation's efforts with moving foster care policy forward in the state. Chaliman said "Family to Family was a really big help. I think Family to Family drove a lot of change. I think the change I've seen more is on the front lines is the engagement of families and how they need to be included in decisions."[29]

The Annie E. Casey Foundation helped mentor Director Udow as she entered her DHS position, and gave her the first training she ever received on foster care. Udow said:

> I didn't know anything about foster care [when I took the position]. Shortly after I came in . . . there was an Annie Casey Family to Family Initiative meeting in New Mexico. That was really my first and biggest learning—hearing from other states, hearing from other staff, shortly thereafter hearing from the kids.[30]

122 *Politics of Foster Care Administration*

This Family to Family pilot has not occurred without some major glitches. One private agency actively involved in the initiative referred to the model as "screwy" and said:

> There used to be a system in place where if a family had a history with an agency, you got the family. Now it works against the family. Now it fits the characteristics of the child instead of [being] family centered. It doesn't allow for [the] history of a child to come into place and enter into their system.[31]

In other words, a foster child could be shifted to a new agency without anyone taking into account the child's long-term relationship with an existing agency. The senior research associate at the Michigan League for Human Services said:

> The Family to Family Initiative has affected a lot—has affected a lot in Wayne County. There are varying reports of it. There are other people concerned about the way it was implemented—families don't really understand [that] what they say in meetings can be used against them. There aren't really strict protocols.[32]

The consensus is that the Annie E. Casey Foundation and its Family to Family Initiative has had a major effect upon Michigan that has been positive overall, but not without glitches.

Udow also partnered with the Jim Casey Foundation[33] to implement the Youth Opportunities Initiative. This initiative develops "youth advisory boards to give youth a voice in the community and develop programs to transition youth from foster care to independence."[34] Udow was perceived as the DHS director behind this Youth Opportunities Initiative during her term (2004–2007).[35] The youth advisory board created the VOICE document, featuring proposals to reform foster care that produced "definite change and major impact."[36] The youth advisory board also spoke to the state cabinet and to the state legislature. Overall, Udow believed this initiative was "very powerful."[37] Director Ahmed said "Jim Casey has been great."[38] Kate Hanley, the director of adoption and permanency services at DHS, said:

> Jim Casey made a big difference—helped to work with the kids on just talking and presenting to the legislature, to the governor. They're on our task force and will be doing another presentation to the legislature again. These kids aren't asking for the world; they're asking for normal teenage things.[39]

The state youth advisory board was so effective that "every county now wants to have a youth board."[40]

Former chief justice Corrigan added, "Jim Casey had the most effect on anything I did (through) the Youth Opportunities Initiative. I'm praying that Jim Casey and Annie Casey will continue their commitment. I think there was great progress."[41] The work resulted in foster children speaking before the legislature, and a five-bill package that passed 48–0 in the Senate.[42]

In addition to the Annie E. Casey and Jim Casey Foundation partnerships, Michigan also had partnerships with the Pew Charitable Trusts and the Skillman Foundation. The Pew Commission work focused primarily on improving the court system as it related to foster care. Udow said, "Michigan Supreme Court chief justice Maura Corrigan and I put a workgroup together which was an outgrowth of the Pew Commission work. There were several states that got together—a lot of exciting work."[43]

DHS director Ahmed cultivated a DHS partnership with the Skillman Foundation, which looked at "an institutional bias in the system that selects out families of color."[44] Ahmed noted, "Michigan is pretty active with fairly breakthrough research with the Skillman foundation."[45] Ahmed was scheduled to present this research to the public one week after our interview.

Ahmed did acknowledge that although the foundations are generally financially supportive, their contributions do not meet the funding levels needed by DHS. He also felt that some of the foundations operate in silos too much in that they need to work together more collectively.

Clearly, the integration of advice from mentors was strong in Michigan. In fact, the advice from mentors was so welcomed that both directors struggled with DHS employees and agencies putting the directives of the foundations ahead of those at DHS. Ahmed acknowledged that the foundations in Michigan have been so powerful that "sometimes the people on our side get confused and may take things [from the foundations] that may not be our directive, and workers go where the foundations want them to go [instead of following DHS leadership]."[46] Udow acknowledged this tension as well. This speaks to the power the foundation community has had in the state of Michigan in shaping initiatives and implementing policies.

Michigan has embraced the use of mentors unlike any other case state. From Annie E. Casey's Family to Family Initiative, to the Jim Casey Youth Opportunities Initiative, to the Pew Commission and the Skillman Foundation, Michigan has been open to experimenting with the advice and research of external mentors.

Building of Community Partners: Significance = Strong

The hypothesis is that the stronger states will have stronger (defined as more or deeper) community partnerships. *Community partnerships are defined here as state and/or local[47] foster care agency relationships with local non-profits, faith-based organizations, and community organizations.* The strong presence of community partners is reflected by a workhorse relationship in which the state has either a large network of community partners or a

124   *Politics of Foster Care Administration*

rigorous relationship with one community partner. Workhorse relationships are deeper relationships in which community partners discuss ideas with the state, and the state then takes action.

A workhorse relationship might include government and community organizations copromoting a conference with mutual organizational roles, or deciding together to more aggressively pursue homes for older female teens. This factor is shown to have a stronger presence when the community partners have significantly shifted the direction of the state's decision-making path regarding the provision of foster care in some area. Basic administrative paperwork or meetings between a community partner and the state do not qualify as a strong presence of this variable.

In Michigan's case, community partners followed the same pattern as relationships with mentors. There are numerous community partnerships between the agency, the courts, and nonprofit and academic institutions in Michigan. Janet Snyder, executive director for the Michigan Federation for Children and Families, said: "Non-profits are very active in Michigan in accomplishing things, and generally at some point they can be listened to."[48] Snyder named a few of them: the Michigan State School of Social Work, Michigan's Children, the Foster Care Review Board, and the Office of the Children's Ombudsman.[49]

Snyder's organization has a mixed relationship with Michigan, sometimes working with the state and other times against it. The Michigan Federation for Children and Families, which has paid lobbyists, is a consortium of the private agencies that lobby the state government on issues related to foster care. Snyder noted, "The federation walks hand in hand with DHS to an extent. If there's an issue that comes up, [we tell them] this is what we're hearing about as a problem or concern."[50]

Udow added that this federation was very active and had been able to push the state in certain directions. The federation lobbied DHS to get a blended rate instead of a two-tier foster care rate. The two-tier foster care rate offered a separate "general per diem child rate" from a "specialized foster care child rate."[51] One foster care agency said, "It was somewhat of a success with DHS/legislature to get a blended rate."[52]

DHS utilizes the member information network both to receive data and to disseminate information on adoption and licensing to the private agencies. DHS representatives also present state developments before the group regularly. The perception was that DHS director Ishmael Ahmed would strengthen this partnership because "Ahmed has been very clear since he took office, to talk about public/private partnerships . . . so we're having quarterly public–private meetings."[53] Vicki Thompson-Sandy, vice president of children and family services for Lutheran Social Services of Michigan, stated: "Michigan is now at the table in those quarterly public–private meetings—talking about how we're not held accountable for any performance measures."[54]

Many of the task forces actively involve community players and have produced results as well. Maura Corrigan, former chief justice of the

Michigan Supreme Court, served on a work group that created the concept of permanent guardianships as an approach to foster care that would reduce the number of state wards and increase the likelihood of reunification. This was an impetus for the 2008 law that would allow the court to appoint a permanent guardian for each foster child, a family that loves the child and is able to provide a permanent, stable home to do so when adoption is not the best option.[55] Corrigan said this new policy will reduce the numbers of children in care and "occurred out of the work group."[56]

In addition, DHS has hosted several work groups that are considering bringing performance-based contracts to the private agencies. Snyder said, "I think change is already underway—more specific goals, more specific outcomes, using benchmarks—performance-based contracting. The state is really taking a hard look."[57] Snyder, who represents the private agencies, affirmed: "Just like everyone else, I want to make sure we're measuring the right way. I don't have the feeling that anyone is afraid of it or [is] reluctant."[58]

Michigan had previously implemented the "One Church, One Child" model in which a congregation would commit to help match a child with an adoptive family. Although Thompson-Sandy did not think that program was very successful, she is implementing a version of the original model at her foster care agency. She has organized the 60 churches in the local Lutheran synod to help find homes for children in foster care who are waiting to be adopted through Lutheran Social Services of Michigan.[59]

The court system created the Foster Care Review Board (FCRB) to partner with the community and operate 30 review boards that evaluate state performance on foster care cases. The FCRB is housed in the judicial department and is state staffed and operated. In addition to recruiting hundreds of volunteers who evaluate state foster care performance, the FCRB also has placed citizens on these boards. The legislative statute only requires that five people serve on a board, but the FCRB frequently seats seven members. James Novell, FCRB program manager, said: "We get amazing volunteers. Kids are a sell. We're part of pushing a boulder up a hill. We've made a difference in cases, I'm certain if we weren't involved a case would go differently."[60] The FCRB recommendations are "advisory only," although Novell commented, "we've got a lot of action on the last report."[61] Novell is also involved with putting together regional training for judges, and he serves on the adoption work group that meets with the courts and DHS to form local teams for adoption placements.[62] The FCRB is an example of a community partnership in which the courts, DHS, and citizens have come together to improve foster care performance.

Michigan also has formed partnerships with members of the academic community. DHS director Ahmed emphasized his desire to build these partnerships, including continuing DHS's association with the Michigan State School of Social Work and creating internships and research partnerships with other schools.[63] During Udow's term, DHS held three summits around

126   *Politics of Foster Care Administration*

the state at different campuses and developed a new relationship with Western Michigan University. Ahmed said, "I want to grow the DHS relationship with universities in particular. A consortium of social work schools is a priority."[64]

Academic partnerships are common in Michigan's foster care system. The state partnered with the largest private foster care agency to administer grants that would pay college tuition for foster children. Through this program, foster children were initially awarded $5,000; by the first quarter of 2008, 250 more awards had been approved than had been approved during the entire first half of 2007. The agency said "we're going to run out of money"[65] due to the popularity of the program. The state also negotiated with a state university to ensure that all former foster youth would be admitted.

Furthermore, when Ahmed entered office in 2007, he immediately created a 1-year community partnership task force so that he would have 2 years to implement recommendations before his position ended. He asked Pat Babcock, former director of DHS, and Carol Gross, executive director of the Skillman Foundation, to co-chair a task force of the 70 best and brightest people in the state, including child welfare policy gurus and university administrators, "to help us define the agenda [for DHS]."[66] This task force integrated community partners and gave them the freedom to find solutions, some of which would not require additional funding.

Ahmed's predecessor, DHS director Marianne Udow, was able to turn an adversarial relationship with the nonprofit agency Children's Rights into a positive community partnership during her time in office. Udow, along with Governor Granholm and other senior staff at DHS, were defendants in a Children's Rights lawsuit that was filed against the state of Michigan. Children's Rights had sued 14 states as of 2008 (including New York, Rhode Island, and Michigan) to encourage better state performance for children in foster care. The plaintiffs in the Michigan state case included a child who was in state custody for the last 14 of her 16 years while being physically and sexually abused and moved through at least 10 different placements. Another child named in the lawsuit, who was 7, had been in eight different foster homes; another plaintiff was 13, had lived in five different foster homes, and had been sexually abused by a foster father. Three siblings named in the lawsuit had either mental retardation, autism, or developmental delays and had been denied access to necessary treatment and services.[67]

Udow worked with Children's Rights to attempt to settle the lawsuit. She spent a significant portion of her time in the office brokering this relationship. Udow said:

> I have great respect for [the organization Children's Rights]. Whether you think litigation is the right strategy, I think it makes sense. In every state [where cases are litigated] more money is given. I understood them. I think Children's Rights is well-intentioned. They're not unreasonable to go through—I think they actually helped the state.[68]

Udow did not negotiate a settlement with Children's Rights in order to buy off the opponent, but rather she used this organization and lawsuit to help achieve their shared goals of obtaining better quality of care and more funding from the state.

Although Udow brokered a deal with Children's Rights, the governor and state legislature did not support this deal or back it with settlement money.[69] At the time of this field research, the settlement deal had failed despite Udow's efforts to build a significant relationship with Children's Rights. It was commonly believed that Udow left her position as DHS director because she did not receive support from the governor and the state legislature on this significant issue.[70]

Following her departure in 2007, Udow said, "I think they will come to a settlement. It took an enormous amount of time. Unfortunately the state backed away from the settlement. Money [is the issue]. They would have to make the financial commitment."[71] This incident shows how a public manager can play a role in turning an adversary into a partner to produce better foster care results.[72]

Clearly, the administrators of Michigan's foster care system have demonstrated their ability to build strong community partners. Leadership from public managers was often the impetus for success with these partners because the state encouraged input and turned external recommendations into action. On many levels, the state of Michigan permitted its community partners to move beyond basic administration tasks with the state and create workhorse relationships.

Leadership from Public Managers: Significance = Strong

The hypothesis is that the stronger states will have more leadership from public managers. *A public manager is shown to evidence leadership when he or she is operating as a "principled agent" in the state or local government or agency responsible for the area of foster care.* In the context of this study, a principled agent is a government employee (public manager) who goes above and beyond his or her public duty to cultivate successful foster care administration. Harvard Kennedy School professor Mark Moore argued that a successful manager "increase(s) the public value produced by public sector organizations in both the short and the long run."[73] A principled agent performs as a workhorse rather than as a standard government employee who is focused on routine functions. The strong presence of leadership from public managers is reflected by a greater presence of principled agents working in foster care in the case state.

Executive Branch Leadership

Michigan governor Jennifer Granholm, a Democrat, succeeded Governor Engler on January 1, 2003. In 2005, *Governing* magazine and the Government Performance Project named Michigan the third best-managed state in the nation and gave Michigan and the Granholm administration high

128   *Politics of Foster Care Administration*

marks in the areas of money, people, infrastructure, and information management.[74] In 2008, the Government Performance Project again recognized Michigan as one of the best-managed states in the nation under Granholm's administration.[75] In the eyes of foster care advocates, "foster care wasn't [Governor Engler's] priority."[76] Udow said that Governor Granholm "has been open to take leadership on this issue [of foster care]. She brought [foster care] kids to cabinet meetings."[77] Interviewees suggested that both Governors Granholm and Engler were supportive of foster care, yet left the bulk of public management activity to their DHS directors.

Michigan has experienced significant upper-staff turnover, including five DHS directors over the 10 year period that preceded this field research. A DHS director prior to the Ahmed–Udow era told Governor Engler, "We [don't] have a children problem in Michigan," meaning child welfare in Michigan was in pretty good shape.[78] But many found the director-level turnover to be problematic. Justice Corrigan stated, "It's enormously frustrating to see turnover. I believe the lack of consistency harms the child welfare endeavor. I think that's a fact of life in every state. I think the frustrating thing is you're starting over every time there's a new director." However, she also noted: "If you have a plan and your strategy is known to the permanent employees, then you can overcome turnover in directors."[79]

The two most recent directors at the time of field research were Marianne Udow and Ishmael Ahmed. Udow served as the DHS director from January 2004 to September 2007. In September 2007, Ahmed took over the position and continued to serve in this position at the time of the field research. In general, private foster care agencies viewed the Ahmed term more favorably than the Udow term. Agency employees viewed Ahmed as "one of them" because he previously had led his own community organization. In 1983, Ahmed cofounded what eventually became the largest Arab-American human services organization in the United States, the Arab Community Center for Economic and Social Services (ACCESS).[80]

Although not every key player supported all the decisions of every DHS director, across key player interviews the overall feeling about both Udow and Ahmed was mostly positive. Udow was perceived to have made lots of changes and "held on longer than we expected [her] to—she only wanted to be there for a short time. She was more responsive than had been the case with previous directors."[81]

On the other hand, there was also some discontent with the Udow administration. The President of Catholic Social Services of Wayne County said "Udow had no experience in child welfare. She was horrible. We were happy to hear she was leaving. Many of the things she dismantled, they're bringing back [under Ahmed]."[82] One key player anonymously commented:

> The previous administration was extremely difficult to work with, we rarely were able to accomplish things working with the Udow administration. I believe fully that this is changing. From what I've seen and

Michigan 129

asked for, there was a quick response. I would say we've been able to change things, to the degree we've been asking.[83]

Udow believed that her biggest accomplishment was expanding the Annie E. Casey initiatives on a statewide basis by focusing on "relative placements, keeping siblings together, placing kids close to their home, and rolling that out statewide."[84]

Udow also led the Skillman Foundation project, which looked at the uneven number of minority children in foster care, as well as practices within DHS that were leading to racial inequality in foster care. The research team found that vendors or partners of DHS were hesitant to travel to certain areas where the majority of African-American families reside. When families would get angry for not getting the help they needed, caseworkers would interpret this as "the families are difficult." Instead, the researchers found it was a simple "contracting out issue that led to institutional racism."[85] At the time of this field research, Udow said that the implementation plan she and her partners identified to resolve this situation "will be carried through."[86]

Udow also altered the child placement system in Wayne County, which represents the Detroit area in which two-thirds of foster children are located. Prior to her tenure, the system rotated agencies so that if one private agency received the last foster care child placement, then the next foster child would be sent to a different private agency.[87] The placements were focused on maintaining equality across foster care agencies, but from Udow's perspective were not in the best interest of the child. She reformed the system via the Family to Family model to focus on the needs of the child first with reference to the biological family.

Udow believes that Wayne County still needs major improvement, because it is a "huge entrenched bureaucracy. Wayne County needed stronger leadership on the child welfare side. [It has had] some success. But the leadership is still not there yet."[88]

Udow also championed kinship care, which is a major component of the Family to Family model. This was considered to be a "massive change in approaching relatives"[89] regarding children in their own families who needed foster care. Although increasing the use of kinship care was a national trend, Michigan was a frontrunner on this issue. In 2002, approximately 28% of Michigan's foster children were placed with relatives;[90] by 2007, approximately 37% of foster children were placed with relatives.[91] Kate Hanley, director of adoption and permanency services at DHS, believed that subsidized guardianship, another benefit for relative caregivers, would also be underway in Michigan by May 2008. Subsidized guardianships "provide financial assistance to caretakers who assume legal guardianship of a child from out-of-home care."[92]

Michigan also adopted a fast track licensing process. One private agency estimated that the licensing period only takes "within 2 to 3 months from [the first] phone call to [the] person being licensed,"[93] compared with Rhode Island's slow licensing time line of 6 months or longer. However, following

130 Politics of Foster Care Administration

Michigan's significant increase in kinship care, many children were placed in relative homes without licensing. In 2008, Thompson-Sandy, a vice president at Lutheran Social Services of Michigan said, "6,000 of the 7,000 relative homes are licensed. Only this year was there funding to license those relatives."[94]

Michigan also addressed some of the concerns that pertain to youths who are aging out of the foster care system, including health insurance. In 2008, Kate Hanley, director of adoption and permanency services at DHS said, "We got Medicaid for Chafee [Foster Care Independence Program[95] eligible youth] to ensure every kid who leaves is signed up for Medicaid. This is a big initiative and just about to go through. By June, we'll have it in place."[96]

Although DHS had authorized the use of the Jim Casey Youth Initiative, Udow was largely responsible for its implementation. Renamed as The Michigan Youth Opportunity Initiative, the program invited foster care youth to participate in a statewide task force. Udow said that when she assumed the director's position, DHS staff did not know what they were going to do with the Jim Casey grant. One county director had no connection to the foster care children that DHS was serving and Udow changed that relationship. She also rolled out the initiative to promote the concept of mentoring because a "mentor solves a lot of problems, even giving advice."[97]

Udow believed that the Family to Family model changed the entire structure of foster care in Michigan. With this shift, the goal became to reunify the child with the immediate biological family first, or if that was not possible, then preferably with relatives second. Private agencies resisted the change because they had built their foundations on residential care:

> As we introduced Family to Family more strongly in the state, we shut shelters because the strong feeling was that children do not belong in shelters. I feel strongly we should do what is right and the best thing for the children and not the best financial model. We had virtually closed all but 10 shelter beds.[98]

With Ahmed as director, Udow believed "the trend [would] be the same, but lesser trajectory. Ishmael made a commitment to open more [shelter] beds."[99]

Director Ahmed was perceived by the private agencies as less of an outsider because he created the nonprofit group ACCESS and turned it into the largest Arab-American human services organization in the United States. Former DHS director Babcock referred to Ahmed's ability to network and connect with people: "It's hard to eat with Ahmed because he knows so many people [in that we're frequently interrupted by his networks of colleagues]. . . . He has an ability to take a position . . . that's strong but provides enough room for people to come together."[100]

Because Ahmed was part of the nonprofit community, he had a long-term relationship with nonprofits and advocacy groups throughout Michigan. Ahmed worked with welfare rights groups and used to "take over welfare offices with children's rights organizations."[101] He said, "I come into [DHS]

Michigan 131

with a good relationship with these groups"[102] since he used to protest alongside them speaking out against DHS's practices. In an effort to build bridges with these groups, Ahmed called the Detroit leaders of the children's rights organizations. He suggested these leaders just call him instead of protesting in the streets about the problems at DHS. But he said that only lasted about 2 months. He received a letter from the leaders, "Dear Brother Ishmael, we RESPECT you, but you are the Director of Hell, so we're going back to the streets."[103] Ahmed laughed and knows the future will be an uphill climb with some of these groups since he is attached to the DHS brand viewed unfavorably by these leaders.

In an increased emphasis on performance measurements, Ahmed wants to lower the average number of foster care cases for each caseworker and "muster [the] strength to meet national standards" regarding caseload numbers.[104] He also wants to build momentum for foster care reform from within the community: "We want to get out more publicly the questions of child welfare reform—press work, electronic work, community level—to create the political will."[105]

Public managers in the state have also championed higher reimbursement rates for Michigan foster parents. As a result, the average day rate at which Michigan reimburses foster families is significantly higher than that of other states. In 2008, when the state of Michigan placed a foster child, the foster family received $50.61 per day, plus county funding for child care.[106] For private agency placements, the reimbursement rate varied.

The state foster care program manager, Mary Chaliman, is a public manager who has been engaged in creating more effective foster care models. One of the bigger initiatives she helped to create was the award-winning Structured Decision-Making Model, which is used to direct foster care caseworkers through a series of decisions regarding a child. Chaliman, who served as a case worker for 7 years, a supervisor for 7 years, and as the state program manager for 5 years, said: "One thing Michigan is very proud of is structured decision making. When I was a worker in the field we had open-ended decision making—no idea how to do things."[107] Structured decision making was created out of Michigan's Family Independence Agency and forces caseworkers to make decisions about when to return a foster child to his or her family, when to permit visitation with the family, and when to offer various benefits to the foster child. Chaliman saw significant results: "I saw it make a huge difference in my unit. Every caseworker utilizes the Structured Decision-Making Model."[108]

The model was so successful that it received national attention and was adopted by other states. The Institute for Government Innovation at Harvard's Kennedy School of Government named Michigan's Structured Decision-Making Model one of their finalists for the Innovations in American Government Award in 2003. Harvard referred to the model as a "widely replicated case management program."[109]

One of the biggest hurdles that Michigan still faces in the area of foster care is its inability to collect strong performance data from private agencies.

132   Politics of Foster Care Administration

At the time of this field research, Michigan had a department of technology that was separate from DHS. DHS had been waiting for a long time for the resources it needed to create databases to collect this data[110] so it could be used to inform future decision making. Chaliman said, "I can't tell you what's better or not—private or public agency"[111] because DHS has no universal system for tracking performance across all placements.

Kate Hanley, director of adoption and permanency services at DHS, believed the future of DHS was bright:

> I think we're moving in the right direction, I guess I feel like Michigan has always had the right intentions. This Adoption Forum taking place with Justice Corrigan where we question everything that happens toward permanency [and] really push ourselves [to find the right permanent solution for these foster children. This also includes] giving staff the resources to find the answers for some of these [foster care] kids.[112]

Although the state has made progress on many fronts, Michigan's foster care system is not without problems. Victoria Tyler, director of child welfare for Catholic Social Services of Wayne, said: "Michigan's abuse and neglect hotline is short-staffed and people won't get their phone calls answered when reporting abuse and neglect about children."[113]

The Judicial Branch and Cross-Branch Collaboration

After what had been a rocky relationship, a stronger agency–judiciary relationship was established in Michigan over time. During the first Child and Family Services Review, DHS did not inform the judicial branch that it was coming inside the courts to review performance measurements. Justice Corrigan said, "The first CFSR took me by surprise."[114] Over time, DHS reached out to the judicial branch and their communication improved. Corrigan stated, "I think now we do have a coordinated strategy—so now we know what's coming. We're better prepared and more organized."[115]

Chief Justice Maura Corrigan was first elected to the Michigan Supreme Court in 1998, served as chief justice from 2001 to 2004, and was reelected in 2006. When she became chief justice, she was appointed to the area of children and families. She was, by far, more active in child welfare than any chief judge in other case states. Like Delaware, Michigan had executive branch public managers that actively worked with judicial branch public managers. DHS director Udow noted, "Michigan was fortunate because [Supreme Court chief justice] Maura Corrigan was in office when I came in. She was really engaged in these issues and wanted to make things better."[116]

It was her service on the Pew Commission that Corrigan says "stirred my involvement [on foster care]." She also weathered a big media crisis hit related to a number of children in foster care who were missing.[117] This experience prompted Corrigan and a team of colleagues to create dockets in all of Michigan's jurisdictions to deal with the problem of runaways.

Michigan 133

While on the Pew Commission, Corrigan joined with agency and judicial branch executives from many states to focus on addressing the problem of court delays. She said the central learning theme from the Pew Commission was the "silo effect," in that there was a tendency to operate in silos in child welfare instead of collaborating across branches. In other words, the judicial branch would operate separately, rather than working alongside the executive branch leadership. They also learned that collaboration needed to start from the leadership at the top of each branch.

In 2005, Corrigan helped to lead a major national conference funded by the National Center for State Courts. This included the very first summit to improve child welfare at the state level. Each state created a team to look at cross-branch collaboration and a federal bill was passed that required collaboration and tied it to federal funding. Iowa Republican senator Charles Grassley was instrumental in this legislation. In 2007, there was an update meeting to assess the performance of how the states were doing.[118] Corrigan's leadership on these foster care issues had a national impact.

Michigan's state foster care manager watched these judicial and agency branch relationships develop. Chaliman said:

> Udow really strengthened our relationship with Maura Corrigan and really ran with youth issues, kids exiting the system. We had legislation to have a task force and she was a very no-nonsense director. [Udow] even brought in the National Governors Association.[119]

The presentation before the National Governors Association was a joint leadership effort by Corrigan and Udow.[120] According to Corrigan, "getting into the organization is greater than getting an individual governor to buy in."[121] Corrigan and Udow also participated on a task force for foster children aging out of the program, and this resulted in a change in philosophy; both women came to believe that jurisdiction should be extended to age 22.[122] Corrigan had this comment:

> A lot of work in the area of adoption [is about how] to take kids to permanency—we have organized teams into 13 large jurisdictions to crash the dockets there. We're taking identified adoptive parents and marrying them to the children. This is a collaboration with DHS—we've called it the adoption forum. We're moving more children to adoption and older children to adoption quickly.[123]

When I asked about whether DHS and the courts have had any disagreements about case placements, the response was startling. Corrigan seemed surprised by the question. Unlike the courts in Rhode Island, the Michigan courts actively worked with DHS recommendations regarding case placements. Corrigan said, "I frankly don't want judges to jeopardize IV-E dollars—don't touch a placement, that's DHS's call."[124] She believed that

134 *Politics of Foster Care Administration*

this philosophy stemmed from the Family to Family model and the Jim Casey Youth Opportunities Initiative.

The Michigan courts recognized that their placement decisions for children would affect how much money the state received from the federal government through Title IV-E. One key player interviewee said, "We had some courts send some kids home and then re-remove them so that they could make the proper IV-E budget. Some courts push their weight around."[125] The Michigan courts worked with the agencies in order to do what was best for foster children including making the best use of maximizing federal Title IV-E funds.

Justice Corrigan also launched an initiative to ensure that all foster children met face-to-face with their lawyers. Corrigan would routinely ask the children if they knew their lawyers, and children often had never met them. Corrigan reorganized the way lawyers were assigned, and required accountability from the lawyers who represented the children. Gayle Robbert of the Lansing Foster Care Review Board said, "Lawyers seeing their children didn't happen before. That has improved. One of the Supreme Court justices is very interested, that's why this has improved. She wanted [the attorneys] to come into compliance."[126] Corrigan said, "I ask kids now if they know their lawyer, [and] they say yes. I want to stand up and cheer."[127] Even though the new chief judge who succeeded Corrigan had the authority to reassign the children and families area to a new judge, the chief judge decided to keep Corrigan in charge of that area. Justice Corrigan said, "If I left, do I think things would be different? I sure do."[128]

Legislative Branch Leadership

Although there is presently no individual state legislator who is known for foster care leadership, the collective Michigan legislature is active on the issue. In the years leading up to this field research, the state was so focused on solving its fiscal crisis that allocating funding for new state programs was infrequent. Yet, foster care is one of the few areas that the legislature has financially prioritized, motivated in part by the Children's Rights lawsuit, as well as a handful of foster care child deaths in Michigan. Mary Chaliman, the state foster care manager said, "I think foster care has [received] attention no matter the budget cuts."[129]

The collaboration between mentors, community partners, and public managers has often been the impetus for legislative action on foster care issues. Corrigan and Udow were heavily involved in the Jim Casey Youth Opportunities Initiative that resulted in legislative activity. Corrigan asked foster children from the initiative to testify in support of the bill. Corrigan said:

> We had a five bill package pass in the Senate 48–0, [meaning] it has five different reforms in foster care. It's now in the house, now waiting for a vote on the floor. Kids believe they have a future. This is getting through to kids. [A] marvelous partnership.[130]

Michigan 135

Two of the bills focused on subsidized guardianship, one focused on concurrent planning, and another bill required a court and a lawyer ad litem to be notified when placement changes.[131] Another bill "would shift the burden back on the state to terminate rights. It gives the state more time to think about it and expands the options available for the child."[132]

"The legislature is all about having a special task force once there's a death or if there's a threat of a find from the federal government, then they get involved. But by and large, they don't," said researcher Zehnder-Merrell.[133] As in other states, the legislature tended to be reactive. The morning of our interview, Zehnder-Merrell had testified before the legislature regarding subsidized guardianship, which could affect 500 children in Michigan. She said "the legislature gets hot when a kid dies and then they're willing to fund something. In this year's budget—fiscal year 2008—I believe they added almost 300 [child welfare workers], and they could lose them if they don't hire people really fast."[134]

One legislator, who came from the private foster care sector, has campaigned to move funding from state foster care agencies to the private sector. Yet, key players revealed in interviews that they tended to view this legislator as self-interested and focused on this one issue, rather than on the collective performance of foster care.

The legislature has joined with the executive branch to strengthen foster care performance. The executive branch has utilized the Office of Children's Ombudsmen (OCO), an independent state agency housed in the executive branch, to monitor foster care performance. In December 2004, the Michigan legislature gave that office additional responsibility to receive and investigate complaints concerning children who are involved with Michigan's child welfare system for reasons of abuse or neglect.[135]

The legislature also helped DHS to collect better performance data from contracting agencies. One interviewee said, "DHS has a bad data system. DHS doesn't measure performance of private agencies. They will now, because it's in the legislature. If you don't perform, you don't get a contract."[136] Corrigan noted:

> I think the legislature has been very receptive. Every 10 years there's a reform movement in Michigan. It's incredibly complex—child welfare. I think it's very difficult in a term-limited legislature to see how complex the system is.[137]

When DHS director Ahmed took office in September 2007, he immediately prioritized his relationship with the state legislature. Ahmed, who created the nonprofit ACCESS, said: "I came with a legislative relationship because I used to have to lobby with both [the] federal and state [governments]. I had a relationship with legislature on both sides of the aisle."[138] Ahmed wanted to continue to cultivate these relationships during his term, and thought the legislature was paying attention to foster care because of the Children's Rights lawsuit.

136 Politics of Foster Care Administration

Overall, Michigan's numerous positive examples of leadership from public managers far outweighed any concerns. Managers attempted new ideas to solve foster care concerns and make improvements for children in care. The Michigan public managers partnered with foundations to pilot and implement foster care improvements. These managers reached out to community partners, including making amends in contentious relationships, such as that with the watchdog group Children's Rights. These managers were open to building cross-branch relationships with the judicial and legislative branches. Finally, these managers tackled issues such as kinship care, the aging out of foster children, child placement and agency restructuring, and other cutting-edge issues. Although the implementation of these projects was not perfect, these managers were committed to improving care for these foster children through new innovations with partners.

AUXILIARY FINDINGS

This research was designed to find out how to improve foster care administration by looking at which variables have been associated with success in states that have performed better on foster care issues. This case research was not designed to track how former foster children fared long term under the current foster care system. Although the Michigan case highlights some of the reasons why Michigan is a top-performing state, the case can provide a glimpse of the limits of long-term foster care outcomes for these former foster children.

The interviews uncovered a disconnect between effective public administration, such as successful outputs defined by the federal performance measures, and the long-term outcomes for former foster care children.

Former Michigan chief justice Corrigan stated:

> I won't even hazard a guess [as to] how these [former foster care] kids [will be] doing in 25 years. In Detroit, we're now at a 90% out of wedlock birthrate. We're only graduating 25% of the kids in Detroit public schools who start as freshman.[139]

Gayle Robbert, the program representative who oversees seven foster care review boards in the state, said: "Children seem to be more disturbed, [compared to] when I first started in child welfare in the 70s. The drug problem has been devastating on the child welfare system."[140] Victoria Tyler, director of child welfare for Catholic Social Services of Wayne in Detroit, stated: "Less than 50% will have jobs and not be homeless or in jail. Nine times out of 10 it's cyclical. The system is in such crisis. It's not focused on the long term."[141] Tyler added her thoughts about foster children: "Their chance of success is very low. I know I wasn't ready to be out there at 17, 18."[142] The State Foster Care Review Board program manager, James

Novell, said "40% of former foster care youth will be okay, not enter the criminal justice system or mental health system, or be homeless."[143] Patrick Okoronokwo, director of the Children's Center in Detroit, stated: "47% of the kids aging out in the system nationally are going into the criminal justice system."[144]

So although Michigan is considered a stronger-performing state according to the federal data, the state's foster care system still has serious limitations in terms of enabling these foster children to experience long-term success throughout their adult lives. In essence, this foster care system needs serious improvement if it is going to produce long-term positive outcomes. The president of Catholic Social Services of Wayne, in Detroit, said: "I believe foster care is the most challenging part of social work—dealing with child, biological family, and foster parents. It would be easier if you just had to work with the kid. But you have to juggle all three of those things."[145]

Both Michigan and Delaware are considered strong states on foster care issues, and yet the future of many of their former foster children looks bleak. Michigan, like other states, receives financial motivation from the federal government to keep foster children in care. The "federal government incentivizes to keep kids in foster care"[146] so that agencies (private and public) are given money based on children in care, and not on actual agency performance designed to shift children out of care.

These auxiliary findings suggest that the state of foster care is much worse nationally than is often acknowledged. If the strongest states acknowledge that their foster children are not headed for long-term success, then troubles abound for foster children in weak or middle-performing foster care states, where abuse while in care is higher, permanency takes longer, and children are shuffled from placement to placement.

CONCLUSION

The hypothesis was that *Michigan became a stronger-performing state in the area of foster care by placing a greater priority on building community partners, integrating the advice of mentors, providing leadership from public managers, and cultivating relationships with the federal government.* This Michigan case research showed that the cultivation of relationships with the federal government was not a major factor, the building of community partners was a strong factor, the integration of advice from mentors was a strong factor, and the leadership from public managers was a strong factor in contributing to the state's success on foster care issues. The most relevant factors were the presence of public managers and the way these public managers brokered relationships across the branches of government and with community partners and foundations.

The federal regional program manager for ACF Region III said, "States that work collaboratively within the states, courts, legislature have

138   Politics of Foster Care Administration

better outcomes."[147] Michigan worked collaboratively and produced better outcomes.

Most field research interviews suggested that Michigan was on a path toward continued improvement, and that Michigan would do much better on the federal 2009 Child and Family Service Reviews. Director Udow said, "In the 2009 CFSR, there will be a trend upward. The budget will be getting better."[148] Janet Snyder, who lobbies for the private foster care agencies, stated: "I think we're going to see a lot of change going on. You'll see a lot of positive change going on in the next 3 to 5 years, being catapulted by a number of dynamics . . . the lawsuit being one of them."[149]

Both Michigan and Delaware placed a heavy emphasis on community partnerships, mentors (Michigan more so than Delaware), and strong public managers. Public management literature (such as DiIulio's *Governing Prisons*[150]) has argued that management matters. This case research recognizes that management mattered in the stronger foster care states, and that good public managers forge partnerships and networks, strategize, and implement policy. As principled agents they strive, support, and sacrifice; one example is Justice Maura Corrigan, who stepped strongly outside of her court responsibilities in order to create better foster care in the state of Michigan.

List of Interviews

Interviewees listed here may have been utilized for quotes, off-the-record data, and/or background data only. Some interviews were conducted specifically for this Michigan case and others served to inform more broadly across many states or across issue areas addressed in this study.

Ishmael Ahmed, Director, Department of Human Services, Michigan, interview, Lansing, Michigan, March 18, 2008. Governor Jennifer M. Granholm appointed Ahmed to this position on September 10, 2007. Ahmed received a bachelor's degree in secondary education and a minor in sociology from the University of Michigan.

Mary Chaliman, Foster Care Program Manager, Department of Human Services, Michigan, interview, Lansing, Michigan, March 18, 2008. Chaliman started in this position in 2003. Chaliman received a bachelor of arts degree in English, language and literature, general, from Michigan State University.

Maura D. Corrigan, Justice of the Supreme Court, Michigan; Chief Justice of the Supreme Court, Michigan, phone interview, April 7, 2008.

Christine Craig, HHS-ACF Region III Program Specialist, federal government, phone interview, June 3, 2008. Craig oversees Delaware in addition to another state. Craig worked on the Title IV-E eligibility review for Delaware from October 2005 to March 2006.

Kate Hanley, Director, Adoption and Permanency Services, Department of Human Services, Michigan, interview, Lansing, Michigan, March 18, 2008.

Patrick Heron, President, Catholic Social Services of Wayne, interview, Detroit, Michigan, March 20, 2008. Wayne County represents the Detroit area.

James Novell, Program Manager, Foster Care Review Board, Courts, Michigan, interview, Detroit, Michigan, March 17, 2008.

Patrick Okoronokwo, Director, The Children's Center, interview, Detroit, Michigan, March 20, 2008. This is a medium-sized private agency with 180 cases.

Lisa Pearson, HHS-ACF Region III Program Manager, federal government, phone interview, June 3, 2008. Pearson reports directly to the HHS ACF commissioner. She is responsible for management of Delaware, the District of Columbia, Maryland, Pennsylvania, Virginia, and West Virginia.

Gayle Robbert, Program Representative, Lansing Foster Care Review Board, Courts, Michigan, phone interview, August 8, 2008. Robbert is also responsible for seven review boards throughout the state.

Janet Snyder, Executive Director, Michigan Federation for Children and Families, phone interview, March 27, 2008. This organization serves as the advocacy group for private nonprofit foster care agencies in Michigan.

Brent Thompson, Director of Communications, William Penn Foundation, informal interview, Philadelphia, Pennsylvania, August 7, 2007. Thompson reported directly to the Penn Foundation's former president and served as a primary contact in the president's absence.

Carole Thompson, Senior Program Officer, Annie E. Casey Foundation, interview, Philadelphia, Pennsylvania, August 16, 2007. The collective Casey family foundations make it the single largest foundation to conduct work in the area of foster care.

Vicki Thompson-Sandy, Vice President, Children and Family Services, Lutheran Social Services of Michigan, phone interview, March 26, 2008. This organization is the largest private foster care agency in Michigan and represents 760 cases.

Victoria Tyler, Director of Child Welfare, Catholic Social Services of Wayne, interview, Detroit, Michigan, March 20, 2008. Wayne County represents the Detroit area.

Marianne Udow, Director, Department of Human Services, Michigan; Director, Center for Healthcare Quality and Transformation,

140　*Politics of Foster Care Administration*

interview, Ann Arbor, Michigan, March 18, 2008. Udow received her master's degree in health sciences administration at the University of Michigan.

Muna Walker, Senior Program Officer, Amachi, Public/Private Ventures, interview, Philadelphia, Pennsylvania, fall 2006. Walker has responsibility for the Mentoring Children of Prisoners program, which has significant client overlap with the foster care system.

Barbara Wilson, Program Officer, Senior Corps, Corporation for National and Community Service (CNCS) federal program, phone and written correspondence with author, fall 2006. Senior Corps provides volunteers in states for foster care.

Harry Wilson, Associate Commissioner, Family Youth and Services Bureau, U.S. Department of Health and Human Services, Administration for Children and Families, Family Youth and Services Bureau, informal background information, dozens of meetings in 2003–2006, Washington, DC.

Jane Zehnder-Merrell, Director, Kids Count in Michigan; Senior Research Associate, Michigan League for Human Services, interview, Lansing, Michigan, March 18, 2008.

NOTES

1. All references in the summary are cited in this chapter. Data refers to the period of research.
2. U.S. Census Bureau, "2003 American Community Survey," http://www.census.gov.
3. The Pew Commission on Children in Foster Care, "Foster Care Population and States Ranked by Total Number of Children in Foster Care. FY2003," http://pewfostercare.org/research/docs/Data091505.pdf.
4. Ibid.
5. Kate Hanley, Director, Adoption and Permanency Services, Department of Human Services, Michigan, interview, Lansing, Michigan, March 18, 2008.
6. State of Michigan, Department of Human Services, *Foster Care Line of Service, Children's Foster Care Fiscal Year 2003 Resources, Presentation to the Executive Council from the State Foster Care Policy Manager* (April 8, 2003). Note: This number should not be compared across case states due to the wide variations in which line items are counted as foster care expenses. This number did not include sources of financing or central office overhead.
7. Kate Hanley, interview.
8. Ibid.
9. State of Michigan, *Foster Care Line of Service*.
10. Mary Chaliman, Foster Care Program Manager, Department of Human Services, Michigan, interview, Lansing, Michigan, March 18, 2008.
11. Janet Snyder, Executive Director, Michigan Federation for Children and Families, phone interview, March 27, 2008.
12. Rochelle Riley, "Need for Good Foster Parents is Increasing," *Detroit Free Press*, May 23, 2010, http://www.freep.com/article/20100523/COL10/5230503/Need-for-good-foster-parents-is-increasing.

Michigan 141

13. National Conference of State Legislatures, "Focusing on Child Welfare Systems: The Role of State Legislators," *Child Welfare: Innovations in State Policy,* http://www.ncsl.org/print/cyf/cwsystems.pdf.
14. State of Michigan, Department of Human Services, "Memo to the House and Senate Appropriations Committee Chairs from Director Ishmael Ahmed (DHS)," http://www.michigan.gov/documents/dhs/DHS-Legislative-Sec271-PA131–2007-CFS-Reviews_229555_7.pdf, 8.
15. Note: At the time of field research, generally, people expected the state to perform very well on the next round of CFSRs.
16. Marianne Udow, Director, Department of Human Services, Michigan; Director, Center for Healthcare Quality and Transformation, interview, Ann Arbor, Michigan, March 18, 2008.
17. Mary Chaliman, interview.
18. Ibid.
19. Maura D. Corrigan, Justice of the Supreme Court, Michigan; Chief Justice of the Supreme Court, Michigan, phone interview, April 7, 2008.
20. Marianne Udow, interview.
21. Jane Zehnder-Merrell, Director, Kids Count in Michigan; Senior Research Associate, Michigan League for Human Services, interview, Lansing, Michigan, March 18, 2008.
22. Ibid.
23. Marianne Udow, interview.
24. Ishmael Ahmed, Director, Department of Human Services, Michigan, interview, Lansing, Michigan, March 18, 2008.
25. Ibid.
26. State of Michigan, *Foster Care Line of Service.*
27. Mary Chaliman, interview.
28. Kate Hanley, interview.
29. Mary Chaliman, interview.
30. Marianne Udow, interview.
31. Confidential remarks.
32. Jane Zehnder-Merrell, interview.
33. Note: The collective Casey foundations are the largest foundation group to be involved in foster care issues.
34. State of Michigan, *Foster Care Line of Service.*
35. Jane Zehnder-Merrell, interview.
36. Marianne Udow, interview.
37. Ibid.
38. Ishmael Ahmed, interview.
39. Kate Hanley, interview.
40. Ibid.
41. Maura D. Corrigan, interview.
42. Ibid.
43. Marianne Udow, interview.
44. Ishmael Ahmed, interview.
45. Ibid.
46. Ibid.
47. Note: Local becomes of particular importance when states have large foster care operations in cities such as Detroit or New York City.
48. Janet Snyder, interview.
49. Ibid.
50. Ibid.
51. Vicki Thompson-Sandy, Vice President, Children and Family Services, Lutheran Social Services of Michigan, phone interview, March 26, 2008.
52. Ibid.

142 *Politics of Foster Care Administration*

53. Ibid.
54. Ibid.
55. State Senator Mark C. Jansen, "Sen. Jansen's Legislation Helping Increase Child Permanency Signed into Law," http://www.senate.michigan.gov/gop/senators/readarticle.asp?id=1630&District=28. Note: This legislation passed July 2008 and was signed into law.
56. Maura D. Corrigan, interview.
57. Janet Snyder, interview.
58. Ibid.
59. Vicki Thompson-Sandy, interview.
60. James Novell, Program Manager, Foster Care Review Board, Courts, Michigan, interview, Detroit, Michigan, March 17, 2008.
61. Ibid.
62. Ibid.
63. Kate Hanley, interview.
64. Ishmael Ahmed, interview.
65. Vicki Thompson-Sandy, interview.
66. Ishmael Ahmed, interview.
67. Children's Rights, "Michigan," http://www.childrensrights.org/site/PageServer?pagename=Michigan_AtAGlance.
68. Marianne Udow, interview.
69. Confidential remarks. Note: Other interviews referred to this as well.
70. Confidential remarks. Note: Other interviews referred to this as well.
71. Marianne Udow, interview.
72. Note: The next DHS director, Ishmael Ahmed, was able to broker a settlement deal based on Udow's preliminary deal. On July 3, 2008, Ahmed reached an out-of-court settlement with Children's Rights Inc. resolving this federal lawsuit over Michigan's child welfare system. Michigan Department of Human Services, "DHS and Children's Rights Reach Out-of-Court Agreement, Agreement Improves Services for Vulnerable Children," http://www.michigan.gov/dhs/0,1607,7-124--195606--,00.html#noprint.
73. Mark Moore, *Creating Public Value: Strategic Management in Government* (Cambridge, MA: Harvard University Press, 1995), 10.
74. State of Michigan, "Office of the Governor: Governor Granholm," http://www.michigan.gov/gov/0,1607,7–168—57920—,00.html.
75. Ibid.
76. Jane Zehnder-Merrell, interview.
77. Marianne Udow, interview.
78. Maura D. Corrigan, interview.
79. Ibid.
80. Note: ACCESS received the Points of Light Award for exemplary nonprofit service from President George H.W. Bush in 1992.
81. Jane Zehnder-Merrell, interview.
82. Patrick Heron, President, Catholic Social Services of Wayne, interview, Detroit, Michigan, March 20, 2008.
83. Confidential remarks.
84. Marianne Udow, interview.
85. Ibid.
86. Ibid.
87. Ibid.
88. Ibid.
89. Mary Chaliman, interview.
90. Child Welfare League of America, "Michigan's Children 2005," http://www.cwla.org/advocacy/statefactsheets/2005/michigan.pdf.

Michigan 143

91. Child Welfare League of America, "Michigan's Children 2010," http://www.cwla.org/advocacy/statefactsheets/2010/michigan.pdf.
92. Child Welfare Information Gateway, "Subsidized Guardianship," U.S. Department for Health and Human Services, Administration for Children and Families, http://www.childwelfare.gov/permanency/guard_sub.cfm#state_ex.
93. Vicki Thompson-Sandy, interview.
94. Ibid.
95. Child Welfare League of America, "Foster Care Independence Act of 1999," http://www.cwla.org/advocacy/indlivhr3443.htm. Note: The Foster Care Independence Act of 1999 permits states to allow current and former foster children to remain eligible for Medicaid up to age 21.
96. Kate Hanley, interview.
97. Marianne Udow, interview.
98. Ibid.
99. Ibid.
100. Jeff Karoub, "Leader Brings Community Activism to State Cabinet," http://www.michigan.gov/documets/dhs/09–04–07_207453_7.pdf.
101. Ishmael Ahmed, interview.
102. Ibid.
103. Ibid.
104. Ibid.
105. Ibid.
106. Mary Chaliman, interview.
107. Ibid.
108. Ibid.
109. "Fifteen Finalists Named for KSG Award," *Harvard University Gazette,* March 20, 2003, http://www.news.harvard.edu/gazette/2003/03.20/15-ksg.html.
110. Note: At the time of field research, DHS stated that this data collection should start in 2009.
111. Mary Chaliman, interview.
112. Kate Hanley, interview.
113. Victoria Tyler, Director of Child Welfare, Catholic Social Services of Wayne, interview, Detroit, Michigan, March 20, 2008.
114. Maura D. Corrigan, interview.
115. Ibid.
116. Marianne Udow, interview.
117. Maura D. Corrigan, interview.
118. Maura D. Corrigan, interview.
119. Mary Chaliman, interview.
120. Maura D. Corrigan, interview.
121. Ibid.
122. Ibid.
123. Ibid.
124. Ibid.
125. Confidential remarks.
126. Gayle Robbert, Program Representative, Lansing Foster Care Review Board, Courts, Michigan, phone interview, August 8, 2008.
127. Maura D. Corrigan, interview.
128. Ibid.
129. Mary Chaliman, interview.
130. Maura D. Corrigan, interview.
131. James Novell, interview.
132. Maura D. Corrigan, interview.

144 *Politics of Foster Care Administration*

133. Jane Zehnder-Merrell, interview.
134. Ibid.
135. State of Michigan, "Office of Children's Ombudsman: Who We Are," http:// www.michigan.gov/printerFriendly/0,1687,7-133—187487—,00.html.
136. Confidential remarks.
137. Maura D. Corrigan, interview.
138. Ishmael Ahmed, interview.
139. Maura D. Corrigan, interview.
140. Gayle Robbert, interview.
141. Victoria Tyler, interview.
142. Ibid.
143. James Novell, interview.
144. Patrick Okoronokwo, Director, The Children's Center, interview, Detroit, Michigan, March 20, 2008.
145. Patrick Heron, interview.
146. Kate Hanley, interview.
147. Lisa Pearson, HHS-ACF Region III Program Manager, federal government, phone interview, June 3, 2008.
148. Marianne Udow, interview.
149. Janet Snyder, interview.
150. John J. DiIulio, Jr., *Governing Prisons: A Comparative Study of Correctional Management* (New York: The Free Press, 1987).

7 Case Research Results and Implications for Increasing Effectiveness

The research design tested the strength of four variables to determine what conditions produced more effective foster care administration. The research was structured to test whether the following hypothesis is accurate: *Delaware and Michigan became stronger-performing states in the area of foster care by placing a greater priority than the lower-performing states of New York and Rhode Island on building community partners, integrating the advice of mentors, providing leadership from public managers, and cultivating relationships with the federal government.*

To recap the findings from the stronger states, for both Delaware and Michigan, the cultivation of federal government relationships was not a major factor; the building of community partnerships was a strong factor; and leadership from public managers was a strong factor. For Delaware, the integration of mentors was a minimal factor, whereas for Michigan it was a strong factor.

To recap the findings from the weaker states, for both New York and Rhode Island, the cultivation of federal government relationships was not a major factor. There was virtually no integration of mentors or leadership from public managers in Rhode Island. For Rhode Island, the building of community partnerships was a minimal factor. In New York, these latter three variables only showed a stronger presence over time, but never approached the levels of Michigan or Delaware.

In other words, the hypothesis was partially correct and partially incorrect. This chapter will take the data generated from the hypothesis and offer theories based upon the case state results. Two major theses are offered; one concerns the role of the federal government in foster care administration, and the second describes the factors that lead to successful foster care programs.

The first thesis integrates the research findings that related to the variable *cultivation of federal government relationships*. My first conclusion is that *the federal government has increased its focus on measuring the performance of state programs while simultaneously decreasing its funding of state foster care programs and offering the states very little management or mentorship.*

146 *Politics of Foster Care Administration*

The other variables of public management, community partners, and mentors are addressed in the second thesis. My second conclusion is that *better foster care administration is produced by public managers who operate as principled agents to develop networks, partnerships, and strategies within and outside their states.* This latter section details what factors strong states utilized to produce higher levels of foster care administration success.

THESIS 1: THE FEDERAL GOVERNMENT ACTS AS A MONITOR, RATHER THAN AS A MENTOR OR MANAGER

The first thesis claims that *the federal government has increased its focus on measuring the performance of state programs while simultaneously decreasing its funding of state foster care programs and offering the states very little management or mentorship.* The integrated state–federal relationship, an outgrowth of federalism, has become more complicated with the onset of increasing levels of government-by-proxy. According to Kettl and Fesler's *The Politics of the Administrative Process*, government-by-proxy is defined as "the use of third party agents to deliver programs that the government funds."[1]

In the last 50 years, the federal government has relied less on direct service provision and more on contracting services out via government-by-proxy. Paul Light exposed the way the federal government hides its workforce under a "shadow of government."[2] Light argued that although there were 1.9 million civil servants in 1996, there were an additional 12.7 million employed in the "shadow of government" who produced goods and services for the federal government under contracts, grants, and mandates.[3] In the case of foster care, the federal government does not directly provide foster care services, but rather offers funding to the states so that they may coordinate services.

A 2003 article in the *Harvard Law Review* by John DiIulio recognized that every federal department depends heavily on government-by-proxy.[4] When referring to the U.S. Department of Health and Human Services (HHS), DiIulio noted that they have "eleven operating divisions, a nearly $500 billion budget and over 65,000 employees whose main work is framing, processing, and monitoring literally hundreds of grant programs."[5] In the case of foster care, the grantor is the federal government (HHS), and the grantees are the state governments that often then contract their obligations out to local government and/or private contractors.

The federal government offers funding to states to cover partial foster care administration costs and requests that the states meet federal standards. States then pay for additional foster care administration expenses and sometimes require local governments to contribute financially as well. This multiple-player, government-by-proxy approach complicates the way that foster care administration is managed, funded, and measured.

Case Research Results and Implications 147

The next sections will detail how the federal government has increased its focus on state performance measurement in the area of foster care, while at the same time offering minimal management/mentorship and decreased federal funding to the states. This thesis developed out of my hypothesis being partially incorrect. My initial hypothesis was that stronger states would have a more active relationship with the federal government. After studying the over $200 million 2003–2008 federal program Mentoring Children of Prisoners, in which the federal government worked closely with local key players, I presumed that the federal government would have paid the same type of attention to a much larger federal program. I was wrong. Rather than acting as a manager of a $4.3 billion annual foster care program, the federal government acted more as a grantor, focusing on performance measurement and data collection. When an organization is spending billions annually, one might presume that a high level of management would be in place to ensure that their money is well-spent. However, that is not the case for foster care administration.

The Federal Government Is Spending Less Money on Overall Foster Care Costs

According to the HHS Office of Human Services Policy, "Federal foster care program expenditures grew an average of 17 percent per year in the 16 years between the program's establishment and the passage of the Adoption and Safe Families Act (AFSA) in 1997."[6] From 1997 to 2002, HHS foster care program growth averaged about 4% per year.[7] In 2005, HHS stated that the "spending growth far outpaced growth in the number of children served."[8] Over recent years, the federal funding of foster care has declined from approximately $4.7 billion to around $4.3 billion (2007: $4.7 billion,[9] 2008: $4.6 billion;[10] 2009: $4.7 billion;[11] 2010: $4.6 billion;[12] 2011: $4.4 billion;[13] 2012: $4.3 billion;[14] 2013: $4.3 billion;[15] 2014: $4.3 billion estimate).[16]

Yet, the federal government has been making significantly fewer foster care cases eligible for federal funding over this same time period. In its FY 2013 report, *Justifications of Estimates for Appropriations Committees*, the HHS noted: "The average monthly number of children for whom states receive federal foster care payments has declined from over 300,000 in FY 1999 to approximately 179,400 in FY 2011."[17] Yet, HHS FY 2011 data reported that 400,540 kids were in foster care in total.[18] In other words, over half of the foster care cases were ineligible for federal funding.

By FY 2014, the number of children for whom states receive federal foster dollars dropped even further. In the HHS FY 2014 "Budget in Brief" report, the proposed level of funding had continued the decline to approximately 147,000 children per month.[19] So, in essence, the federal government is spending less money on overall foster care costs by funding significantly fewer cases.

148 *Politics of Foster Care Administration*

The FY 2013 report explained the reasons for the significant decrease in the number of cases eligible for federal funding: "Title IV-E caseloads have been declining, which can be attributed to several factors, including a reduction in the overall foster care population, increased adoptions, and, notably, the erosion of eligibility."[20] The FY 2014 report found that

> some of the decline can be attributed to the erosion of eligibility under statute, as children's eligibility for federal foster care is tied to the former Aid to Families with Dependent Children income eligibility standards, which are increasingly outdated as they were not indexed to account for inflation.[21]

Due to the erosion of eligibility, the federal government is spending less money on overall foster care costs. According to the FY 2013 report released on January 30, 2011:

> Fewer and fewer families meet these static income standards over time thereby reducing the number of children who are title IV-E eligible. The federal IV-E participation rate stood at approximately 51.8% in FY 2000. Currently, the participation stands at approximately 43% of all children in foster care nationally.[22]

In essence, HHS stated that 51.8% of all foster care cases nationwide received federal funding and this number dropped to 43% in slightly over a decade. The states, and often their localities, become responsible for *any* costs not covered by the federal government on the 43% of eligible nationwide cases. Additionally, the states and often their localities become responsible for *all* costs on the remaining 57% of nationwide cases.

The Urban Institute had similar findings covering an earlier period when they conducted an analysis and determined that in state fiscal year (SFY) 2000, 58% of cases were eligible for Title IV-E funding in all 36 states reporting; in SFY 2002, 55% of cases were eligible in the 36 states reporting; and in SFY 2004, 52% of cases were eligible in all 46 states reporting.[23] This data shows that the states' eligibility for federal funding reimbursement dropped from approximately 58% to 52% in 4 years, which helps to explain the rising burden of foster care costs on the states.[24]

This decrease in overall federal funding affects state foster care programs. The interviewees suggested that states are struggling to meet their foster care costs because the federal government is now giving them less money for their overall foster care expenses. In 2007, the director of the Division of Family Services in Delaware said that there has been shrinkage of Title IV-E funds, and as a result Delaware has provided an infusion of money to offset federal losses.[25] Delaware Department of Services for Children, Youth and Their Families (DCYF) cabinet secretary Cari DeSantis said, "Federal Title IV-E has been declining. As the 1996 AFDC [Aid to Families with Dependent

Children] dollars change in value, there are fewer and fewer people that meet that [requirement to obtain federal funding for foster care]."[26] Delaware made the choice to maintain the same level of funding for its foster care population despite the federal decrease in funding. In 1996, the state of Delaware provided 68% of the funding for overall child welfare (which included foster care plus other programs) while the federal government provided 32% of the funding for overall child welfare.[27] By 2007, the state of Delaware was spending more money on foster care ($15.9 million)[28] than it was receiving from the federal government for foster care ($2.5 million).[29] This equates to only 16% federal funding for Delaware foster care and 84% state funding.

The result is that the cabinet secretary of this top-performing state is even considering rejecting the federal money because it comes with strings attached. DeSantis asked, "Should states participate in federal money [programs], for what we're getting any more?"[30] DeSantis added emphatically, "Hello folks. Wake up. This is a Big Problem. It keys up a conversation that is worth having on a national level."[31]

This foster care financing structure is fairly consistent with the changes in overall child welfare financing. "The share of federal funds as a percentage of all child welfare expenditures decreased each biennium between 2002 and 2008, while the share from state funds increased over that time period."[32] The American Reinvestment and Recovery Act (ARRA) stopped this trend in 2010 by infusing a large amount of nontraditional dollars into child welfare for a temporary period.[33] In SFY 2010, states spent approximately $13.6 billion in federal funds, $12.5 billion in state funds, and $3.3 billion in local funds on child welfare activities.[34] Similar to the pattern of foster care financing, the states and their localities spent more on child welfare, while the federal government's share of overall child welfare costs decreased apart from the ARRA exception.

According to case interviews, the primary reason for the shift in decreased federal funding for overall foster care costs is not a reduced caseload, but rather the income eligibility requirements and the federal penalties that states face. Interviewees noted that there are *fewer* Title IV-E cases now eligible for federal reimbursement because of the need-based requirements. Title IV-E, an open-ended entitlement,[35] is the primary vehicle for federal reimbursement to states for a portion of their foster care costs. Title IV-E eligibility is linked to a child's eligibility for AFDC as it existed in their state's plan on July 16, 1996.[36] As these income requirements become outdated and inflation rises, fewer children are eligible for federal assistance. A survey of 26 states found that 40% of Title IV-E cases in 2010 were deemed ineligible due to the income of parents.[37] The New York state foster care program manager, Nancy Martinez, said: "fewer and fewer [foster care] cases are eligible for federal standards [reimbursement for federal money]."[38] For instance, Martinez added, "In 1996, 80% of [New York] foster care cases were federal government Title IV-E eligible and in 2007 only 40% of [New York] foster care cases are IV-E eligible."[39]

150   *Politics of Foster Care Administration*

As a result, the financial burden to fund these noneligible Title IV-E foster care children shifts to the state governments. Furthermore, the federal government's auditing tactics have led New York State to stop reporting potentially eligible cases. Martinez said, "The federal government started auditing on Title IV-E and won't even allow cases that are potentially eligible. This reduced funding."[40]

Michigan also has had to contend with the federal government shifting the cost of foster care to their state. Former Michigan DHS director Marianne Udow referred to this shift as "a huge issue: how arcane Title IV-E is."[41] Further, when states do not meet federal benchmarks they are frequently penalized. Chief Supreme Court Justice Corrigan said, "The federal government audits you. They try to take money away from you. The penalty environment I find difficult: 'We're going to assess penalties if you haven't accomplished the impossible.'"[42] Michigan has had to find money within their state to make up for the decreased amount of federal funding for Title IV-E cases.

Figure 7.1 shows that with the passage of time, fewer foster care cases have been eligible for Title IV-E funding. The U.S. Department of HHS Office of the Assistant Secretary for Planning and Evaluation noted in 2005 that "funding levels and caseloads have not closely tracked one another for over a decade, and indeed since 1998 have been moving in opposite directions."[43]

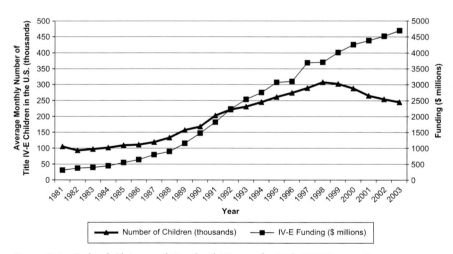

Figure 7.1   Federal Claims and Caseload History for Title IV-E Foster Care
Source: U.S. Department of Health and Human Services, Office of the Assistant Secretary for Planning and Evaluation, Office of Human Services Policy, "APSE Issue Brief: Federal Foster Care Financing," http://aspe.hhs.gov/hsp/05/fc-financing-ib/ib.pdf, 4.

Case Research Results and Implications   151

Although the HHS Office of the Assistant Secretary for Planning and Evaluation has not released an official graph showcasing data beyond 2003, the average monthly number of Title IV-E children would trend downward over recent years while the federal funding levels would hover around $4.3 to $4.7 billion.

Shifting the burden of foster care costs can have a domino effect. Nicholas Pirro, who served as the former president of the New York State Association of Counties as well as the former president of the County Executive Associations, said: "The state of New York has consistently tried to push off their responsibility for funding to county and local governments [for foster care, as well as other areas]."[44] Pirro, who also served as the Onondaga County executive and as the chairman of the Onondaga County Legislature representing the Syracuse area of New York, added: "When the state budget comes out, there's always some attempt to shift some of the cost to the local programs. This is a constant battle."[45] In 2004, Pirro fought New York State when the state attempted to change the foster care funding formula and the state retroactively reduced the amount of funding that its counties would receive for their previous 10 months of expenses. His county would have lost $727,000, although it only carries an average caseload of 250 to 300 foster care children.[46] In New York, the federal–state funding battle has trickled down to the county level.

In sum, federalism masks the way that foster care funding is shifted among and between the federal, state, and local governments. Currently, the federal government spends less on overall foster care program costs and funds fewer foster care cases, while states and their localities are expected to make up the shortfall.

The Federal Government Has Increased Performance Measurement in the Area of Foster Care

The federal government has also increased the use of performance data collection in many areas of government, including foster care. This increased use of performance measurement is an outgrowth of the overall federal trend toward implementing performance measurement in the 1990s. Compared to the private sector, the federal government was slow to adopt performance measurements. However, during the 1990s, President Clinton was credited with implementing Osborne and Gaebler's "reinventing government" concept that was designed to have government "cost less and do more."[47] Osborne was a senior advisor to Vice President Gore on the "reinventing government" task force.[48] One outcome of this task force was the 1993 Government Performance and Results Act (GPRA), which marked the first time that the federal government measured program performance annually and tied these measures to objectives. A bipartisan effort, GPRA was initiated by Republican legislators, including Senator Roth, and was also strongly supported by the Clinton administration. GPRA required

152   Politics of Foster Care Administration

each federal agency to develop a 5-year strategic plan (with updates every 3 years) and an annual performance plan that provided objective, quantifiable criteria by which to measure the success of each program activity.[49] GPRA required the first strategic plans to be completed by September 30, 1997. There remained outstanding questions about reporting mechanisms, including how the federal government could be held accountable for state performance. Yet overall, the implementation of federal government performance data collection was well-received. Political scientist Don Kettl spoke before the House Committee on Government Reform and Oversight and the Senate Committee on Governmental Affairs and stated that "performance is not what it could be [in the federal government] and the performance measurement required by the act is the keystone for solving this problem."[50]

The increased use of performance measurement by the federal government spilled into foster care administration in the late 1990s. The Adoption and Safe Families Act, signed into law on November 19, 1997, required the collection of data on foster care and child welfare.[51] This requirement was the impetus for the annual "Child Welfare Outcomes: Annual Report" beginning in 1998. This research design utilized child welfare performance data from these reports for the years 2000 to 2003.

The trend of federal performance measurement continued with President George W. Bush and his administration's Program Assessment Rating Tool (PART), developed by the Office of Management and Budget (OMB). The PART evaluation examines federal programs' purpose and design, strategic planning, management, results, and accountability in order to "enrich budget analysis."[52] Beryl Radin noted:

> While PART shares some perspectives with GPRA, it does differ from the earlier effort in a number of ways. Its focus is different; it is located only in the executive branch; it has more of a top-down than a bottom-up approach; it does not attempt to include all programs every year; it focuses only on performance measures; and it emphasizes efficiency approaches.[53]

Like GPRA, PART received mixed reviews of its data collection methods, yet the overall concept of stronger federal government performance data collection was well-received. From 2002 to 2008, PART evaluated every federal program and suggested management, legislative, and regulatory improvements. In 2002, over 50% of the programs analyzed "received a rating of Results Not Demonstrated because of the lack of performance measures and/or performance data."[54] At the outset, "the vast majority of programs [had] measures that emphasize[d] inputs [such as the number of brochures printed] rather than outcomes or results."[55] By 2008, less than 20% of the federal programs were ranked as Results Not Demonstrated.[56] Robert Shea, OMB's former associate director of administration and government performance and one of the creators of PART, said in 2008: "More

Case Research Results and Implications   153

and more, programs are meeting their goals and measuring success today better than they were five or seven years ago."[57]

Foster care was one of the programs assessed under the PART policy in 2007. While the "Child Welfare Outcomes: Annual Report" measures actual state performance on child welfare measurements, the PART policy measured federal foster care administration across program purpose and design (80% out of 100%), planning (88% out of 100%), management (100% out of 100%), and results (67% out of 100%) and concluded that the foster care program was "moderately effective."[58] Regarding foster care performance measurement during the Obama administration, the "Child Welfare Outcomes Report to Congress" serves as the primary document.[59]

President Obama and his administration did not continue PART and did not immediately embrace improved mechanisms for measuring performance during the initial period in office. Philip Joyce wrote *Governing*, in reference to Obama's performance agenda, that "there is less apparent progress two years into Obama's presidency than was made at a comparable point in the last two administrations."[60] Over time, however, the Obama administration focused efforts on performance measurement (www.performance.gov) and through annual reports such as the "Fiscal Year 2013: Annual Performance Report and Performance Plan."[61] Many of these overall efforts are driven by the Office of Performance and Personnel Management (OPPM), which "leads the effort to drive mission-focused performance gains across the Federal government."[62]

Over the last decade, the federal government also measured state foster care performance via the Child and Family Service Reviews, as well as two rounds of Program Improvement Plans and financial audits for each state. Foster care program managers and policy creators in Delaware, New York, and Rhode Island showed me hundreds of pages of forms that had to be completed for the federal government. This show-and-tell of federal requirements was each state's way of saying "enough is enough." Several of the Delaware case interviews noted that the various measures of federal reporting regarding performance, audits, and improvement were time consuming. Even the nonstate foster care employees were affected by the federal requirements. One Delaware nonstate foster care provider commented that his job involved "lots of paperwork for [the] federal government."[63]

Although the paperwork is burdensome, states acknowledge that the federal government's performance measurement system inspires improvement. Delaware DFS director Carlyse Giddens expressed a desire to be challenged by the federal standards, while honestly recognizing that Delaware's performance on foster care was not where she wanted it to be. Giddens added, "I don't disagree with the federal standards. The standards should be high."[64] Michigan DHS director Marianne Udow responded to my question about whether federal performance measures were too high by saying: "No, I would never say the bar is too high, because we have to do better by our children."[65] Mary Chaliman, Michigan's foster care program manager

154   *Politics of Foster Care Administration*

said, "I think the CFSR has been referenced more and more as an impetus for change."[66] She went on to affirm that, "Permanency [getting kids into permanent placements] has improved as a result of the CFSR."[67] Dorothy Hultine, the chief policy creator for DCYF in Rhode Island stated, "The Program Improvement Plan has driven activity in a lot of different areas."[68] Rhode Island DCYF director Patricia Martinez said, "Any framework that you have to improve your services is good."[69]

Yet, when states do not meet federal benchmarks they are frequently penalized. As previously noted by Michigan Chief Supreme Court Justice Corrigan, the federal government will "take money away" from the state foster care program when penalties are assessed.

Although continuing use of federal performance measure data for foster care is expected, how foster care performance data will be collected and assessed in the future is unknown. What is known is that the performance measurement collection methods outlined in this research are burdensome on the states.

The Federal Government Is Providing States with Minimal Management and Mentorship in the Area of Foster Care

The federal government's Corporation for National and Community Service (CNCS) has been very active in providing volunteers and training mentors for the newer (post-2003) and smaller (over $200 million) Mentoring Children of Prisoners (MCP) federal program.[70] Yet, the case state interviews did not suggest that CNCS has been similarly active in the multibillion dollar foster care program.[71]

Rarely did an interviewee mention that the federal government had been helpful with training. Interviewees from state child and family departments were asked questions along the lines of "Who is helping you?" or "Who is mentoring you?" or "Who do you look to for guidance?" Questions were also asked about the nature of the relationship with the federal government. The federal government was rarely mentioned as an active trainer, mentor, or advisor in relation to foster care programs.

This is consistent with the heavy workload that is placed upon the federal government personnel who have been appointed as liaisons to the states. Christine Craig is the HHS-ACF Region III program specialist for the federal government appointed to oversee Delaware. She was hired to monitor only Delaware, but due to staff vacancies is now assigned to two states. For both states, she handles all of the following initiatives: foster care, CASA, child abuse prevention, adoption, independent living, education and training vouchers, family preservation, safe and stable families, and reunification, as well as technical matters relating to the state's financial report, audit, training for staff, and preplacement costs. After realizing that only one person was responsible for foster care in two states on behalf of the federal government, while at the same time responsible for a dozen other

Case Research Results and Implications   155

federal initiatives for those two states, I stated, "That's a lot for one person" and she responded, "Yes, it is."[72] In other words, the federal representatives for the states are involved in so many policies that they have minimal time to assist the states in the area of foster care administration.

In this study, the federal government has been repeatedly mentioned in the context of its aforementioned reduced funding to states and increased monitoring of performance measures. It could be argued that increasing attention to performance measurement *is* management by the federal government. However, the interviews did not suggest that state employees felt as though they were being managed by the federal government; rather, the states were required to report data to the federal government in exchange for partial foster care funding. There was virtually no mention among interviewees of federal training being offered as an impetus to improve foster care programs. Instead, improvements in foster care were tied to the involvement of foundations, state and local public managers, and community partners.

The federal government has increased the use of state performance measurement reporting while paying less of the overall foster care bill. DiIulio added in his *Harvard Law Review* article, "Federal and local officials each try to get some benefit while passing on to the other side most of the costs."[73] This push–pull relationship between the federal government and the states encapsulates foster care administration.

In *The Next Government of the United States* (2009), Donald F. Kettl said that "we can also think about American government as a pendulum swinging between extremes: between centralized power (in the hands of the national government) and decentralized action (dominated by state and local governments)."[74] This pendulum of foster care administration swings back and forth between the states (who administer the programs and create policy) and the federal government (which monitors the programs and creates policy).

In *Government by Proxy* (1988), Kettl referred to grants to state and local governments as one of the four mechanisms that the federal government utilizes to administer its program goals. Kettl found that the federal government also faces the task of "synchronization of goals" such as getting its proxies to behave as the federal government wants. It also faces the "problem of feedback," or understanding what proxies are accomplishing with the programs.[75] Currently, the federal government has chosen to monitor the foster care programs that are implemented by states through performance measurement collection. This is their primary method for getting states to align with federal government goals.

In sum, the states complain that now they must pay a larger portion of the cost of providing foster care for each child and that fewer children are meeting the federal guidelines to become Title IV-E eligible. At the same time, the federal government has increasingly chosen to focus upon monitoring performance data from the states, as opposed to providing management or mentorship.

156 *Politics of Foster Care Administration*

THESIS 2: BETTER FOSTER CARE ADMINISTRATION IS PRODUCED BY PUBLIC MANAGERS WHO OPERATE AS PRINCIPLED AGENTS TO DEVELOP NETWORKS, PARTNERSHIPS, AND STRATEGIES WITHIN AND OUTSIDE THEIR STATES

Although the federal government has not been involved in management or mentorship of foster care programs, the stronger states have utilized strong public management and a network of mentors and/or community partners. The second and final thesis purports that better foster care administration is produced by public managers who operate as principled agents to develop networks, partnerships, and strategies within and outside their branch in their state. This section will detail how the states with stronger foster care programs had multiple public managers who operated as principled agents.

The concept of strong public management leading to better results is not new to the public administration field. As Kettl and Milward stated in *The State of Public Management* (1996), "Public management matters, and it matters because the quality of public management shapes the performance of public programs."[76] In *Governing Prisons* (1987), DiIulio downplayed the role of "violent characteristics of the inmates, low level of expenditures, crowding, high inmate-staff ratios, little formal staff training" and instead argued that "prison management leads to increased administrative success."[77]

The public administration literature includes many examples of successful public managers and the functions that they perform. Doig and Hargrove offered the case of Gifford Pinchot as an entrepreneurial manager of the forest service who created dedication in his recruits and "dreamed dreams."[78] Chester Barnard explained the functions a public manager can perform via *The Functions of the Executive* (1938) and claimed that corporate culture can be managed by the top executive.[79]

In *Leadership in Administration* (1957), Selznick argued that "leadership is not equivalent to office-holding or high prestige or authority or decision-making"[80] but rather, "the executive becomes a statesman."[81] The position title alone lacks the ability to define a leader; rather, it is the leader that defines the position. Along the same lines, the interviews in this study reflected a pattern of public managers going above and beyond their job requirements in the stronger foster care states.

Strong Public Management Produces Better Foster Care Administration

Within foster care administration, strong public management can increase the quality of foster care. Evidence from both strong states, Michigan and Delaware, showed that strong public management led to more effective administration. The lack of strong public management in Rhode Island

Case Research Results and Implications   157

helped explain why Rhode Island suffered as a weak state. In the weak case state of New York, public management improved over time and insiders recognized an improvement, particularly in New York City.

Public administration literature often suggests that better public management leads to more effective administration. In addition, some research has sought to identify the overall goal of a strong public manager. Mark Moore's *Creating Public Value* (1995) argued that a successful public sector manager "increase(s) the public value produced by public sector organizations in both the short and the long run."[82] My case research confirmed the public administration body of work, which asserts that "public management matters." The public administration field has demonstrated that management matters and includes many case studies of effective public managers. However, there is minimal public administration research that identifies what tasks effective public managers perform. This case research helps to identify what these public managers do that increases their effectiveness.

The next sections will offer insight into the roles that public managers played in the foster care system and the tasks they performed that achieved administrative success. There appeared to be a link between the public management variable and the community partners/mentors variables. The latter hypotheses were that stronger states would utilize more community partners and mentors. These cases suggest that those hypotheses are true. Moreover, as these sections will demonstrate, it was the public managers that chose whether to build relationships with community partners and mentors. Also, the data confirmed that public managers in stronger states did significantly more networking and strategizing. Public managers successfully developed partnerships within their own state governments in some of the following combinations: court to agency, agency to legislature, director to cabinet secretary, cabinet secretary to governor, and agency executive team to agency staff.

A strong public manager was defined as a "principled agent" in a public management position. John DiIulio has argued that principled agents are those who "strive [work hard and go 'by the book'], support [put public and organizational goals ahead of private goals], and sacrifice [go 'above and beyond the call of duty'] on the job."[83] Mark Moore has identified this same "principled agent" as a public manager that "creates value."

In the strong state of Delaware, public managers operated as principled agents. Interviewees made statements that described the qualities of principled agents when they spoke about Carlyse Giddens, the director, and John Bates, the foster care program manager, of the Division of Family Services: "Carlyse legitimately cares for the kids." "DFS has adoptions hold—they prepare people well." "DFS works hard at reunification." "A lot of people move up [in government] and tend to lose sight of the kids, but that's not true for [John Bates, the program manager]."[84] In addition, several interviewees offered off-the-record comments along the same lines: "There are extraordinarily dedicated welfare professionals in DFS." And

158 Politics of Foster Care Administration

"[these leaders are] outstanding, amazing people."[85] Giddens also viewed the federal government performance measures as a criteria she needed to meet, rather than as an annoyance, and she was proud of being the "longest-serving DFS director ever in any agency in any state."[86] In another example, Tania Culley, executive director of the Office of the Child Advocate in Delaware, acquired significantly more child advocate lawyers than the law required because she believed this was in the best interest of foster children.

Both the Delaware cabinet secretary, Cari DeSantis, and Giddens were responsible for reducing staff turnover and the "turnover ratio is a national standard."[87] The governor, the cabinet secretary, and the director were involved in creating and implementing the model "Think of the Child First." The Delaware foster care program manager, John Bates, oversaw mandatory supervisor training that was so effective that he has frequently been asked to speak about Delaware as a model state.[88]

In the strong state of Michigan, public managers at multiple levels also operated as principled agents. The Michigan director of the Department of Human Services, Marianne Udow, led a race equity campaign in foster care, emphasized relative placements and grouping siblings together, and changed the child placement system in Wayne County (Detroit) to focus on the child rather than the foster care agency. Udow also closed many shelters in an effort to get foster children into families.

The next Michigan director of the Department of Human Services, Ishmael Ahmed, was viewed favorably by private foster care agencies for his work in reaching out to them. The Michigan state foster care program manager, Mary Chaliman, helped to create the award-winning Structured Decision-Making Model, which is used to direct foster care caseworkers through a series of decisions regarding a child.

On the other hand, as anticipated, the weak state of Rhode Island lacked strong public management. Almost every interview offered evidence of a public management disaster related to Rhode Island foster care. The state lost foster care parent records, made children sit in shelters for months on end while they waited for the state to approve their foster parent matches, and placed foster children in unlicensed kinship foster care. DCYF chief casework supervisor Maureen Robbins stated, "No legislators are really active on this issue [of foster care]."[89] The Rhode Island DCYF policy officer in central management stated there is a "lot of animosity between the family courts and the state. There is a fight going on."[90] Additionally, the courts lost my interview requests multiple times after repeatedly committing to follow up on these requests.

The DCYF agency suffers from a lack of professionalism as well. A DCYF worker said her 10-person foster care unit is "really bad and embarrassing and I can only chalk it up to the union."[91] DCYF workers have been unwilling to place a child on a Saturday and as a result the kids sit in shelters over weekends. "The workers will state, 'I don't work on a Saturday.'"[92] DCYF foster care case workers even "sold" their right to reduce caseloads. DCYF offered to give each caseworker a "$4,000 bonus per year in return for no limits on caseloads."[93]

The case of New York is a little more complicated. Although the New York case is classified as a weak state, public management has increased in New York City over time, and foster care workers acknowledged a corresponding improvement in the system. When Scoppetta was commissioner of the NYC ACS (1996–2001), he came into the system at "one of its lowest ebbs; it had been neglected by New York City Mayor Guiliani during the first few years of his administration and he was forced to pay attention to it."[94] There was nearly universal consensus among the interviewees that NYC ACS commissioner Mattingly, who began his post in 2004, has been the strongest administrator and has initiated improvements. As a result, there is now more systematic change, which has been associated with the presence of best practices from former Casey employees now serving in New York. Richard Hucke, program director of Foster Family Services at the Jewish Child Care Association noted that "half of the staff at ACS are people [Mattingly has] pulled in from Casey."[95] Key players acknowledge that Mattingly and Mayor Bloomberg have a "tight relationship"[96] and that Mattingly has been able to convince the mayor to increase resources when needed.[97] One key indicator of this shift toward stronger public management was that during the first three years of the Scoppetta administration, 12,000 children a year were removed, whereas during the first full year of the Mattingly administration in 2004, only 4,800 were removed.[98] There was a major effort to solve family problems via preventative measures so fewer children would be placed in foster care. In general, public management increased in New York City, and at the same time, insiders recognized an improvement in foster care.

In both states where there was strong foster care administration (Delaware, Michigan), there were higher levels of public management. In states where there was weaker foster care administration (Rhode Island, New York), there were lower levels of public management. When there was increased public management, the perception of New York foster care improved. In other words, when public managers operate as principled agents, foster care reaches higher levels of success.

Strong Public Managers Utilize Community Partners and Mentors

This case research confirms the existing thesis in the literature that public management matters, yet it adds to that thesis by showing the patterns of how strong public managers operate to create more effective foster care administration. I hypothesize that better foster care administration is produced by public managers who operate as principled agents to develop networks, partnerships, and strategies within and outside their states. In other words, strong public managers utilize community partners and mentors to increase the effectiveness of foster care administration.

160 Politics of Foster Care Administration

Community Partners

The hypothesis was that stronger states would utilize more community partners. Strong states Michigan and Delaware utilized community partners the most, whereas weak state Rhode Island utilized community partners in a minimal capacity. New York utilized some community partners as the perception of the New York foster care system improved.

There is a link between the mentor/community partner hypotheses and the public management hypothesis, in that public managers were primarily responsible for permitting mentors and community partners to play a role in creating more effective foster care administration. In strong states Michigan and Delaware, community partners were welcomed by public managers. The Michigan director of the Department of Human Services, Ishmael Ahmed, attempted to build relationships with the leaders of Detroit's children's advocacy organizations and encouraged them to phone him directly.

In Michigan, DHS director Marianne Udow even reached out to a community partner that was suing her and the state of Michigan for mistreatment of children in foster care! Udow said:

> I have great respect for [the organization Children's Rights]. Whether you think litigation is the right strategy, I think it makes sense. In every state [where cases are litigated] more money is given. I understood them. I think Children's Rights is well-intentioned. They're not unreasonable to go through—I think they actually helped the state.[99]

In this case, a director took a problematic situation and spent countless hours turning it into a positive community partnership.

Delaware and Michigan both partnered with the faith-based community and the academic community. During Udow's term, DHS held three summits across the state at different campuses and developed a new relationship with Western Michigan University. Michigan director Ahmed also said, "I want to grow the DHS relationship with universities in particular. A consortium of social work schools is a priority."[100] The director of DFS, Carlyse Giddens, said that one "can't forget the role of FBOs [faith-based organizations]. Several churches allow us to have meetings, provide money,[101] and allow us to recruit foster parents there."[102] Giddens added, "FBOs have been successful in helping them to find permanency for kids."[103]

The Delaware foster care program manager, John Bates, created a plan to recruit 360 faith-based organizations in calendar year 2007 to partner with the agency on foster care.[104] As of mid-August 2007, Bates and his team had already made 178 contacts with churches that resulted in 26 partnerships.[105]

Most foster care committee meetings in Delaware included community partners who joined the state in problem-solving roles. Bates noted that these partners played a significant role in oversight, and said, "I combine them together—oversight and partnership."[106]

Case Research Results and Implications   161

As the perception of the foster care system in New York City improved, there was increased use of community partnerships in the city. Francis Ayuso, operating as an employee of NYC ACS, set out to repair the government's scarred relationship with the community. He said "we know there's baggage [from the government] and we want you to be part of the solution."[107] Ayuso attempted to repair the tarnished reputation of the foster care system by reaching out to the community. The former director of social service policy for the New York State Council of Family and Child-Caring Agencies and a former director at Harlem's Children's Zone stated that there was a "dramatic shift" in ACS's relationship with the city neighborhoods over time.[108] Commissioner Mattingly even came out to visit a community partnership in the Bronx, whereas previous commissioners had been reluctant to go into the communities.[109]

The state of Rhode Island, as expected, had a rocky relationship with community partners. Rhode Island hosted a foster planning task force for which all agencies met together once a month, but there was little evidence that it fostered collaboration. One attendee stated, "once the issues are presented to DCYF [in that meeting], they are slow to change. I've been very shocked about how DCYF handles things. It makes you laugh—'Are you serious?'"[110]

One community partner, the Rhode Island Foster Parents Association, battled with the state government on a wide range of issues: rates of reimbursement to parents for boarding foster children, the court system, the application process by caseworkers, and the change in eligibility from age 21 to 18.

In Rhode Island, public managers were not open to community partnerships, so tension grew between the community and the state. In Michigan and Delaware, public managers sought out community partners to solve problems and hence experienced higher levels of foster care administration success.

One of the recommendations from DiIulio, Kettl, and Garvey in *Improving Government Performance* (1993) was to create a personnel system that gave managers the flexibility to manage creatively.[111] In 2009, Kettl's *The Next Government of the United States* found that great public managers (aka "rocket scientists") coupled with institutional flexibility are both necessary in order for government to fix "a growing class of wicked problems that pose especially difficult puzzles."[112]

As this research showed, the best public managers crossed boundaries and built partnerships across branches and between private and public organizations. Public managers cultivated mentors and integrated community partners into the system. Kettl described "rocket scientists" as public managers who were able to "seek results through interrelated partnerships" and those who "created relationships of trust before the relationships are needed."[113] For instance, Delaware public managers partnered with faith-based organizations in order to be prepared for current, as well as future,

162 Politics of Foster Care Administration

foster care needs. The strong public managers in these state case studies fostered long-term relationships with both community partners and mentors.

Mentors

The hypothesis was that stronger states would utilize more mentors. Strong state Michigan utilized mentors the most; weak state Rhode Island utilized mentors the least; and strong state Delaware utilized mentors minimally. New York utilized some mentors as the perception of the New York foster care system improved.

Public managers in Michigan sought out mentors and allowed them to significantly shift the policy direction of the state. Michigan DHS director Marianne Udow rolled out Annie Casey Initiatives, which focused on child-centered, relative placement, and concern for the birth family approach.[114] Annie E. Casey's "Family to Family" model shifted foster care placements away from strangers as a first option and, in Michigan, redirected thousands of placements toward the extended family of the foster child.

Moreover, the Annie E. Casey Foundation helped to mentor Director Udow as she entered her DHS position and gave her the first training she ever received on foster care. Udow said:

> I didn't know anything about foster care [when I took the position]. Shortly after I came in . . . there was an Annie Casey Family to Family Initiative meeting in New Mexico. That was really my first and biggest learning—hearing from other states, hearing from other staff, shortly thereafter hearing from the kids."[115]

In addition, Udow partnered with the Jim Casey Foundation[116] to implement the Youth Opportunities Initiative. This initiative developed youth advisory boards and assisted foster care youth transitioning to independence. Udow was perceived as the DHS director behind this Jim Casey Youth Opportunities Initiative during her term, which spanned 2004 to 2007.[117] The work resulted in foster children speaking before the legislature, and a five-bill package that passed 48–0 in the Senate.[118]

Referring to the relationships with the foundation community, such as Jim Casey, Annie E. Casey, Kellogg, Skillman, and community foundations, DHS director Ishmael Ahmed shared the same sentiment: "Generally speaking the foundation community has been really good—they've given us the ability to try new things, to draw on a wealth of knowledge from across the country with best practices."[119]

Although Delaware's public managers utilized the resources that they gained from national mentors, they did not have active mentor relationships similar to those in Michigan. Many Delaware case interviews cited both the Annie E. Casey Foundation and Casey Family Services as excellent resources for learning about effective foster care practices, yet their relationships with

Case Research Results and Implications   163

these foundations did not seem to transcend the typical transactional relationship. Delaware public managers worked alongside the Pew Commission to propel foster care reforms. Yet, Delaware seemed to utilize community partners rather than foundations for learning and problem solving.

New York began to utilize mentors more as observers of New York City's foster care system began to notice improvements. NYC ACS commissioner Mattingly has had an active relationship with the Annie Casey family. As ACS has focused more on community partnerships, "Casey has been involved in a lot of the workgroups and has helped agencies collaborate," according to Richard Hucke, program director of Foster Family Services at the Jewish Child Care Association.[120]

Rhode Island case interviews suggested that the state was essentially not using mentors in its foster care system. A community partner in the state, the Foster Parents Association, did however rely upon the Annie E. Casey Foundation as a mentor for its programming, and Rhode Island DCYF was hesitant to join this collaborative effort.

To recap, in the strong state of Michigan, public managers significantly reached out to both mentors and community partners. In the strong state of Delaware, public managers prioritized community partnerships and learned from the materials of mentor organizations. Both strong states had public managers who "reached out" to partners to problem solve. This was not the case for either weak state, where public managers often choose not to partner with others. When improvement in the New York State foster care system became noticeable, New York started to utilize more mentors and community partners.

Strong Public Managers Develop Strategies and Build Networks

Public managers in the strong states reached out to external partners, such as mentors and/or community organizations, but these public managers also built strategies and built networks internally. This concept of strong managers utilizing networking and collaborative techniques is a fairly recent development in public administration literature. The December 2006 issue of *Public Administration Review* included a call from the members of the Collaborative Democracy Network to integrate deliberative and participatory governance processes, which included "collaboration among private, public, and nonprofit organizations" and could include "issue forums and collaborative policy making."[121]

Don Kettl has described how 21st century public administration has shifted from the Gulick era of "administrative boundaries [that were used] to control and manage important problems" toward a need for fewer "boundary-based solutions," which can be "out of sync with 21st century problems."[122] Kettl added, "It is hard to use vertical structures to hold individuals accountable when they are working in increasingly horizontal partnerships." Goldsmith and Eggers have referred to this "governing by

164　*Politics of Foster Care Administration*

network" as the result of the rise of third-party governance, streamlining processes, technology breakthroughs, and demands for greater choices.[123] Like Kettl, Goldsmith argued that government must adapt from the days of horizontal structures and create ways to govern by network.

Eugene Bardach has even offered a computer simulation for interagency collaboration. Bardach defined this interagency collaboration as one subprocess that is "collective craftsmanship by a large number of players" and another that is "an evolutionary process in which various capacities and opportunities that contribute to the overall result do or do not emerge from the interaction of the craftsmen and in turn condition the emergence of still other capacities and opportunities."[124]

Robert Agranoff stated that "operating in networks is changing the nature of government organizations," and the "public agency representative does not have nearly the monopoly or the corner on technical expertise that previous public administrators possessed."[125] Agranoff coauthored *Collaborative Public Management: New Strategies for Local Governments* (2004), which found that one sector of public managers spent approximately 20% of their time in collaborative activity outside their home agencies.[126] Many of these boundary-crossing public managers documented in this research performed public management network functions found in Agranoff's 2007 book. Robert Agranoff's *Managing within Networks* recognized that public management networks performed these seven key functions: problem identification and information exchange, identification of extant technologies, enhancement/development of merging technologies, improving knowledge infrastructures, mutual capacity building, reciprocal strategies and programming, and joint policymaking/programming.[127]

This research on foster care found that in addition to external collaboration with community partners and mentors, the strong public managers also used collaboration and networking inside the government.

Judicial Branch

In both Delaware and Michigan, public managers in the agency branch established relationships with strong judges in the judicial branch. In Delaware, there was an effort by the judiciary and the executive to have a "very improved" relationship with "natural tension [over cases]—and to agree to disagree."[128] As the relationships between the judicial and executive branches improved in Delaware, one member of one branch noted, "I trust [the other] with my life."[129]

After what had been a rocky relationship, a stronger agency–judiciary bond developed over time. During the first Child and Family Services Review, DHS did not inform the judicial branch that it was coming inside the courts to review performance measurements. Justice Corrigan said "the first CFSR took me by surprise."[130] Over time, DHS reached out and prepared the judicial branch. Corrigan stated, "I think now we do have a coordinated strategy—so now we know what's coming. We're better prepared and more organized."[131]

Case Research Results and Implications   165

DHS director Udow said, "Michigan was fortunate because [Supreme Court chief justice] Maura Corrigan was in office when I came in. She was really engaged in these issues and wanted to make things better."[132] The Michigan state foster care manager watched the judicial and agency branch relationships develop and credited Udow with building this cross-branch collaboration. Chaliman said, "Udow really strengthened our relationship with Maura Corrigan and really ran with youth issues, kids exiting the system."[133]

In the weak state of Rhode Island, DCYF and the courts operated as opponents. Dorothy Hultine, the Rhode Island DCYF policy officer in central management, noted that there was a "lot of animosity between the family courts and the state. There is a fight going on."[134] There was so much animosity between the two branches that they could not even agree upon whether 19-year-old children under state care were under the jurisdiction of DCYF or the courts.

In both Michigan and Delaware, strong public management led to cross-sector collaboration with the judicial branch. Beryl Radin described in *Federal Management Reform in a World of Contradictions* (2007) that "Unlike the United Kingdom, the US system is designed both to avoid concentrated power and to fragment decision making in a way that makes it difficult to establish clear goals, values, and approaches."[135] Amongst the backdrop of this fragmented checks and balances system, the public managers in these two states networked and strategized with the judicial branch and were unafraid to work through cross-branch problems.

Legislative Branch

Case research suggested that the legislative branch was more involved with foster care issues in Michigan and Delaware than in New York and Rhode Island. In Michigan, strong public managers reached across the aisle to the state legislative branch. Both Udow and Corrigan were heavily involved in the Jim Casey Youth Opportunities Initiative, which resulted in foster care youth legislation. Mary Chaliman, the Michigan state foster care manager, said: "I think foster care has been paid attention to no matter the budget cuts."[136] Michigan's DHS asked the legislature to approve 300 additional foster care workers, and they were approved in the budget for state fiscal year 2008. When DHS director Ahmed took office in September 2007, he immediately prioritized his relationship with the state legislature. Ahmed, who created the nonprofit group ACCESS, said: "I came with a legislative relationship because I used to have to lobby with both [the] federal and state [government]. I had a relationship with legislature on both sides of the aisle."[137] Ahmed desired to continue to cultivate these relationships during his term, and thought the legislature was paying attention to foster care because of the Children's Rights lawsuit.

In Delaware, the organization CPAC, formed by the legislature, worked actively with the agency branch. CPAC executive director Tania Culley

166 *Politics of Foster Care Administration*

sets the agenda and "throw issues on the table" without "many political restraints." She was working on the hottest issue of the day, which was the "age of kids in family court, extending services to kids 18 to 21 years old."[138]

In one of the two strong states, I asked a public manager whether their "agency plants ideas" in one of its review boards in order to get legislation passed. The public manager smiled and said "I can't comment on that."[139]

In the weak state of Rhode Island, DCYF and the legislative branch did not work together effectively to solve problems. DCYF chief casework supervisor Maureen Robbins stated, "No legislators are really active on [this] issue [of foster care]."[140] The executive director of the FCPA added that the General Assembly "is not really active" on foster care, with "everything being dictated by a dollar."[141]

To recap, public managers in both of the strong states strategized and networked across branches, even at times when there was "natural tension" over cases. In other words, the branches served as checks and balances, while at the same time showing respect for one another's functions.

One of the greatest public administration failures in the last decade was the coordination during the immediate aftermath of Hurricane Katrina. Vicki Bier noted in *On Risk and Disaster: Lessons from Hurricane Katrina* that "My contention here, in particular, is that many of the problems observed in the aftermath of Katrina were not due to any one person or organization, but rather were problems of coordination at the interfaces between multiple organizations and multiple levels of government."[142] The public managers in strong case states did not fall into this noncoordination post-Katrina aftermath trap. Rather, they leveraged these cross-sector partnerships across branches, with partners, and between various levels of government to produce stronger foster care administration.

Finally, state size was unrelated to the ability to leverage these cross-sector partnerships. Rhode Island (a weaker-performing state) is the smallest state in the United States (37 miles by 48 miles), and Delaware (a stronger-performing state) is the second smallest (35 miles by 96 miles). Yet, Rhode Island failed to build strong relationships between state and local administrators while Delaware utilized these methods to improve performance. Conversely, Michigan (386 miles by 456 miles) and New York (285 miles by 330 miles) are both large states, and yet Michigan (a stronger-performing state) utilized collaboration and worked with state and local administrators to a much larger degree than their smaller New York peer choose to do (weaker-performing state). Both two-state scenarios show that size was unrelated to the ability to build strong relationships between state and local administrators.

CONCLUSION

After completing this original research, I reviewed how each of the four case states had performed on the 2008 Government Performance Project (GPP) rankings. Their independent state rankings perfectly aligned with my

Case Research Results and Implications   167

research for these case states on foster care. The rankings assessed how well state governments perform their basic management functions.[143] Of the two strong states, both Michigan and Delaware received a B+. This ranking placed Michigan and Delaware among a group of the eight top states.[144] Of the two weak states, New York received a B– and Rhode Island received a C–. I did not look at the GPP data prior to conducting this study, but these rankings concerning overall state government management were consistent with my findings concerning foster care administration in these states.

Original data from over 55 key player and key player elite interviews provided the research base that was supported by two theses: (1) *the federal government has increased its focus on measuring the performance of state programs while simultaneously decreasing its funding of state foster care programs and offering the states very little management or mentorship*, and (2) *better foster care administration is produced by public managers who operate as principled agents to develop networks, partnerships, and strategies within and outside their states.* The next chapter uses these findings to discuss the future of foster care in the United States.

NOTES

1. Donald F. Kettl and James W. Fesler, *The Politics of the Administrative Process*, 4th ed. (Washington, DC: CQ Press, 2009), 41.
2. Paul Light, *The True Size of Government* (Washington, DC: Brookings Institution, 1999), 1.
3. Ibid., 3. Note: When Light adds in military and postal service workers, the number nears 17 million in 1996.
4. John DiIulio, "Government by Proxy: A Faithful Overview," *Harvard Law Review*, Vol. 116, No. 5 (March 2003): 1271–1284.
5. Ibid., 1272.
6. U.S. Department of Health and Human Services, Office of the Assistant Secretary for Planning and Evaluation, Office of Human Services Policy, "ASPE Issue Brief: Federal Foster Care Financing: How and Why the Current Funding Structure Fails to Meet the Needs of the Child Welfare Field," http://aspe.hhs.gov/hsp/05/fc-financing-ib/ib.pdf, 4.
7. Ibid.
8. Ibid.
9. The White House, Office of Management and Budget, "Program Assessment Rating Tool (PART): FY2009 Budget and Spring Update," http://www.whitehouse.gov/omb/assets/omb/expectmore/part.pdf.
10. Ibid.
11. U.S. Department of Health and Human Services, "Administration for Children and Families All-Purpose Table—FY 2009–2011," http://www.acf.hhs.gov/sites/default/files/olab/fy2011allppurposetable.pdf.
12. U.S. Department of Health and Human Services, "Administration for Children and Families All-Purpose Table—FY 2010–2012," http://www.acf.hhs.gov/sites/default/files/assets/fy2012apt.pdf.
13. Ibid.
14. U.S. Department of Health and Human Services, Administration for Children and Families, "Payments for Foster Care and Permanency, FY2012–FY2013," http://www.acf.hhs.gov/sites/default/files/assets/FCAA%20final.pdf, 318.

168 *Politics of Foster Care Administration*

15. U.S. Department of Health and Human Services, "Fiscal Year 2014 Budget in Brief. Administration for Children and Families: Mandatory Programs," http://www.hhs.gov/budget/fy2014/fy-2014/fy-2014-budget-in-brief.pdf, 101.
16. Ibid.
17. U.S. Department of Health and Human Services, Administration for Children and Families, "Fiscal Year 2013, Justifications of Estimates for Appropriations Committees," http://www.acf.hhs.gov/sites/default/files/assets/FCA Afinal.pdf, 325.
18. U.S. Department of Health and Human Services, Administration for Children and Families, Administration on Children, Youth, and Families, Children's Bureau, "The AFCARS Report: Preliminary FY 2011 Estimates as of July 2012, No. 19," http://www.acf.hhs.gov/programs/cb/resource/afcars-report-19.
19. U.S. Department of Health and Human Services, "Fiscal Year 2014 Budget in Brief."
20. U.S. Department of Health and Human Services, "Fiscal Year 2013."
21. U.S. Department of Health and Human Services, "Fiscal Year 2014 Budget in Brief."
22. U.S. Department of Health and Human Services, "Fiscal Year 2013."
23. Cynthia Andrews Scarcella et al., "The Cost of Protecting Vulnerable Children V: Understanding State Variation in Child Welfare Financing," http://www.urban.org/publications/311314.html, vi.
24. Note: The number of states reporting data varied across the time period.
25. Carlyse Giddens, Director, Division of Family Services, Delaware, interview, Wilmington, Delaware, August 15, 2007.
26. Cari DeSantis, Cabinet Secretary, Department of Services for Children, Youth and Their Families, Delaware; Chair, National Council State Human Service Administrators, phone interview, December 19, 2007.
27. Rob Green, Shelly Waters Boots, and Karen C. Tumlin, "The Cost of Protecting Vulnerable Children: Understanding Federal, State and Local Child Welfare Spending," *The Urban Institute,* Occasional Paper Number 20 (January 1, 1999), http://www.urban.org/publications/308046.html.
28. Carlyse Giddens, interview.
29. Cari DeSantis, interview. Note: The comparison between 1996 and 2007 is based on two different sources for the data.
30. Ibid.
31. Ibid.
32. Kerry DeVooght et al., "Federal, State, and Local Spending to Address Child Abuse and Neglect in SFYs 2008 and 2010," *The Annie Casey Foundation, Child Trends* (June 2012): 6, http://www.childtrends.org/Files/Child-Trends-2012_06_20_FR_Casey CWFinancing.pdf.
33. Ibid.
34. Ibid.
35. Green, Boots, and Tumlin, "The Cost of Protecting Vulnerable Children."
36. Scarcella et al., "The Cost of Protecting Vulnerable Children V," 2.
37. DeVooght et al., "Federal, State, and Local Spending," 18.
38. Nancy Martinez, Director, Strategic Planning and Policy Development, New York State Office of Children and Family Services, interview, Rensselaer, New York, November 30, 2007.
39. Ibid.
40. Ibid.
41. Marianne Udow, Director, Department of Human Services, Michigan; Director, Center for Healthcare Quality and Transformation, interview, Ann Arbor, Michigan, March 18, 2008.

Case Research Results and Implications   169

42. Maura D. Corrigan, Justice of the Supreme Court, Michigan; Chief Justice of the Supreme Court, Michigan, phone interview, April 7, 2008.
43. Ibid.
44. Nicholas Pirro, Former Onondaga County Executive (Syracuse, New York, area); Former President of New York State Association of Counties; Former President of County Executive Association for New York; Former Chairman of the Onondaga Legislature, phone interview, October 14, 2008.
45. Ibid.
46. Ibid.
47. David Osborne and Ted Gaebler, *Reinventing Government: How the Entrepreneurial Spirit is Transforming the Public Sector* (Reading, MA: Addison-Wesley, 1992).
48. Elizabeth Newell and Robert Brodsky, "Obama Reform Plan Bears Traces of Clinton and Bush Efforts," http://goexec.com/story_page_pf.cfm?articleid=41039&printerfriendlyvers=1.
49. NPAction, "Government Performance and Review Act," http://www.npaction.org/article/articleprint/360/-1/%7Bcategory_id%7D/.
50. "Implementation of the Government Performance and Results Act of 1993," testimony by Donald F. Kettl, Nonresident Senior Fellow, Governance Studies, Brookings Institution. Presented to the House Committee on Government Reform and Oversight; Senate Committee on Governmental Affairs, March 6, 1996, http://www.brookings.edu/testimony/1996/0306governance_kettl.aspx?p=1.
51. U.S. Department of Health and Human Services, Administration for Children and Families, Administration on Children, Youth, and Families, Children's Bureau, "Statistics and Research," http://www.acf.hhs.gov/programs/cb/stats_research/index.htm.
52. The White House, Office of Management and Budget, "Rating the Performance of Federal Programs," http://www.whitehouse.gov/omb/budget/fy2004/performance.html.
53. Beryl Radin, *Challenging the Performance Movement: Accountability, Complexity, and Democratic Values* (Washington, DC: Georgetown University Press, 2006), 122.
54. The White House, "Rating the Performance of Federal Programs."
55. Ibid.
56. Ibid.
57. Robert Brodsky, "Bush Performance Rating Tool Draws Plaudits, Pans," http://www.govexec.com/story_page.cfm?articleid=41219&dcn=todaysnews.
58. The White House, "Program Assessment Rating Tool (PART)." Note: These are percentages assigned by PART regarding scores on individual areas out of a possibility of 100%. The federal government took the individual score calculations and deduced that the foster care program was "moderately effective."
59. U.S. Department of Health and Human Services, "Statistics and Research: Child Welfare Outcomes," http://www.acf.hhs.gov/programs/cb/research-data-technology/statistics-research.
60. Philip Joyce, "Obama's Performance Measurement Agenda," *Governing* (March 23, 2011). http://www.governing.com/templates/gov_print_article?id+118465734.
61. U.S. Department of Health and Human Services, "Fiscal Year 2013: Annual Performance Report and Performance Plan," www.hhs.gov/budget/performance-appendix-fy2013.pdf.
62. The White House, The Office of Management and Budget, "Performance and Personnel Management," http://www.whitehouse.gov/omb/performance.

170 Politics of Foster Care Administration

63. Del Failing, Director of Children's Services, People's Place, interview, Milford, Delaware, August 24, 2007.
64. Carlyse Giddens, interview.
65. Marianne Udow, interview.
66. Mary Chaliman, Foster Care Program Manager, Department of Human Services, Michigan, interview, Lansing, Michigan, March 18, 2008.
67. Ibid.
68. Dorothy Hultine, Policy, Central Management, Department of Children, Youth and Families, interview, Providence, Rhode Island, January 23, 2008.
69. Patricia Martinez, interview.
70. Note: This program was launched through HHS, but now receives its funding through DOJ.
71. Barbara Wilson, Program Officer, Senior Corps, Corporation for National and Community Service (CNCS) federal program, phone and written correspondence with author, fall 2006. Note: Wilson stated that CNCS was planning to become more active on foster care and hoped to provide 3,000 volunteers dedicated to the issue.
72. Christine Craig, HHS-ACF Region III Program Specialist, federal government, phone interview, June 3, 2008.
73. DiIulio, "Government by Proxy."
74. Donald F. Kettl, *The Next Government of the United States: Why Our Institutions Fail Us and How to Fix Them* (New York: W.W. Norton and Co., 2009), 133.
75. Donald F. Kettl, *Government by Proxy: Mis?Managing Federal Programs* (Washington, DC: CQ Press, 1988).
76. Donald F. Kettl and H. Brinton Milward, *The State of Public Management* (Baltimore: Johns Hopkins University Press, 1996) 1.
77. John J. DiIulio, Jr., *Governing Prisons: A Comparative Study of Correctional Management* (New York: The Free Press, 1987).
78. Jameson W. Doig and Erwin C. Hargrove, *Leadership and Innovation: Entrepreneurs in Government* (Baltimore: Johns Hopkins University Press, 1987).
79. Chester Barnard, *The Functions of the Executive* (Cambridge, MA: Harvard University Press, 1938).
80. Philip Selznick, *Leadership in Administration: A Sociological Interpretation* (New York: Harper and Row, 1957). Note: See Chapter 1.
81. Ibid.
82. Mark Moore, *Creating Public Value: Strategic Management in Government* (Cambridge, MA: Harvard University Press, 1995), 10.
83. John DiIulio, Jr., "Principled Agents: The Cultural Bases of Behavior in a Federal Government Bureaucracy," *Journal of Public Administration Research and Theory*, Vol. 4, No. 3 (1994): 277–318.
84. Vincent Giampeitro, Program Director, Children and Families First, interview, Wilmington, Delaware, August 24, 2007.
85. Confidential remarks.
86. Carlyse Giddens, interview.
87. John Bates, Foster Care Program Manager, Division of Family Services, Delaware, foster care general statistics letter to author, August 2007.
88. Ibid.
89. Maureen Robbins, Chief Casework Supervisor, Adoption and Foster Care Preparation and Support Unit, Department of Children, Youth and Families, interview, Providence, Rhode Island, January 24, 2008.
90. Dorothy Hultine, interview.
91. Sarah St. Jacques, Junior Human Services and Policy Systems Specialist, Department of Children Youth, and Families, Rhode Island, phone interview, February 11, 2008.

Case Research Results and Implications 171

92. Confidential remarks.
93. Maureen Robbins, interview.
94. John Courtney, Co-Director of the New York City Partnership for Family Supports and Justice; Senior Advisor to both the Child Welfare Fund and FAR Fund, phone interview, November 20, 2007.
95. Richard Hucke, Program Director of Foster Family Services, Jewish Child Care Association, phone interviews, December 6, 2007, and December 14, 2007.
96. Michael Arsham, Director of the Child Welfare Organizing Project (CWOP), interview, East Harlem, New York, November 8, 2007.
97. John Courtney, interview.
98. Ibid.
99. Marianne Udow, interview.
100. Ishmael Ahmed, Director, Department of Human Services, Michigan, interview, Lansing, Michigan, March 18, 2008.
101. Note: Churches have provided direct donations to foster care organizations.
102. Carlyse Giddens, interview.
103. Ibid.
104. John Bates, interview.
105. Ibid.
106. Ibid.
107. Francis Ayuso, New York City Administration for Children's Services (ACS) Neighborhood-Based Services Coordinator; Project Director of Bridge Builders, interview, Highbridge section of Bronx, New York, November 2, 2007.
108. Michael Arsham, interview.
109. Francis Ayuso, interview.
110. Confidential remarks.
111. John J. DiIulio Jr., Gerald Garvey, and Donald F. Kettl, *Improving Government Performance: An Owner's Manual* (Washington, DC: Brookings Institution Press, 1993). Note: See Chapter 9.
112. Kettl, *The Next Government of the United States,* 133.
113. Ibid., 210–211.
114. Marianne Udow, interview.
115. Ibid.
116. Note: The collective Casey family foundations constitute the single largest foundation to conduct work on foster care.
117. Jane Zehnder-Merrell, Director, Kids Count in Michigan; Senior Research Associate, Michigan League for Human Services, interview, Lansing, Michigan, March 18, 2008.
118. Maura D. Corrigan, interview.
119. Ishmael Ahmed, interview.
120. Richard Hucke, interview.
121. Anonymous, "A Call to Scholars and Teachers of Public Administration, Public Policy, Planning, Political Science, and Related Fields," *Public Administration Review,* Vol. 66 (Dec. 2006): 168.
122. Donald F. Kettl, "Managing Boundaries in American Administration: The Collaboration Imperative," *Public Administration Review,* Vol. 66 (Dec. 2006): 10.
123. Stephen Goldsmith and William D. Eggers, *Governing by Network: The New Shape of the Public Sector* (Washington, DC: Brookings Institution, 2004).
124. Eugene Bardach, "Developmental Dynamics: Interagency Collaboration as an Emergent Phenomenon," *Journal of Public Administration Research and Theory,* Vol. 11, No. 2 (April 2001): 149–164.
125. Robert Agranoff, "Leveraging Networks: A Guide for Public Managers Working across Organizations," in *Collaboration: Using Networks and*

172 *Politics of Foster Care Administration*

Partnerships, ed. John M. Kamensky and Thomas J. Burlin (Lanham, MD: Rowman & Littlefield, 2004), 65.

126. Robert Agranoff and Michael McGuire, *Collaborative Public Management: New Strategies for Local Governments* (Washington, DC: Georgetown University Press, 2003).

127. Robert Agranoff, *Managing Within Networks: Adding Value to Public Organizations* (Washington, DC: Georgetown University Press, 2007), 222.

128. Confidential remarks.

129. Confidential remarks.

130. Maura D. Corrigan, interview.

131. Ibid.

132. Marianne Udow, interview.

133. Mary Chaliman, interview.

134. Dorothy Hultine, interview.

135. Beryl A. Radin, *Federal Management Reform in a World of Contradictions* (Washington, DC: Georgetown University Press, 2012), 43.

136. Mary Chaliman, interview.

137. Ishmael Ahmed, interview.

138. Tania Culley, Executive Director of the Office of the Child Advocate; Executive Director of Child Protection Accountability Commission, interview, Wilmington, Delaware, September 6, 2007.

139. Confidential remarks.

140. Maureen Robbins, interview.

141. Lisa Guillette, Executive Director, Rhode Island Foster Parents Association, interview, East Providence, Rhode Island, January 23, 2008.

142. Vicki Bier, "Hurricane Katrina as a Bureaucratic Nightmare" in *On Risk and Disaster: Lessons from Hurricane Katrina,* ed. Ronald J. Daniels, Donald F. Kettl, and Howard Kunreuther (Philadelphia: University of Pennsylvania Press, 2006), 243.

143. The Government Performance Project, "Grading the States 2008," http://www.pewstates.org/research/reports/grading-the-states-2008-report-85899379355

144. Note: These top eight ranked states were all given A– or B+ grades.

8 Improving Foster Care

"Foster care is not something that you deal with [which then] goes away, because you have a whole new clientele every day; it never ends. If you allow the program to slip, then you start falling backward. The better you can make the program, the better your future can be. You can never let up on this."

—Nicholas Pirro, former president of New York State Association of Counties and former president of the County Executive Association for New York

THE FUTURE OF FOSTER CARE

On October 7, 2008, President George W. Bush signed into law a major federal foster care policy, the Fostering Connections to Success and Increasing Adoptions Act (Public Law 110–351).[1] This bill has increased the options that are available to foster care children by recognizing the significant number of relative caregivers who are raising foster children and the need for additional foster care support for children between the ages of 18 and 21. The U.S. Department of Health and Human Services, the agency tasked with implementing the new law, stated that this federally subsidized guardianship bill would "create an option to provide kinship guardianship assistance payments" and will "create an option to extend eligibility for title IV-E foster care, adoption assistance, and kinship guardianship payments to age 21."[2] The bill also offers states higher adoption payment incentives, in an effort to financially motivate states to seek out adoptions for their children in care.[3]

Early versions of this law were defined and drafted with input from strong public managers from Delaware and Michigan, along with the Pew Charitable Trusts. This law was influenced by the efforts of chief justices and foster care directors in multiple states who worked together across the branches of government to create more effective foster care policy. The law was also the product of what seems to be increasingly rare collaboration between the U.S. Senate, the U.S. House, and the president, who worked across party lines to improve foster care.

174   Politics of Foster Care Administration

If implemented according to plan, this legislation should significantly improve foster care. Even so, foster care administration still has a long road ahead in order to effectively administer "24-hour substitute care for all children placed away from their parents or guardians and for whom the State agency has placement and care responsibility."[4] This chapter utilizes results gleaned from the case research to offer a few suggestions that state and federal governments, as well as policy and program entrepreneurs, might consider implementing in order to improve foster care.

How the State Governments Can Improve Foster Care

One concluding thesis maintained that *better foster care administration is produced by public managers who operate as principled agents to develop networks, partnerships, and strategies within and outside their states.* States need public managers that network, partner, and strategize within and outside their states. The methods by which public managers in Michigan and Delaware improved foster care can serve as guidelines for future public managers. In other words, states should hire strong public managers who cross boundaries to form partnerships with foundations, community organizations, faith-based organizations, the state judicial branch, the state agency branch, and the state legislative branch.

How the Federal Government Can Improve Foster Care

The other concluding thesis claimed that *the federal government has increased its focus on measuring the performance of state programs while simultaneously decreasing its funding of state foster care programs and offering the states very little management or mentorship.* In other words, the federal government operates as a monitor of foster care, rather than as a mentor or manager for the states as they provide foster care services.

What was the result, then, of this federal emphasis on monitoring? Did the monitoring improve performance? Generally, both strong and weak case states reported that federal monitoring (the collection of performance measurement data via "Child Welfare Outcome: Annual Reports") encouraged them to improve and served as a benchmark. However, the audits (both financial and administrative) were frustrating even for the strong states because they were penalized for not itemizing cases according to federal standards. Even strong states felt repeatedly penalized by the federal government. The federal government's intention to collect strong performance data and hold states to high standards is admirable. However, the federal government should look at the impact of its performance measurement collection process on the states, while balancing the need for rigorous data and financial accountability.

This research finding regarding a need for improved foster care performance measurement collection is consistent with public administration

Improving Foster Care   175

scholars' viewpoints regarding a need for improving performance measurement collection overall. David G. Frederickson and H. George Frederickson noted in *Measuring the Performance of the Hollow State*:

> The problems with performance measurement in government have to do with two key points: (1) expecting too much from it and (2) attempting performance measurement without understanding the third-party nature of the modern federal government and accommodating performance measurement to that reality.[5]

Beryl Radin stated in *Challenging the Performance Movement: Accountability, Complexity, and Democratic Values*:

> In a sense, one could argue that the performance movement is constructed on false or, at least, unrealistic assumptions. These assumptions make up what I call the "unreal or naïve approach." They are: Information is already available. . . . Information is neutral. . . . We know what we are measuring. . . . We can define cause-effect relationships in programs. . . . Baseline information is available. . . . Almost all activities can be measured and quantified.[6]

This finding that foster care performance measurement needs to be tweaked is consistent with overall findings that performance measurement needs to be measured correctly across all policy or program areas, including foster care.

A second question that arises from the thesis statement is whether something is lost if the federal government doesn't offer mentoring or management to the states as they implement foster care programs. Should the federal government expend effort and resources to more closely manage foster care? Or, drawing from the lessons learned in this case study, is there another way the federal government could improve foster care?

Instead of the federal government mentoring or managing the states' foster care programs, I propose that the federal government *network* with the states. The federal government should leverage its networks to bring about greater state performance. Just as the strong public managers in the research cases were able to use those relationships to increase the effectiveness of the foster care programs for which they were responsible, the federal government could use a similar approach to achieve better outcomes for foster care children. First, the federal government should maximize its connections with the Corporation for National and Community Service, the Mentoring Children of Prisoners (MCOP) program and other overlapping at-risk youth federal programs, and the White House Faith-Based and Neighborhood Partnerships Office.[7]

In the last few years, the Corporation for National and Community Service (CNCS) has begun to take a more active role on the foster care

176 *Politics of Foster Care Administration*

issue. Yet, there is still a mismatch between CNCS's strong volunteer base and expertise on youth programs and the actual use of CNCS resources within the states. Not once was CNCS mentioned in state-level key player interviews as an active partner on foster care, through either Senior Corps or AmeriCorps. The federal government could utilize the knowledge and resources of CNCS to offer volunteers and other resources to the state foster care programs.

Second, the federal government should connect state foster care programs with other programs for at-risk youths that share mutual clients. The federally funded MCOP program, created in 2003, was designed to provide children of prisoners with a mentor for at least 1 hour per week for 1 year. The program successfully connected 100,000 mentors with mentees, with the goal of reducing drug and alcohol use, improving school performance, and directing the child of the prisoner away from a path toward prison. When the states struggled with administering the MCOP programs, the federal government was able to coordinate mentorship and training and provide a significant volunteer workforce through CNCS. A large percentage of children of prisoners are foster care children, and there is significant overlap between the goals of the two federal policies. For instance, when a foster care child is identified as the child of a prisoner, he or she could simultaneously be sent to a matching MCOP program. This win–win scenario would reduce costs for MCOP programs as they attempted to track down children of prisoners,[8] and the simultaneous mentoring would ensure a higher rate of success for the foster child.

Finally, the federal government can leverage the resources of the White House Office of Faith-Based and Neighborhood Partnerships to improve foster care. Delaware's success was partially related to its active recruitment of faith-based and community partners. One Delaware foster care provider said, "A large percent of families who become foster parents have faith-based connections. We sometimes go through faith-based connections to recruit [foster care parents] for kids."[9] The federal government should utilize the resources of this White House office in order to develop stronger faith-based and neighborhood partnerships for the foster care community.

These are only a handful of the resources that the federal government can utilize to improve foster care. The strong public managers in the strong states demonstrated that utilizing networks will improve foster care, and the federal government should heed this advice.

How the Policy and Program Entrepreneurs Can Improve Foster Care

Strong foster care administration does not necessarily equate to effective policy, long-term success, or the intended program outcome. The strong states measured high on reducing levels of abuse for foster children while in care, as well as increased success in reaching permanency for children.

Improving Foster Care 177

However, it does not follow that Michigan and Delaware foster children turn out to be more well-balanced, self-sufficient adults. Rather, case interviews painted a bleak outlook for adults who were former foster children.

Interviews uncovered poor long-term outcomes for adults who were foster children in both strong states. Delaware provided numerous examples of poor outcomes for their foster children. The executive director of a Delaware foster care provider said, "Only 50% of my kids will make it. Not homeless, not in jail. The rest is really a crapshoot."[10] The director of children's services for another Delaware foster care provider stated, "A lot of what we [foster care programs] do is a band aid. Former foster kids end up homeless [or in the] criminal justice [system]. Thirty percent of the general homeless population is from foster care.[11]

In response to a question about how Delaware's foster children would succeed in life once they left foster care, Vincent Giampeitro, program director of Children and Families First, asked: "When you were 18, were you able to make it on your own without the support of your parents?"[12] He went on to talk about how foster children leave the foster system, have no support network, and struggle to make it on their own.

Michigan offered examples of the bleak futures that were expected for many of its foster care children. Former Michigan chief justice Corrigan stated:

> I won't even hazard a guess [as to] how these [former foster care] kids [will be] doing in 25 years. In Detroit, we're now at a 90% out of wedlock birthrate. We're only graduating 25% of the kids in Detroit public schools who start as freshman.[13]

Gayle Robbert, the program representative overseeing seven foster care review boards in the state, said: "Children seem to be more disturbed from when I first started in child welfare in the 70s until now. The drug problem has been devastating on the child welfare system."[14] Victoria Tyler, director of child welfare for the Catholic Social Services of Wayne in Detroit, stated: "Less than 50% will have jobs and not be homeless or in jail. Nine times out of 10 it's cyclical. The system is in such crisis. It's not focused on the long term."[15] Tyler added her thoughts about foster children: "Their chance of success is very low. I know I wasn't ready to be out there at 17, 18."[16] The State Foster Care Review Board program manager, James Novell, said: "40% of former foster care youth will be okay, not enter the criminal justice system, mental health system, or be homeless."[17] Patrick Okoronokwo, director of the Children's Center in Detroit, stated: "47% of the kids aging out in the system nationally are going into the criminal justice system."[18]

The data is significant, because it shows that even foster children from the stronger-performing states have grim prospects for well-balanced, self-sufficient adult lives. Even stronger states are producing foster children that enter the criminal justice system, fall into homelessness, become single parents, and live in poverty.

178   Politics of Foster Care Administration

These findings on the long-term outcomes of former foster children corresponded to findings from the largest longitudinal study of former foster youth regarding their transition to adulthood since the passage of John Chafee Foster Care Independence Act in 1999. The Chapin Hall Center for Children at the University of Chicago followed approximately 700 former foster youth from three states from 2002 to 2011 and matched them to a control group for outcomes when possible.[19] The report identified the following results for former foster youth at the age of 26:

- Approximately 20% did not have a GED/high school diploma (compared to 6% of the control group)[20]
- Less than 3% had completed a 4-year college degree (compared to nearly 24% of the control group)[21]
- Approximately 46% were employed (compared to nearly 80% of the control group)[22]
- Nearly 28% reported not having enough money to pay rent (compared to nearly 6% of the control group)[23]
- 38% reported that they were "sometimes or often worried about running out of food"[24]
- 31% reported being homeless or couch surfing since being interviewed at age 23–24[25]

According to testimony by the study's author, Mark Courtney, before the Committee on Ways and Means in the U.S. House of Representatives on July 12, 2007, "Thirty percent of the males and 11 percent of the females reported being incarcerated at least once between 17 and 19. Many more had been arrested."[26] Almost 50% were pregnant by age 19 (compared to approximately 25% of the control group).[27]

Casey Family Programs conducted "The Casey Young Adult Survey," which tracked 1,000 alumni of Casey Family Programs foster care.[28] Because Casey produces most of the research on foster care program effectiveness and then integrates the best practices into its foster care programs, it follows logically that Casey program foster alumni should have higher success rates than those of other programs, on average. In the areas of birth certificates, health insurance, reduced drug use, and educational outcomes, the Casey alumni fared better than other former foster care youth. Yet, over 80% of these Casey former foster youth had household incomes three times below the poverty line; 32% had been arrested since leaving foster care; and approximately 20% had been homeless, with the majority of those having been homeless for "substantial periods of time." An October 20, 2011, article about New York City foster care in *New York Times* stated: "Previously, the city's Department of Homeless Services and the City Council estimated that more than a quarter of youths discharged from foster care because of their age end up homeless almost immediately."[29] Based on this case data and studies like these, it appears that a large percentage of adults who were former foster children are either homeless, incarcerated, or living in poverty.

Because the case interviews show that even stronger states produce high levels of former foster children who struggle as adults with homelessness, incarceration, or poverty, the success of foster care administration is *not* linked to effective long-term outcomes for foster care children. The goals, or performance targets, for effective foster care administration need to be more closely aligned with what will serve these children over the long term. Quick placements, minimal transfers, good permanency strategies, and minimal abuse do *not* always equate to foster care children ultimately having successful adult lives—growing up with jobs, staying out of correctional systems, and not being homeless.

There are many potential entrepreneurial approaches that could align effective foster care administration with long-term success for former children in foster care. Policies and programs should be designed to help these children develop into self-sufficient, well-balanced adults.

One starting point is addressing the problem of instability for foster care children. Foster care children are routinely bounced among agencies, courts, and CASA workers, and between parents, foster parents, and permanent guardians. New policies have shifted foster care children between different agencies, and caseworker turnover means that children may have no reliable adult advocate. These at-risk youth need stability instead of the current revolving door of state/private social workers, lawyers, foster parents, and guardians.

I propose that an organization should conduct a pilot project to create greater stability for foster care children in order to improve short-term, as well as long-term, outcomes for these children. The focus of the pilot would be establishing a human link that mitigates the upheaval that the children experience in the foster care system. In order to best test this program, it should be implemented in a heavy foster care area, such as a large city. This cost-effective program would train unpaid volunteers to be *child liaisons*. Each child liaison would make a commitment to partner with one foster care child for a 5-year period, assuming the child remained within a 60 mile radius of the volunteer. The liaison would be matched to the child once the child entered the foster care system and remain with the child as the child navigated the legal system; multiple placement options (shelters, residential treatment, unlicensed guardians); possibly multiple foster care homes; and even *after* the child had achieved permanency.

The child liaison would serve as a reliable and stable mentor, advocate, and problem-solver that understood the foster child's history. In an environment of revolving door foster care caseworkers, changing guardians, and programmatic uncertainty, this liaison would function as a stable, reliable adult in the foster care child's life for 5 years. This liaison would be trained to be familiar with the resources that should be available to a child and the warning signs of hazards in the child's life. For instance, these liaisons would make sure the child has access to any potential government resources such as Medicaid, tuition, or a clothing stipend. They would navigate the legal system, ensuring that foster children meet their various CASA workers, attend

180 Politics of Foster Care Administration

court dates, and receive placement options aligned with the child's interests. Their presence in the children's lives would be another check, watching to see that the children are receiving proper medical care and mental health services and are protected from abuse. They would track important developmental points, such as seeing that the child received driver's education and obtained a license and had the resources to succeed in high school, such as a computer and homework support. They would broker relationships between foster care families, birth families, and caseworkers, in order to consider every serious placement option for the child. Because foster children are often shuffled through case workers and various guardians, including multiple foster care parent placements, the liaison would most likely be the *only* stable adult in the foster child's life over a 5-year period. The volunteer would serve as an addendum to any work already being completed by CASA volunteers, foster care parents, and social workers.

This pilot borrows from the lessons learned via the U.S. Department of Health and Human Services[30] and the U.S. Department of Justice[31] Mentoring Children of Prisoners (MCOP) program,[32] including the following: that a loving, caring mentor can have significant impact on the life of an at-risk youth; that long-term mentoring produces better outcomes; and that the cost of matching a child to a volunteer mentee is only a few thousand dollars per match annually. This low-cost, high-impact model makes it a well-positioned candidate for foundation or corporate financial support.

Furthermore, there are differences between this volunteer child liaison and what foster children are already receiving via their caseworkers. Paid caseworkers have high turnover both in the public and private sectors, so rarely are these child advocates consistent in the life of a foster child. Also, caseworkers often have no time or only a few minutes each month to spend with each foster care child. Experiencing such high turnover and a lack of interaction with an adult advocate only adds to the trust issues that these foster children face.

Child liaisons solve this problem, because they would be trained to navigate the foster care system for the child. The liaison might even hunt down a potential foster family, or, as in the case of Delaware, they might utilize the faith-based community to increase a child's emotional health, provide more community connections, and showcase positive role models. Instead of the revolving door of CASA workers, agency social workers, and private agencies, children would have one consistent adult who would navigate the foster care system for them. Because the average foster child will wait 39 months before being adopted and have three foster care placements,[33] the volunteer can provide stability for the children prior to and during their foster care, as well as for up to a 1-year period after reunification or adoption occurs. The liaison would also be encouraged to maintain some form of communication with the foster child beyond the 5-year period, so that children do not feel that their liaisons were also revolving door adults in their lives.

Improving Foster Care 181

The pilot would most likely work best in a city with a heavy foster care caseload that is in an entrepreneurial state that is willing to work with unconventional partners (such as Michigan). This pilot is one potential policy solution to create better long-term success for foster children.

How the Policy and Program Entrepreneurs Can Improve Transitioning Out of Foster Care

I propose the creation of another pilot project for older foster youth transitioning out of foster care that incorporates the aforementioned *child liaison* concept. Foster children aged 18 to 21 would be matched with a youth liaison that would follow the young adult until the age of 25. Foster children who aged out of the system or those who remained in the system but had yet to achieve permanency would be eligible. The youth liaison would serve the same function as a child liaison, but would be trained to deal specifically with life issues that older children face.

The impetus for this pilot is the reality that older youth encounter unique issues and face a plethora of major decisions in their twenties, such as choosing a college, finding a job, securing housing, and often starting a family. Youth liaisons would advocate for the children as they accept independent living funds, state grants for education, and any eligible Medicaid/medical services. Pilot program success could be measured by a child graduating with a technical institute certificate/associate's degree/bachelor's degree, as well as obtaining a safe independent living environment with a stable source of income. The goal would be to reduce the number of former foster children that are homeless, carrying unplanned pregnancies, living in poverty, or incarcerated. The youth liaison would serve to direct the former foster child during this crucial decision-making period.

There is a precedent for targeting programs and policies to this specific age group, such as the federal government's Independent Living Program. And, the poor long-term outcomes for foster children suggest that these are critical years in which these emerging adults struggle with significant life choices. This pilot is designed to have mentors for the older youth as they make major life decisions.

CONCLUSION

This case research presents strengths and weaknesses of foster care administration and the findings offer some useful tools for improvement in foster care. State and local governments should hire pubic managers who are effective at networking, partnering, and strategizing within and outside their states. Public managers who hinder the effectiveness of foster care administration or refuse to network, partner, and strategize should be removed.

182   *Politics of Foster Care Administration*

In addition to revising the performance measurement collection process, the federal government should first leverage its networks, such as CNCS, to bring about greater success for state performance. Second, the federal government should connect state foster care programs with other at-risk youth policies that share mutual clients. Finally, the federal government should leverage the resources of the White House Faith-Based and Neighborhood Partnerships Office to improve foster care.

Furthermore, this case research has shown that strong foster care administration does not necessarily equate to effective policy or achieving intended program outcomes. In order to better align foster care administration with long-term success for former foster children in adulthood, the two pilot projects that would establish a 5-year mentoring program for foster children should be created.

If individuals are interested in improving foster care, they should consider adopting all of the aforementioned concepts, as well as developing entrepreneurial policy approaches or programs that stem from the findings in this research. Efforts to improve foster care help not only foster children but also their biological and foster parents, as well as taxpayers and citizens.

NOTES

1. U.S. Department of Health and Human Services, Administration for Children and Families, Administration on Children, Youth and Families, "Program Instruction: New Legislation—The Fostering Connections to Success and Increasing Adoptions Act of 2008 (Public Law 110–351)," http://www.cwla.org/advocacy/adoptionhr6893hhs.pdf.
2. Ibid.
3. Child Welfare League of America, "Summary of Fostering Connections to Success and Increasing Adoptions Act, H.R. 6893," http://www.cwla.org/advocacy/adoptionhr6893summary.htm.
4. U.S. Department of Health and Human Services, Administration for Children and Families, Administration on Children, Youth, and Families, Children's Bureau, "Child Welfare Policy Manual," http://www.acf.hhs.gov/j2ee/programs/cb/laws_policies/laws/cwpm/policy_dsp.jsp?citID=207.
5. David G. Frederickson and H. George Frederickson, *Measuring the Performance of the Hollow State* (Washington, DC: Georgetown University Press, 2006), 170.
6. Beryl Radin, *Challenging the Performance Movement: Accountability, Complexity, and Democratic Values* (Washington, DC: Georgetown University Press, 2006), 184–185.
7. Note: During President George W. Bush's term, this office was called The White House Office of Faith-Based and Community Initiatives. During President Barack Obama's term, this office is called The White House Office of Faith-Based and Neighborhood Partnerships.
8. Note: The primary method for finding children of prisoners is for grantees to enter prisons and ask prisoners directly to identify their children for program consideration. Complications arise with getting access to prisons and prisoners, as well as prisoners incorrectly identifying children for whom they are technically not the guardian and disconnected phone numbers or outdated contact information. As a result, MCOP programs spend a portion of their federal grant money on tracking down these children of prisoners.

Improving Foster Care 183

9. Vincent Giampeitro, Program Director, Children and Families First, interview, Wilmington, Delaware, August 24, 2007.
10. Michael Kersteter, Executive Director, People's Place, interview, Milford, Delaware, August 24, 2007; Del Failing, interview.
11. Del Failing, Director of Children's Services, People's Place, interview, Milford, Delaware, August 24, 2007.
12. Vincent Giampeitro, interview.
13. Maura D. Corrigan, Justice of the Supreme Court, Michigan; Chief Justice of the Supreme Court, Michigan, phone interview, April 7, 2008.
14. Gayle Robbert, Program Representative, Lansing Foster Care Review Board, Courts, Michigan, phone interview, August 8, 2008.
15. Victoria Tyler, Director of Child Welfare, Catholic Social Services of Wayne, interview, Detroit, Michigan, March 20, 2008.
16. Ibid.
17. James Novell, Program Manager, Foster Care Review Board, Courts, Michigan, interview, Detroit, Michigan, March 17, 2008.
18. Patrick Okoronokwo, Director, The Children's Center, interview, Detroit, Michigan, March 20, 2008.
19. Mark E. Courtney et al., *Midwest Evaluation of the Adult Functioning of Former Foster Youth: Outcomes at Age 26* (Chicago: Chapin Hall at the University of Chicago, 2011).
20. Ibid, 21.
21. Ibid, 21.
22. Ibid, 28.
23. Ibid, 39.
24. Ibid, 41.
25. Ibid, 12.
26. Mark E. Courtney, "Children Who Age Out of the Foster Care System." Presentation before the Subcommittee on Income Security and Family Support, Committee on Ways and Means, United States House of Representatives, July 12, 2007, http://www.gpo.gov/fdsys/pkg/CHRG-110hhrg43505/pdf/CHRG-110hhrg43505.pdf, 74.
27. Ibid, 74.
28. Anne Havalchak, Catherine Roller White, and Kirk O'Brien, "The Casey Young Adult Survey: Findings Over Three Years," Casey Family Programs, March 26, 2008, http://www.casey.org/Resources/Publications/CaseyYoungAdultSurvey ThreeYears.htm.
29. Mosi Secret, "A Deal to Help Foster Youths Find Housing," *New York Times*, October 20, 2011, http://www.nytimes.com/2011/10/21/nyregion/nyc-agrees-to-find-housing-for-ex-foster-youths.html.
30. U.S. Department of Health and Human Services, "Reauthorization of Three Programs: The Mentoring Children of Prisoners Program, The Promoting Safe and Stable Families Program, and the Court Improvement Program," testimony by Joan E. Ohl, Commissioner, Administration on Children, Youth and Families, ACF, HHS. Presented to The Committee on Finance, U.S. Senate, May 10, 2006, http://www.hhs.gov/asl/testify/t060510.html.
31. U.S. Department of Justice, Office of Justice Programs, "FY 2014 Performance Budget," http://www.justice.gov/jmd/2014justification/pdf/ojp-justification.pdf, 74.
32. Thomas J. Smith, "The Least of These: Amachi and the Children of Prisoners," *Public/Private Ventures*, http://www.issuelab.org/resource/least_of_these_amachi_and_the_children_of_prisoners_the.
33. Kids Are Waiting: Fix Foster Care Now, "510,000 U.S. Children in Foster Care Are Waiting for Reform," http://www.kidsarewaiting.org/publications/statefacts. Note: Data is from federal government AFCARS database for 2006.

Appendix
Explanation of "Child Welfare Outcomes 2003: Annual Report"

The following questions were posed to the states to determine information about each outcome measurement in the U.S. Department of Health and Human Services "Child Welfare Outcomes 2003: Annual Report. Safety, Permanency, Well-Being."[1]

OUTCOME 1—REDUCE RECURRENCE OF CHILD ABUSE AND/OR NEGLECT

Outcome measure 1.1—Of all children who were victims of substantiated or indicated child abuse and/or neglect during the first 6 months of the reporting period, what percentage had another substantiated or indicated report within a 6-month period? (N = 34 States).

OUTCOME 2—REDUCE THE INCIDENCE OF CHILD ABUSE AND/OR NEGLECT IN FOSTER CARE

Outcome measure 2.1—Of all children who were in foster care during the reporting period, what percentage was the subject of substantiated or indicated maltreatment by a foster parent or facility staff member? (N = 27 States).

OUTCOME 3—INCREASE PERMANENCY FOR CHILDREN IN FOSTER CARE

Outcome measure 3.1—Of all children who exited foster care during the reporting period, what percentage left either to reunification, adoption, or legal guardianship (i.e., were discharged to a permanent home)? (N = 44 States).

Outcome measure 3.2—Of all children who exited foster care and were identified as having a diagnosed disability, what percentage left either to

186 *Politics of Foster Care Administration*

reunification, adoption, or legal guardianship (i.e., were discharged to a permanent home)? (N = 37 States).

Outcome measure 3.3—Of all children who exited foster care and were older than age 12 at the time of their most recent entry into care, what percentage left either to reunification, adoption, or legal guardianship (i.e., were discharged to a permanent home)? (N = 40 States).

Outcome measure 3.4—Of all children exiting foster care to emancipation, what percentage was age 12 or younger at the time of entry into foster care? (N = 50 States).

Outcome measure 3.5—Of all children who exited foster care, what percentage by racial/ethnic category left either to reunification, adoption, or legal guardianship?

Author's note on Outcome measure 3.5: This is a neutral outcome measure in that there was not a directional (increase/decrease) goal for this outcome. The report noted that "in almost all of the States, Black (non-Hispanic) children, Hispanic children, Alaskan Native/American Indian children, and White (non-Hispanic) children exiting foster care were about equally likely to be discharged to a permanent home." Although this outcome was collected from the states, this outcome measure was not used as part of my research design for this reason.

OUTCOME 4—REDUCE TIME IN FOSTER CARE TO REUNIFICATION WITHOUT INCREASING RE-ENTRY

Outcome measure 4.1—Of all children who were reunified with their parents or caretakers at the time of discharge from foster care, what percentage was reunified in less than 12 months from the time of entry into foster care? (N = 43 States).[2]

Outcome measure 4.2—Of all children who entered foster care during the reporting period, what percentage re-entered care within 12 months of a prior foster care episode? (N = 46 States).[2]

OUTCOME 5—REDUCE TIME IN FOSTER CARE TO ADOPTION

Outcome measure 5.1—Of all children who exited foster care to a finalized adoption, what percentage exited foster care less than 24 months from the time of the latest removal from home? (N = 34 States).[2]

OUTCOME 6—INCREASE PLACEMENT STABILITY

Outcome measure 6.1—Of all children served who had been in foster care for less than 12 months, what percentage had no more than two placement settings during that time period? (N = 51 States).[2]

Appendix 187

OUTCOME 7—REDUCE PLACEMENTS OF YOUNG CHILDREN IN GROUP HOMES OR INSTITUTIONS

Outcome measure 7.1—Of all children who entered foster care during the reporting period and were age 12 or younger at the time of their more recent placement, what percentage was placed in a group home or institution? (N = 49 States).

NOTES

1. U.S. Department of Health and Human Services, Administration for Children and Families, Administration on Children, Youth, and Families, Children's Bureau, "Child Welfare Outcomes 2003: Annual Report. Safety, Permanency, Well-Being," http://www.acf.hhs.gov/programs/cb/pubs/cwo03/cwo03.pdf.
2. This outcome question referenced several time periods but the time period mentioned was the one HHS primarily utilized for performance improvement comparison.

Index

administrative federalism 2
adoption: Delaware 28, 55, 58, 157;
  federal government 49, 154; law
  173; Michigan 27; New York
  29; Rhode Island 28–9, 124;
  timeline 180; Title IV-E 148
Adoption and Foster Care Reporting
  System (AFCARS) 9
Adoption and Safe Families Act (AFSA)
  9, 147, 152
Adoption Forum 132
agency-centered change 35
agency staff turnover 57
Agenda for Children Tomorrow (ACT)
  77, 80–3
aging out 56, 95, 130, 133, 137, 177,
  181
Agranoff, Robert 164
Ahmed, Ishmael 119, 121–5, 128,
  130–1, 135, 158, 160, 162, 165
Aid to Families with Dependent
  Children (AFDC) 9, 48, 148–9
American Political Development 36
American Reinvestment and Recovery
  Act (ARRA) 149
AmeriCorps 176
Ann Arbor, Michigan 118
Annie E. Casey Foundation Family to
  Family Initiative 32; involvement
  with foster care 50, 74, 95;
  kinship care 56; Mattingly 82,
  Michigan 115, 121–3, 129;
  thesis 162–3
Arab Community Center for Economic
  and Social Services (ACCESS)
  128, 130, 135, 165
Arsham, Michael 78–81, 161
at-risk youth 56, 182
Ayuso, Francis 76–7, 83, 161

Babcock, Pat 126, 130
Bane, Mary Jo 34
Bank of America 51, 53
Bardach, Eugene 164
Barnard, Chester 156
Bates, John 54–5, 57, 60, 157–8, 160
Bedford, Brooklyn 77
Bell, William C. 71, 74, 78, 80
Bier, Vicki 166
Bloomberg, Michael 81, 159
boroughs 68–9
Bridge Builders 76–7, 83
Bronx, New York 68, 70, 161
Brown, Nixzmary 81
Budget in Brief report 147
Burns, James MacGregor 33
Bush, President George W. 152, 173

California 25
Carcieri, Donald 97, 105, 107–8
caseloads: better standards 52;
  Delaware 45; IOC 82; lighter
  4; Michigan 116–17; per capita
  26; Rhode Island 90, 92, 100,
  102–3, 106, 158–9; size 25;
  standards 53, 57, 58
case management 34
case selection 8
Casey family foundations 50, 74–5, 84,
  159
Casey Family Services 50, 74, 95, 162,
  178
Casey Young Adult Survey 178
Casey Youth Opportunities Initiative 95
Catholic Social Services of Wayne
  County 128, 132, 136–7, 177
Chafee Foster Care Independence
  Program for Youth in Transition
  115, 117, 130

190 *Index*

Chaliman, Mary 119, 121, 131–4, 153–4, 158, 165
Challenging the Performance Movement: Accountability, Complexity, and Democratic Values 175
Chapin Hall Center for Children at the University of Chicago 178
child abuse prevention 49, 154
child advocacy organizations 10
child advocate 55, 158, 97, 180
Child Advocate of Rhode Island 105, 108
Child and Family Services Review (CFSR) 9; Delaware 46; federal government 153–4; Michigan 34, 117, 119, 132, 138, 164; New York 69; Rhode Island 92, 94
child liaisons 179–81
child protection 82
Children and Families First 53, 55, 58, 60, 177
Children at Risk Evaluation (CARE) Program at Alfred I. duPont Hospital for Children 52
children of prisoners 176
Children's Bureau 9
Children's Center 137
Children's Friend and Service 100–1
Children's Rights 29, 105, 126–7, 134–6, 160, 165
child welfare agencies 2, 27–9
child welfare agency administrators 10
Child Welfare Organizing Project (CWOP) 70, 77–81
"Child Welfare Outcomes 2003: Annual Report": Delaware 46; federal data from 26; federal monitoring 174; Michigan 117; New York 69; overview 10–11; requirements for 49; Rhode Island 92
Child Welfare Outcomes Reports 9, 152–3
child welfare researchers 10
churches 53–4, 125, 160
civil servants 146
claiming practices 10
Clinton, President Bill 151
cluster groups 56
cluster support communities 34
cluster system 47
Cohen, Steve 33

Collaborative Democracy Network 163
Collaborative Public Management 164
Colorado 26
community foundations 121, 162
community organizations: Delaware 51; hypothesis 31; Michigan 123; New York 75–6; Rhode Island 95–6, 98; thesis 174
community partners: building of 4, 8; Delaware 51–4, 57, 59; explanation of 31–2; hypothesis 46–7, 60, 68, 145; improvement 155–7, 176; Michigan 116–17, 123–7, 134, 136–8; New York 75–6, 79–80, 83–4, 161; Rhode Island 91, 95–8, 107–8; thesis 146, 159–62; variable 30
Community Partnership Initiative 77, 81
Congress 10
contracting services out 146
Corbin, Juliet 38
corporate culture 156
Corporation for National and Community Service (CNCS) 35, 48–9, 154, 175–6, 182
Corrigan, Maura 115, 119, 123–5, 128, 132–6, 138, 150, 154–5, 164–5, 177
County Executive Association of New York 70, 72, 83, 150, 173
Court Appointed Special Advocates (CASA) 49, 90, 100, 105, 154, 179–80
Courtney, John 79, 81, 83
Courtney, Mark 178
Craig, Christine 39, 49, 72, 94, 154–5
Creating Public Value 157
criminal justice system 137, 177
Culley, Tania 45, 52, 158, 165–6

DeJong, Allan 52
Delaware 176, 180; background 28; Delaware case 45–61; federal government 148–9, 153–4; hypothesis 40, 68, 145; law 173–4; versus Michigan 116, 119, 137–8; versus New York 71–3; outcome performance 15, 20–5; performance 8–9; score 13; versus Rhode Island 93–4, 96, 98–100, 108; thesis 156–67

Delaware Child Protection Accountability Commission (CPAC) 52, 165
Delaware Community Foundation 52
Delaware Department of Services for Children, Youth, and their Families (DCYF) 33, 48, 148
Delaware Division of Family Services (DFS): Delaware 57–8; employees 157–8; federal standards 153; Giddens 160; responsibility for 45–6; 48–9; 51–5; Title IV-E 148
Delaware Foster Care Task Force 55
Delaware Office of the Child Advocate 52, 158
DeSantis, Cari 48, 57, 148–9, 158
Detroit, Michigan 116, 118, 129, 131, 136–7, 158, 160, 177
DiBari, Julie 97
DiIulio, Jr., John J.: *Governing Prisons* 138, 156; *Government Performance* 161; *Harvard Law Review* 146, 155; leadership 33; principled agent 157; prison management study 3–4
direct provider 69
direct service provision 146
Doig, Jameson W. 33, 156
Dunkin' Donuts 102

East Providence, Rhode Island 93
Eggers, William D. 163–4
Ellen Roche Relief Foundation 80
Engler, John 121, 127–8
Executive Office of Health and Human Services 105

Failing, Del 53, 55, 177
faith-based organizations: Delaware 51, 160–1; hypothesis 31; major community partner 53–4; Michigan 123; New York 75, Rhode Island 95; thesis 174
faith-based partners 54, 176
faith-based services 54
family preservation 49, 154
Family to Family foster care initiative 74, 121–3, 129–30, 134, 162
Federal Emergency Management Agency 3
federal funding decline 48, 149
federal government: administration of programs 2; changing role

4; procurement 3; relationship to states 146–56, 158; thesis 174–6, 181
federal government, cultivation of relationships: collection of data 9; Delaware 48–50; explanation of 34–6; hypothesis 46–7, 60, 68, 145; Michigan 116–17, 119–20, 137, 156; New York 72–3, 84; performance 8; Rhode Island 91, 93–4, 107; variable 30
federalism 146, 151
federalist system 59
federal performance data 9, 154
federal performance reviews 107
Federal Reserve 1
federal standards 146, 149
Fenno, Richard 30
Fesler, James W. 1, 146
Fiscal Year 2013: Annual Report and Performance Plan 153
Forest Ranger, The 33
Fortier, Anne 104–5
foster care: definition of 1; spending 2; U.S. birth of 9
foster care administration: better 2, 4; Delaware 45–7, 54, 96; effective 145–7; knowledgeable about 36; Michigan 115–18, 127; New York 29, 68, 70–1, 74, 79, 84; Rhode Island 90, 99, 107–8; state performance 39; success 26, 32–3, 36; thesis 152–3, 155–6, 159, 161, 167, 173, 176, 179, 181–2
foster care administrative efficiency and effectiveness 27
foster care administrative systems 3
foster care administrators 4
foster care agencies 2–3; Delaware 47; Michigan 118, 123, 125, 158; New York 75, Rhode Island 95, 97
foster care caseload 20, 26–30, 45–6, 79, 94, 150–1
foster care employees 2, 153
foster care entry 2
foster care exit 2
foster care financing 149
Foster Care Independence Act 56
foster care licensing 28, 45
foster care outcomes 2; conditions to improve 39; data 10; Delaware 46–7; improvement of 8; Michigan 117, 136; New York 69–71, 73

192 *Index*

foster care performance 11, 97, 135
foster care policy 10, 173
foster care population 25–6, 45, 67, 70, 90, 116, 148
foster care programs 8, 145–8, 154, 167, 175–7
Foster Care Review Board 118, 124–5, 136, 177
foster care services 4, 146
foster care system 2, 3, 59, 60; Delaware 46, 56, 177; liaison 179; Michigan 117, 126, 130, 132, 157; New York 67–8, 73, 79, 93, 95, 162–3; operating 37; Rhode Island 91, 108, 163; stronger 8
Foster Family Services for the Jewish Child Care Association 70, 82, 159
Fostering Connections to Success and Increasing Adoptions Act 173
Foster Parents Association 95–9, 100–2, 105–7, 163
foundation: Delaware 50; government 155; mentors 32; Michigan 120–1, 123, 136; New York 73–4, 76–7; relationships with 4; Rhode Island 95; thesis 163, 174
Frederickson, David G. 175
Frederickson, H. George 175
Functions of the Executive, The 156

Gaebler, Ted 151
Garvey, Gerald 161
Garvey, Kelly 82
General Assembly 99
Gerstenzang, Sarah 83
Giampeitro, Vincent 53–5, 57–8, 60, 177
Gibbs, Linda 81
Giddens, Carlyse 48, 53–5, 57, 153, 157–8, 160
Giuliani, Mayor Rudy 79–80, 159
Global Youth Help 51, 53, 55
Goldsmith, Stephen 163–4
Gonzales, Logino 34
Goode, Sr., W. Wilson 61
Gore, Vice President Al 151
Governing (magazine) 127, 153–4
Governing by Network 163–4
Governing Prisons 2, 138, 156
government by proxy 2, 39, 146
Government by Proxy 155
Government Performance and Results Act (GPRA) 151–2

Government Performance Project (GPP) 127–8; 2008 GPP 166–7
Granholm, Jennifer 118, 126–8
Grassley, Charles 133
Gross, Carol 126
group homes, Rhode Island 91, 97, 104
guardianships 125
Guillette, Lisa 90, 95–8, 101, 105
Gulick, Luther 163

Hanley, Kate 122, 129–30, 132
Hargrove, Erwin C. 33, 156
Harlem, New York 70
Harlem Children's Zone 161
Harvard Kennedy School 54, 78, 99, 127, 131
Harvard Law Review 146, 155
Harvard University 53, 131
Harvard University Innovations in American Government Awards 27–8
Harvard University Institute for Government Innovation 34, 131
Hayward, Jane A. 105
Highbridge, Bronx 68, 76–7, 83
Horn, Wade 10, 60
House Committee on Government Reform and Oversight 152
Howard, Douglas E. 34
Hucke, Richard 74, 82 159, 163
Hultine, Dorothy 94, 106, 154, 165
Hurricane Katrina 3, 166

Implementation 36
implementation of public policy 2, 36, 39
Improved Outcomes for Children Initiative (IOC) 82–3
Improving Government Performance 161
independent living 49, 154, 181
Independent Living Program 181
ING Direct 53
interagency collaboration 164
intergovernmental relations 2
issue networks 39

Jamaica, Queens 77
Jewish Child Care Association 74, 82, 163
Jim Casey Foundation 115, 121–3, 162

Index   193

Jim Casey Youth Opportunities
Initiative 122–3, 130, 134, 162,
165
John Chafee Foster Care Independence
Act 178
Joyce, Philip 153
Judge Jeremiah 100
*Justifications of Estimates for
Appropriations Committees* 147

Kaufman, Herbert 1, 33
Kellogg Foundation 121, 162
Kelman, Stephen 3
Kersteter, Michael 60, 177
Kettl, Donald F.: his books 3, 34, 161;
boundary-based solutions 163–4;
*The Next Government of the
United States* 155; performance
measurement 152; *The Politics of
the Administrative Process* 146;
public administration 1; *The
State of Public Management*
156
kinship care 30, 56, 103, 128, 130,
158, 173
kinship caregivers 56, 99
Kuhlmann, Arkadi 38

Lansing, Michigan 118
Lansing Foster Care Review Board 134
leadership 2–4, 39
Leadership in Administration 156
legislation 35
Light, Paul 34, 146
Lutheran Social Services of Michigan
124–5, 130

management: federal government
152–6; foster care administration
2; little of 4, 145–7; prison
administration 3; thesis 167,
174–5; USCG 3; variables 4
managers 4, 174
Managing within Networks 164
mandates 146
Manhattan, New York 70
Martinez, Nancy 72–3, 84, 149–50
Martinez, Patricia 94, 97, 101, 104–6,
154
Mattingly, John B., service dates 71,
74–84, 159, 161, 163
Mead, Lawrence 3
*Measuring the Performance of the
Hollow State* 175

Medicaid 84, 94, 130, 179, 181
Meek, Jack W. 34
Meier, Kenneth J. 33
mental health system 137, 177
Mentoring Children of Prisoners
(MCOP) 4–5, 8–9, 49, 147, 154,
175–6, 180
mentors: Delaware 50–1, 55;
explanation of 32–3; hypothesis
46–7, 60, 68, 145; integrating
the advice of 8; Michigan
115–17, 120–1, 130, 134,
137–8; network of 4; New York
73–5, 84; Rhode Island 91, 95,
107; thesis 146, 156–7, 159–61,
163, 173, 176, 179–80; variable
30
mentorship 4, 145–7, 154–6, 167, 174,
176
Michigan: background 27–8; children
177; hypothesis 40, 68, 145; law
173–4; Michigan case 115–38;
outcome performance 15, 20–5;
performer 8–9; role of federal
government 150, 153; score 11;
unconventional partners 181;
variables 156, 159–60, 162,
164–7
Michigan Department of Human
Services (DHS) 115, 117–18,
121–33, 135, 150, 158, 160–2,
164–5
Michigan Family Independence Agency
34, 131
Michigan Federation for Children and
Families 124
Michigan League for Human Services
120, 122
Michigan Program Improvement Plan
34
Michigan's Children 124
Michigan State School of Social Work
124–5
Michigan Supreme Court 125, 134
Michigan Youth Opportunity Initiative
130
Milward, H. Brinton 156
Mink, Janice 52
Minner, Governor Ruth Ann, 28, 33–4,
47–8, 54–9, 158, 107
minorities in child welfare 27
monitor of foster care 174
Moore, Mark 33, 54, 78, 99, 127,
157

194 *Index*

Mullen, Dana 100
Mulligan, Heidi 104

National Center for State Courts 133
National Child Abuse and Neglect Data
System (NCANDS) 9
National Governors Association 133
neglected children 5, 29, 97, 108, 132
neighborhood-based services 77, 80
networks thesis 146, 156, 159, 163,
167, 174–6, 181
New Jersey 3, 58
New Jersey Division of Youth and
Family Services (DYFS) 58
New Mexico 162
New York: background 29–30;
federal funding 72; hypothesis
40, 145; lawsuit 126; versus
Michigan 116; New York case
67–85; performance 15, 20–5;
performer 8–9; relationship to
government 149–51, 153; versus
Rhode Island 93–4; score 13;
thesis 157–63, 166–7
New York City Council 178
New York City Department of
Homeless Services 178
New York City Partnership for Family
Supports and Justice 70
New York City's Administration for
Children's Services (ACS) 29,
67–71, 74–7, 79–84, 104, 159,
163
New York City's Child Welfare
Administration 79, 81
New York Nonprofit Press 77
New York State Association of
Counties 70, 72, 83, 151, 173
New York State Citizens' Coalition for
Children 69–70, 83
New York State Council of Family and
Child-Caring Agencies 161
New York State Office of Children and
Family Services 67–70; 72, 84
New York State Office of Strategic
Planning 67
New York Times 3, 29, 82, 178
*Next Government of the United States,
The* 3, 155, 161
nonprofit organizations 2; community
partners 54; Delaware 50–1;
hypothesis 32; Michigan 120,
123, 130; New York 69, 73–6;
Rhode Island 95
no reject, no eject policy 58, 59

North Providence, Rhode Island 93, 97
Novell, James 125, 137, 177

Obama, President Barack 153
Office of Management and Budget
(OMB) 152
Office of Performance and Personnel
Management (OPPM) 153
Office of the Children's Ombudsman
(OCO) 124, 135
Okoronokwo, Patrick 137, 177
One Church, One Child model 125
Onondaga County, New York 151
Onondaga County Legislature 151
*On Risk and Disaster: Lessons from
Hurricane Katrina* 166
open-ended entitlement 149
Osborne, David 151
O'Toole Jr., Lawrence J. 33
outcome assessment 9
outcome indicators 10, 60
outcome measurement 12, 20
outcomes: cases 100; child welfare
28; long-term 60; Mattingly
on 77; no relationship between
10; obtainment of 177–81;
tabulation of 11
outsourcing 2

partnerships thesis 146, 156, 159, 167,
174, 181
Pascoag, Rhode Island 93
Pasricha, Meghan 53, 55
Pearson, Lisa 94
peer organizations 51
People's Place 53, 55, 60
per capita budgets 4
performance audits 49
performance indicator 25
performance measurement: assessment
of 9; federal 60; federal
government 49; increase of 4;
Michigan 131–2; outcomes
50; Rhode Island 94, 106, 119;
thesis 145–7, 151–3, 155, 158,
167, 174–5, 182
permanency 82, 97–8, 101, 119, 125,
132–3, 137; CFSR 154, 160,
176, 179
personnel per capita 4
Pew Charitable Trusts: Delaware
51; grantmaker 38; law 173;
Michigan 121, 123; New York
74; program staff member 4;
Rhode Island 95

Index 195

Pew Commission on Children in Foster Care 32–3, 51, 123, 132–3, 163
Philadelphia 61
Pinchot, Gifford 33, 156
Pirro, Nicholas 67, 72, 83, 151, 173
police administration 2
policy and program entrepreneurs 174, 176, 181
policy implementation 38
Politics of the Administrative Office, The 1, 146
Pressman, Jeffrey L. 36
preventative services 77, 80, 82
principled agents: Delaware 54–5, 58–9; description 33; Michigan 127, 138; New York 78–9, 83; produced better foster care 4; Rhode Island 98–9; thesis 146, 156–9, 167
prison administration 3
prison management 156
private agencies 47
privatization 2
Program Assessment Rating Tool (PART) 152–3
Program Improvement Plan (PIP) 49, 94, 106, 119, 153
program measurement 39
program outputs 28
Providence, Rhode Island 93
public administration: definition of 1; of foster care 2; after Hurricane Katrina 166; Michigan 136, newer literature 60; public management 157, studies 2, 4; synonyms for 2; thesis 174
Public Administration Review 163
public bureaucracy 1
public management 1, 85, 128, 138; variable 146, 156, 158–60, 164
public manager leadership: Delaware 54–9; explanation of 33–4; hypothesis 46–7, 60, 68, 145; Michigan 116–17, 127–38; New York 78–84; provision of 8; Rhode Island 91, 98–108; role 155–7, 173–5, 181; thesis 146, 161–7; variable 30

qualitative research 8, 36
quantitative data 9, 25

Radin, Beryl 152, 175
Real Connections 95–6, 98

reinventing government 151
remove the child philosophy 79–80
residential placements 68–9
reunification 49, 55; Delaware 157; federal 154; Michigan 125, 130; New York 76, 78–80, timeline 180
Rhode Island: background 28–9; federal government 153; hypothesis 40, 68, 145; lawsuit 126; versus Michigan 116, 129, 133; performance 15, 20–5; performer 8–9; relationship to variables 156–63, 166–7; Rhode Island case 90–108; score 13
Rhode Island 2008 State of the State address 97, 108
Rhode Island 2008 State of the State report 107
Rhode Island Department of Children, Youth, and Families (DCYF) 28; 90–1, 93–7, 99–108; PIP 154, 158, 161, 163, 165–6
Rhode Island Family Court 100
Rhode Island Foster Parents Association 90, 93, 161, 166
Rhode Island General Assembly 165
Robbert, Gayle 134, 136, 177
Robbins, Maureen 90, 98–100, 102, 106–7, 158, 166
Robert Sterling Clark Foundation 80
Roth, Senator William 151

safe and stable families 49, 154
St. Jacques, Sarah 103, 107
St. Mary's Home for Children 97, 104, 107
Sam and Tony M. v. Carcieri 105
Savage, Kevin 93–4, 102, 104, 106
Scoppetta, Nicholas: philosophy 78–81, 159; service dates 71; his term 74
Securities and Exchange Commission 1
Selznick, Philip 156
Senate Committee on Governmental Affairs 152
Senior Corps 35, 176
service districts 68–9
service-planning areas (SPAs) 77
service quality 10
shadow of government 146
Shea, Robert 152
shelters 69, 91, 97–9, 104, 130, 158
show horses 31

196   *Index*

Skillman Foundation 121, 123, 126, 129, 162
Snyder, Al 52
Snyder, Janet 124–5, 138
soak and poke 30
state child protective services 53
state child welfare systems 9
state claims 10
State of Public Management, The 156
state sizes 25
Steiner, Philip 100, 102–3
strategies thesis 146, 156, 159, 163, 167, 174, 181
Strauss, Anselm 38
structural change 35
structured decision-making case management 28, 34, 131, 158
subsidized guardianship 129, 135, 173
subsidy rates 29
Syracuse, New York 151

Tannerhill Specialized Foster Care 103
technical assistance 72–3
Texas 26
Think of the Child First model 57, 59, 158
think tanks 32, 50, 73, 95, 120
third party agents 146
third-party government 2
Thompson, Brent 38
Thompson, Carole 38
Thompson-Sandy, Vicki 124–5, 130
Thurmaier, Kurt 34
Title IV-E Foster Care of the Social Security Act: since 1980 9; Delaware 45–6, 48; federal guidelines 155; law 173; Michigan 115, 117, 120, 133–4; New York 67, 69, 72–3, Rhode Island 92, 94; role of 148–51
Tyler, Victoria 132, 136, 177

Udow, Marianne 119–23, 125–6, 128–30, 132–4, 139, 150, 153, 158, 160, 162, 165
unions 101–2
University of Chicago 178
Urban Institute 148
Urban League of Rhode Island 105–6
U.S. Coast Guard 3
U.S. Congress 108

U.S. Department of Health and Human Services (HHS): defining foster care 1; executive summary 15; housing of agencies 9; input from 10; large role 2; MCOP 180; Michigan 119; rearrangement of agency units 36; Rhode Island 108; structure 146
U.S. Department of Health and Human Services (HHS), Administration for Children and Families (ACF) 9; Delaware 49; 60, 137, 154, 173
U.S. Department of Health and Human Services (HHS), Administration on Children, Youth, and Families (ACYF) 9
U.S. Department of Health and Human Services (HHS), Family Youth and Services Bureau 71
U.S. Department of Health and Human Services (HHS), Office of Human Services Policy 147
U.S. Department of Health and Human Services (HHS), Office of the Assistant Secretary for Planning and Evaluation 150–1
U.S. Forest Service 1
U.S. House of Representatives 173; Committee on Ways and Means 10, 60, 178
U.S. military operations 2
U.S. military special operations forces 1
U.S. Senate 173
Utah 26

variables: Delaware and federal government 48–50; federal government, mentors, community partners, leadership 8, 69; hypothesis 145; New York 71; Rhode Island 119
Varieties of Police Behavior 2
Verizon 53
VOICE 122
vulnerable children 3

Walker, Muna 38
Wayne County, Michigan 118, 122, 129, 158
welfare-to-work programs 3
Western Michigan University 126, 160

Index 197

White House Faith-Based and
    Neighborhood Partnerships
    Office 175–6, 182
Wildavsky, Aaron 36
Wilson, Barbara 38
Wilson, Harry 38
Wilson, James Q. 1, 2

workhorses 31
wrap-around communities 106
wrap around services 58

Yin, Robert 38

Zehnder-Merrell, Jane 120, 135